Discrimination American Style

Discrimination American Style

institutional racism and sexism

Joe R. Feagin
Clairece Booher Feagin

Second Edition

ROBERT E. KRIEGER PUBLISHING COMPANY
MALABAR, FLORIDA

Original Edition 1978
Second Augmented Edition 1986

Printed and Published by
ROBERT E. KRIEGER PUBLISHING COMPANY, INC.
KRIEGER DRIVE
MALABAR, FLORIDA 32950

Library of Congress Cataloging-in-Publication Data

Feagin, Joe R.
    Discrimination American style.

    Reprint. Originally published: Englewood Cliffs, N.J. :
Prentice-Hall, c1978.
    Includes bibliographical references and index.
    1. Discrimination—United States. 2. Affirmative action
programs—United States. 3. Civil rights—United States.
I. Feagin, Clairece Booher. II .Title.
JC599.U5F38 1986   305.8'00973   85-24195
ISBN 0-89874-915-8

10 9 8 7 6 5 4 3

JOE R. FEAGIN is currently Professor of Sociology at the University of Texas, Austin. He is the author of eight books, including *Ghetto Revolts* (Macmillan, 1973) and *Racial and Ethnic Relations* (Prentice-Hall, Inc., 1978), as well as forty articles on race relations and urban problems. In addition, he served as Scholar-in-Residence with the U.S. Commission on Civil Rights (1974–75).

CLAIRECE BOOHER FEAGIN, an experienced public school teacher, holds a master's degree in education from Harvard University.

For Michelle and Trevor

Contents

Preface
and
Introduction

As this goes to press, concern over discrimination against non-white minorities and women has receded substantially into the background. The publicly expressed concern of the 1960s over such matters seems to have evaporated. The current public concern is over the treatment of white males in "affirmative action" programs. Hand-wringing pronouncements are made about the threat that affirmative action and other anti-discrimination programs pose to such sacred ideas as "merit" and "individual opportunity." Yet, the agitation against affirmative action is less serious in our view than the neglect ("malign neglect") by the powers that be of the serious patterns of discrimination still afflicting minorities and women throughout the United States. The Richard Nixon and Gerald Ford presidencies saw a pulling back by the executive and legislative branches, as well as the mass media, from probing and investigating forays into the problems of race and sex discrimination. This pulling back, hopefully, is temporary, but it is nontheless tragic. A basic problem here is that of perspective. Many whites, or white males, seem to feel that the old problems of discrimination, such as that against black Americans, have been solved by the Great Society efforts of the 1960s. The new white male concern over affirmative action is doubtless, at least in part, legitimate. New government remedial programs can create bureaucratic problems. But the old discrimination problems have *not* been solved. A renewed investigation of and attack on discrimination against millions of minority persons and women are far more important tasks for this nation than actions to protect white males from the abuses, real and alleged, of affirmative action.

In this book we focus on this "old-fashioned" discrimination against minorities and women. A few notes on the book's organization seem appropriate at this point. Chapters One and Two look at traditional views of prejudice and discrimination, with a focus on recent conceptions of institutionalized discrimination. Chapter Two provides a typology of four basic but somewhat different types of discrimination, which we here term isolate, small-group, direct institutionalized, and indirect institutionalized discrimination. These latter two types, distinguished by intent or lack of intent, then provide a conceptual framework used in exploring specific examples of institutionalized discrimination in a broad range of areas from employment to the courts. Thus Chapter Three probes deeply into a range of employment discrimination problems, ranging from recruiting practices, to employment screening practices, to tracking systems, promotion actions, and layoff practices. Discriminatory mechanisms and results are both analyzed. Chapter Four explores institutionalized discrimination in housing—in the real estate industry and in lending and insuring organizations, as they affect homeowners and renters, minorities and women. In Chapter Five we assess the mechanisms and effects of discrimination in a number of different societal sectors, including the widely divergent areas of education, health care, politics, and the judicial system. In conclusion, Chapter Six briefly explores significant remedies for discrimination, both traditional remedies and innovative approaches which have been developed in recent years by victims, as well as by established private and public organizations. We conclude with an assessment of the future of anti-discrimination efforts.

A year as Scholar-in-Residence (1974–75) at the U.S. Commission on Civil Rights provided the time for the senior author to begin the research that eventually led to this book; and an early version of Chapters Two to Four appeared as a working paper for the use of commissioners there. Comment and criticism by various people at the U.S. Commission on Civil Rights helped to stimulate the more thoroughgoing and, hopefully, more useful analyses presented here. A summary article based on an earlier version of Chapter Two also appeared in the *American Politics Quarterly* in the spring of 1977; we have also found useful the critical responses of readers to that piece.

We cannot possibly name all those who have helped us in the research and writing of this book, but we are particularly grateful for the probing suggestions and critical comments of the following: Nijole Benokraitis, Charles Tilly, Paula Miller, John A. Buggs, Gene Mornell, Ed Dean, Gregg Jackson, Mark Yudof, Nestor Rodriguez, Barbara Romzek, Wess Robinson, John S. Butler, S. Dale McLemore, and Beryl Radin. Many of their insightful criticisms and comments, however disguised and altered, have found their way into our text. It is our hope that those concerned with researching and fighting discrimination will find this book both provocative and useful. The necessary work, however much the "malign neglect" advocates argue to the contrary, has just begun. There is much left to do in exposing, documenting, and eradicating the discriminatory mechanisms generating race and sex inequality in this society.

Discrimination
American Style

Theories of Discrimination

chapter one

Traditionally discrimination has been viewed as a creature of prejudice.* Until the late 1960s the dominant perspective among popular and social science analysts of discrimination underscored prejudice and intolerance as the causes underlying discriminatory actions. Some analysts have focused on individual racists and sexists, viewing the fundamental problem as the individual motivated by hatred of a given "outgroup." For others operating within the traditional perspective this emphasis on the individual has been coupled with a concern for patterns of segregation in the form of community practices, particularly racial practices—usually in the American South. Here prejudice, manifested in the guise of numerous racist (or sexist) individuals, is perceived as the motivation for both the

---

*For the moment, *discriminatory acts* can be viewed as acts that have a negative impact on minorities or women. *Prejudices* will be taken to mean negative and/or hostile attitudes toward a sexual or race/ethnic outgroup.

1

origin and continuation of these patterns. The prevailing model has thus been a prejudice-causes-discrimination model.

In addition, much traditional analysis before the late 1960s and early 1970s was optimistic, although sometimes cautiously so, tending to view prejudice as an archaic survival of an irrational past which could and would disappear as this society became more industrialized, rational, and progressive. This view has been coupled with the commonplace idea that the eradication of prejudice will lead to the progressive eradication of discrimination.

Social Science Perspectives

The traditional orientation toward discrimination described above has been at the center of much social science analysis, as well as of popular and media analysis. Most social science analysis until recently has adopted a prejudice→discrimination (prejudice-causes-discrimination) model and has tended to be optimistic about the assimilation of nonwhite minorities into the fabric of the society. The greater part of the sociological and social psychological literature on discrimination, particularly in mainline journals and influential books, has been preoccupied with issues tied to prejudice and prejudice-motivated discrimination. For example, the monumental and still influential work in race relations by Gunnar Myrdal, *An American Dilemma*, tied racial discrimination closely to racial prejudice. Myrdal defined *race prejudice* as "the whole complex of valuations and beliefs which are behind discriminatory behavior on the part of the majority group" and which contradict the "equalitarian ideas of the American Creed." Thus both individual acts of discrimination and the segregation patterns implemented by a large number of individuals in the South reflected local prejudices. Because, in Myrdal's view, prejudice and the discrimination it provokes contradict the fundamental American Creed emphasizing freedom and equality, their continued existence results in a basic moral conflict or dilemma for Americans and their society. Changes will come only when the "century-long lag of public morals" can be overcome; "in principle the Negro problem was settled long ago."[1] Here Myrdal eloquently summarized the thinking of the small group of social scientists working on these discrimination problems in the 1940s, views whose influence has persisted well into the present.

Myrdal's influence on such subsequent analysts as Merton and DeFleur and Westie was substantial. In the late 1940s Robert K. Merton carried the discussion of the gap between the American Creed and discriminatory conduct one step farther with the innovative suggestion that knowing a person's prejudices may or may not enable you to predict the actions. Thus Merton suggested a four-fold typology of prejudiced discriminators, prejudiced nondiscriminators, unprejudiced discriminators, and unprejudiced nondiscriminators. Merton's influential discussion of the critical type, the unprejudiced discriminator, is, unfortunately, very brief; he views such discrimination as intentional, but motivated by the social pressures of prejudiced family members, friends, fellow workers, or customers rather than by personal prejudices.[2] Subsequent researchers, as a result, have been particularly interested in individuals whose attitudes (prejudices) and behavior (discrimination) are inconsistent—the cases of Merton's prejudiced nondiscriminator and the unprejudiced discriminator.

Since Myrdal's and Merton's time, social science researchers have also framed their research hypotheses in terms of the prejudice → discrimination model. There have been several dozen studies of the prejudice → discrimination linkage. One typical approach has been to measure the extent of verbally expressed prejudices of a number of people by means of a written test and then to relate this measure to some type of discriminatory behavior considered relevant to the prejudices expressed (or not expressed). The discriminatory behavior measured has been of a very limited sort—such as a white subject's willingness or reluctance to sign a release to be photographed with blacks, or to sign an endorsement of open housing as public policy. The findings of the studies of this sort have varied considerably. Several have found that prejudice is correlated with the limited discriminatory actions assessed, although a few have found *no* correlation between prejudice and discrimination as measured. Most have been concerned with explaining why prejudice does not consistently predict discrimination. In the 1950s two pioneer researchers, DeFleur and Westie, suggested that the discrepancy between attitudes and behavior might be explained for the majority of subjects by their attempts to do or say what their social reference groups wished them to do or to say. That is, reference groups were suggested to be mediators of the linkage of racial or ethnic prejudice to behavior.[3]

Subsequent research substantiated this hypothesis. Pressures in the social environment, particularly those of family and friends, have been shown to have a strong impact on behavior, somewhat apart from the impact of personal prejudices. The views of reference group members have been found to be important in proportion to the visibility of an individual's discriminatory act. The model implicit in this later research has been one of individuals linked to primary groups, to family and friends, whose effects on a person's behavior can be somewhat independent of the prejudices of that person. Prejudice is still a central concern of this later research, the focus still on individuals and their discriminatory behavior, but with the prejudices of others in informal social contexts introduced to explain inconsistencies found in studies relating attitudes to behavior. Serious attention to what social scientists call the secondary group, to the organizational or institutional context in which most individuals find many of their actions shaped, is generally missing from this tradition of research on prejudice and discrimination. Missing too is measurement of serious discriminatory practices.[4]

In addition to this empirical literature, there are a number of more theoretical social science analyses which continue to accent prejudice as the prime determinant of discrimination. A few contemporary examples of the prevalent prejudice⟶discrimination model will suffice. In a still widely cited analysis, Allport has suggested that few prejudiced "people keep their antipathies entirely to themselves," but act their feelings out in a variety of ways, ranging from the least energetic to the most energetic—from commenting unfavorably about the outgroup to discriminating violently against the outgroup. Simpson and Yinger have seen discrimination as flowing from unfair distinctions, from stereotyped views of outgroup characteristics. In his recent general text Tumin defines *discrimination* as "the translation into consequential behavior of prejudicial beliefs." Kinloch views discrimination as "applied prejudice in which negative social definitions are translated into action and political policy." And in his 1975 critique of institutional racism models, Butler vigorously argues that discrimination involves only the conscious actions of racially prejudiced people, of intolerant bigots. While this prejudice ➤ discrimination perspective has seen a growing number of critics in the last few years, it remains a common view among contemporary analysts, be they journalists or social scientists.[5]

In addition to emphasizing prejudice, many social scientists have, explicitly or implicitly, viewed racial discrimination as "an aberration rather than a fundamental principle of American society."[6] Economic analysts such as Gary Becker have viewed discrimination as motivated by an irrational "taste" for discrimination, and as allegedly representing greater economic costs to the society than benefits. From the perspective of a number of leading economic analysts, greater awareness and rationality in the economic sphere should lead to the eradication of prejudice-generated discrimination and to great social, if not economic, benefits to the society.[7] Sociological analysts operating in the dominant assimilationist tradition, men such as Robert Park in the past and Milton Gordon, Talcott Parsons, and Nathan Glazer in the present, have underlined the importance of the ongoing assimilation or inclusion process in which every outgroup, white or nonwhite, has suffered some degree of discrimination; thus they often view race discrimination as different only in degree from problems suffered earlier by white European immigrant groups. For many who take this perspective, the inevitable decline in prejudice will lead to opportunities for significant minority advancement, and probably to full assimilation and inclusion. Prejudice and the discrimination it generates are typically viewed as irrational elements which will eventually wither away in the normal societal processes of urbanization and industrialization. Many still view traditional remedial techniques for discrimination optimistically. Prejudice and prejudice-generated discrimination, being essentially irrational, are not so basic to American society that they will not soon be eradicated.[8]

The literature we have just discussed focuses heavily on nonwhite minorities, with little more than hints or implications for prejudice and discrimination affecting women, especially nonminority women. Until quite recently social science and popular literatures have been silent on the issues of sex prejudice and sex discrimination, as well as the related questions of female upgrading and inclusion. It would have been logical to extend the empirical research on race prejudice and discrimination to women, focusing on such things as inconsistencies in attitudes and behavior and the progressive inclusion of women into all aspects of the society. Yet a traditional literature analogous to that on nonwhites has not yet emerged. A few brief analyses of the position of women have assumed, implicitly or explicitly, a prejudice ──➤ discrimination model.

A pioneering analysis in the 1940s by the Myrdals pointed up the importance of prejudices and stereotypes* concerning the intellectual and emotional inferiority of women in fostering discrimination; the situation of women and blacks was seen as similar in this regard. Another author, Helen M. Hacker, developed a view of women as a minority group analogous to nonwhites, a group whose barbed stereotypes as the weaker, more irresponsible, sex played an important role in shaping and rationalizing the discrimination they encountered. And Allport, in his classic study *The Nature of Prejudice*, argued, rather briefly, that inaccurate stereotypes about women were tied to discrimination against them.[9] There is a concern here with prejudiced individual discriminators, with subordinate group self-conceptions, and with the analogous victimized circumstances of women and blacks. As in the case with the traditional race discrimination model, a serious concern with institutions, organizations, and bureaucracies, as well as with covert and subtle types of discrimination, is usually missing. In any event, sex prejudice and sex discrimination were not major foci of analysis until the late 1960s.

Movement toward an Institutional Emphasis

It is not surprising that prejudice has received so much emphasis in conventional assessments of discrimination, particularly race discrimination, for such attitudes have been both blatant and conspicuous in the United States. The negative racist and sexist attitudes of individuals and the consequent prejudice-generated discrimination have long been very serious societal problems. Yet numerous recent public opinion polls have shown a sharp decline in,

---

Stereotypes have often been viewed as synonymous with prejudices, although some accent the cognitive aspect of stereotyping, the uncritical beliefs about the hated outgroup.

for example, white prejudice and stereotypes concerning blacks (and to some extent other nonwhites) compared to opinions several decades ago.[10] While this decline in prejudice may to some extent reflect a subtle concealment of rank-and-file attitudes from interviewers, it is so steep a decline that it almost certainly reflects some change from the blatantly racist and nearly universally hostile white prejudices of the recent past. Over the same period the economic, social, and political positions of nonwhites have improved much more slowly. Prejudiced attitudes of whites seem to have lessened substantially more rapidly than discrimination has declined. Such conflicting trends also seem to be the case for women, although the limited data we have on the decline in prejudice are impressionistic. In addition, the growing view among white males that they are not prejudiced, that they are not intolerant "Archie Bunker" types, supports the contention that they are no longer responsible for the oppressive subordinate conditions of women or nonwhites. From the vantage point of the conventional prejudice —➤ discrimination model, most rank-and-file whites (or white males) can argue that they are not prejudiced and, therefore, that their actions are no longer discriminatory. This points up the critical policy implications of one's view of discrimination—a point we will return to later.

Primarily since the 1960s three formidable streams of thought relevant to a systematic rethinking of discrimination have emerged in the literature. All point to the importance of the social and organizational environment. One stream can be termed the *interest theory* of discrimination; the second is usually called *internal colonialism;* the third stream has been termed *institutional racism* (or *institutional sexism*). All three streams will here be drawn on to flesh out a more adequate conceptualization of discrimination. All three raise questions as to whether subordinate groups can be viewed simply in terms of a model which assumes a progressive, gradual process of inclusion into the dominant society and as to whether a prejudice—➤discrimination model is adequate for a thorough analysis of discrimination patterns. Let us briefly examine the contributions of these three perspectives.

First, we can note the development of an *interest theory of discrimination.* The basic idea here is that the motivating force behind discrimination can be the desire to protect one's own privilege and power. As we have previously noted, a number of the authors whose work falls more or less in line with the conventional prejudice—➤discrimination model have pointed up the importance of the social context, suggesting that people may discriminate out of fear of the prejudices of relevant others. Myrdal and Merton on occasion briefly noted the role of such reference group pressure, as have numerous researchers gathering empirical data on behavior and attitudes; a few of these even hinted at the possibility that the motivating force behind discrimination may not always be linked to prejudice and intolerance. But there were a few who were pressing for a different emphasis. As early as the 1950s Rose groped toward a better conceptualization of discrimination, suggesting that one should not focus on attitudes but on structural features of the society in order to understand the nature of race relations. In the early 1960s Antonovsky suggested the importance of vested interest as a driving force. Antonovsky advocated distinguishing between prejudice-motivated discrimination and gain-motivated discrimination, the latter referring to the actions of persons discriminating solely because of the economic or political gains redounding to them.[11]

Very important in the development of this interest (intent-to-harm) perspective have been authors such as Herbert Blumer, Robin Williams, and David Wellman. In the late 1950s Blumer argued that race prejudice was better viewed as a "sense of group position" rather than as a set of hostile feelings toward an outgroup. In his view the dominant group's race prejudice is but a mask, or rationalization, for protecting the dominant group's position.[12] In the mid-1960s Robin Williams pointed up the importance of race discrimination as a way of perpetuating a white group's current privileges. In a fashion similar to that of the internal colonialism analysts we will examine in a moment, Williams has argued that the colonial expansion of mercantilist European powers overseas created the great racial inequality in North America. Racial ideologies developed to rationalize the social, economic, and political domination initially developed to enhance the resources and privileges of white Europeans. This colonial expansion established structured-in privileges persisting to the present day. Protection of white privilege is critical to patterns of discrimination: "Whenever a number of persons within a society have enjoyed for a considerable period of time certain opportunities for getting wealth, for exercising power and authority, and for successfully claiming prestige and social deference, there is a strong tendency for these people to feel that these benefits are theirs 'by right.'" Those who have greater privilege will vigorously defend "their established system of vested interests."[13]

More recently, Wellman has cogently argued that discrimination against nonwhites is a "rational response to struggles over scarce resources."[14] Racial stratification is a critical feature in the operation of American society. In the struggle over resources a system of stratification was established in which whites benefited economically, politically, socially, and psychologically. Indeed, "without the notion of privilege, the concept of discrimination is static; it just refers to blocked access. When you introduce the idea of privilege you have a much more dynamic relationship involved: one group is 'fat' because the other is 'skinny.'"[15] Discrimination is more than the imposition of barriers at a given point in time; it entails a process of constantly defending one group's privileges gained at the expense of another. Thus race discrimination (and by extension sex discrimination, although this view has yet to be systematically developed) can be seen as behavioral processes aimed at maintaining the privileges of the dominant group. There may be a social "law of inertia" here—a "law of inertia of privilege"—guaranteeing that the privileges or resources gained at the expense of another group remain massed in the hands of the dominant group unless acted on by that other group. In the world of race and sex privilege, as well as in the world of physics, there is a tendency for things to stay the same without outside pressure. Moreover, actions are taken to protect that privilege, actions falling under the rubric of discrimination.

A closely related perspective, the *internal colonialism* interpretation of privilege, has been persuasively argued in recent years. Internal colonialism theorists have placed less emphasis on prejudiced individuals; they have underscored the way in which privilege was created in the process of white European groups taking by force resources such as land (for example, of Native Americans) and labor (for example, of African Americans) and using those resources for their own advantage. Unequal life chances by race in the Americas (and elsewhere) originated in the European colonization beginning in the fifteenth century. The uneven spread of technological development and industrialization resulted in technologically advanced and less advanced groups, particularly in the sphere of military technology and firepower. This in turn created critical power imbalances. In newly colonized societies the unequal distribution and control of economic and political resources, initially established by force, was institutionalized: "The super-ordinate group, now ensconced as the core, seeks to stabilize and monopolize its advantages through policies aiming at the institutionalization and perpetuation of the existing stratification system."[16] The historical conquest or enslavement of predominantly non-European groups such as blacks, Mexican Americans, and Native Americans ("Indians") provided the underpinning for institutionalized arrangements that became a structure of *internal* colonialism. Nonwhite workers were brought in as cheap labor, or their land was stolen. Industrialization in the late nineteenth and early twentieth centuries saw the incorporation of racial discrimination into a sophisticated economic system. A critical, persisting racial division of labor, labor colonialism, was set up, at first by force, then by law and more informal mechanisms. This situation is one of internal colonialism. From this perspective, racial stratification can exist where there are currently few prejudiced people because "the processes that maintain domination—control of whites over nonwhites—are built into the major social institutions."[17] Subordination is built into the warp and woof of the societal fabric.

Only a few analysts have begun the potentially fruitful assessment of sexual colonialism in analogous terms. Examining the current scene, Millett has noted that "what goes largely unexamined, often even unacknowledged (yet is institutionalized nonetheless) in our social order, is the birthright priority whereby males rule females." She further notes that "through this system a most ingenious form of 'interior colonization' has been achieved."[18] The exact origin of this ancient type of internal colonialism is apparently lost in the distant past, but a rigid form of sex subordination, the patriarchal family structure, characterized the North American colonies from the earliest decades. In an earlier stage of European society the concentration of subsistence activities in a larger household or clan and the relative absence of individually controlled private property seem to have made the work of women considerably more important than in later periods. Engels and neo-Marxist writers in his tradition have argued that the emergence of commercial and industrial capitalism in the Western world actually made for a *worsening* of the subordinate situation of women.[19]

Yet most would argue that women were never equal. Nevertheless, changes in resources, private property, and capitalist technology in the eighteenth and nineteenth centuries did bring changes in the hierarchical nature of the household and the significance of men's and women's work. Increasingly, women in nuclear families were more subordinated than before; they now worked specifically for their employed husbands rather than for the larger extended family group.[20] A rigid sexual division of labor developed, a familial colonialism of the most intimate, internal type. Men went into higher-status, socially "productive" work. Responsibility for low-status, and private, domestic work became the material basis of female subordination both in Europe and the far-flung North American colonies. A man's home became *his* castle. Moreover, in the ever-increasing industrialization process both male employers and male workers shaped sex segregation outside the home in the labor market, utilizing both traditional patriarchal family techniques and the new techniques of bureaucratic organization to keep women in a subordinate position outside the home. "Thus, the hierarchical domestic division of labor is perpetuated by the labor market and this domestic division of labor, in turn, acts to weaken women's position in the labor market."[21] Since working women had been relegated to domestic work and childrearing, when they entered the larger labor market they did so with handicaps which made competition with men difficult. Male-dominated workers' movements and unions also kept women down. The hierarchical system favored by employers, the patriarchal family, and male-dominated unions reinforced one another.[22] Labor market colonialism and familial colonialism became twin burdens for women.

Sexual colonialism in the United States is similar in many—*although by no means all*—important ways to race colonialism, for both involve control defined by birth. In both cases the relationship is one of dominance and subordination. Today the hierarchy in the typical sexual division of labor indicates that this type of internal colonialism is still similar to that of racial minorities. Racial and sexual hierarchies both have a *material* basis, the former in the sexual division of labor in the family and in the economy, the latter in the racial division of labor in the economy. Homemaking, in which a large proportion of adult females are still engaged full-time or part-time, is unpaid, although economically essential. Outside the home women workers still are typically in domestic, clerical, and other service positions that confer relatively low status and pay.[23] Basic to patriarchal stratification is family subordination, and this distinguishes sex from race subordination, but the broader economic and political situations of women and minorities are strikingly similar. Indeed, sexual colonialism in the family may be the most ancient prototype of internal colonialism. Even such Marxist analysts as Friedrich Engels have underscored the point that historically the "first class oppression" was that of "the female by the male sex."[24]

We can now turn to the third important perspective enlarging our understanding of discrimination—that of *institutional racism/ institutional sexism*. As we have seen, once a colonial system is established historically, those in the superior position seek to monopolize basic resources. In this process, privilege becomes institutionalized, that is, it becomes imbedded in the norms (regulations and informal rules) and roles (social positions and their attendant duties and rights) in a variety of social, economic, and political organizations. We should note here that *institution* is a word used in several different senses. One common usage is in regard to specific organizations such as a business, a corporation, a union, a school, a hospital, and so on. These are formally, legally constituted organizations, with written and unwritten rules governing the conduct of those who fill positions therein, such as supervisor or teacher. *Institution* is also a term used for larger sets or combinations of organizations such as "the economy" or "the family." In institutionalized racism and sexism the concept can be applied in both senses. Just how the imbalance in privilege gets incorporated in the first place is a major concern of internal colonialism theorists. Note too that a major concern in much institutional analysis is with the effects and mechanisms (methods) of contemporary discrimination, an emphasis more on different *types* of discrimination than on the *origins* of discrimination.

Writing in the mid-1960s, Charles Hamilton and Stokeley Carmichael were apparently the first to systematically probe the concept of institutional racism. Contrasting "individual racism"— illustrated, for example, by the actions of a small band of white terrorists bombing a black church—with "institutional racism"— illustrated by the practices which lead to many black children dying each year because of inadequate food, medical facilities, and shelter—Hamilton and Carmichael attempted to move beyond a focus on prejudiced white bigots acting out racist attitudes.[25] Yet even for them prejudiced attitudes ultimately underlay institutions. They were among the first to link institutional racism, seen as discriminatory mechanisms and effects, to the concept of internal colonialism: "Black people in the United States have a colonial relationship to the larger society, a relationship characterized by institutional racism."[26] In a 1969 book Knowles and Prewitt (and their associates) utilized institutional racism for their conceptual framework. In their view individual acts of racism and racist institutional policies can "occur without the presence of conscious bigotry, and both may be masked intentionally or innocently."[27] Here was the suggestion that institutional mechanisms need not be intentional, although this important point was not developed. Their subsequent analysis of institutional areas such as the economy and housing combined many examples of the effects of intentional discrimination with a few examples of the effects of unintentional discrimination. Their major emphasis was on racial differentials in the *effects* of societal operations.

Since the appearance of these pioneering books modest amounts of analytical attention have been given to institutional racism and the broader concept of institutional discrimination. A few social science and legal researchers have preferred the conceptual approach which emphasizes the unequal consequences or effects of institutional operations, whatever their intent, but underplaying the mechanisms or practices that led to those effects. The emphasis on effects has led to useful operational (statistical) indices of institutional racism and to the pioneering empirical research of Butler and Nordlie on patterns of racial inequality in the armed forces, on which we will draw in a later chapter.[28] Others have dealt more directly with the concept. In a probing analysis Downs has elaborated on the point that institutional racism can involve actions where people have "no intention of subordinating others because of color, or are totally unaware of doing so." Downs has also suggested the concept of "institutional subordination," which refers to subordination "by means of attitudes, actions, or institutional structures which do not use color itself" but "mechanisms indirectly related to color."[29] In a recent analysis of racism and mental health Pettigrew briefly explored these issues, distinguishing between direct racial discrimination and indirect racial discrimination, where restrictions in one area are shaped by direct racial discrimination in another.[30]

Social scientists are not the only ones who have contributed to broadening the concept of discrimination in the institutional direction. By the late 1960s legal researchers and practicing lawyers, such as those in the federal government's Equal Employment Opportunity Commission (EEOC), were pressing to extend the traditional prejudice → discrimination concept of discrimination underlying earlier court decisions. These developments, which focused primarily on discrimination in employment practices, were apparently independent of social science analysis. Blumrosen has charted this shift from a concern with what lawyers quaintly term "evil-motive" discrimination (actions which are intended to have a harmful effect on minority group members) to "effects" discrimination (actions which have a harmful effect whatever their motivation).[31] The EEOC view emphasizing "effects" discrimination was accepted by several federal judges in the late 1960s and early 1970s. Increasingly, until about 1974, employment discrimination decisions in the federal courts frequently emphasized the *consequences* of employment practices, rather than the motivation lying behind those practices. Here was a practical application of a concept of institutional discrimination which stresses the "effects" aspect. More recently, however, the Supreme Court has been moving back to a position recognizing "evil-motive" (intentional) discrimination as the only type prohibited by law.

As for institutional sexism, social science analysts have done little more than use the concept occasionally in sorting out empirical analyses of the situation of women in the United States. None has developed a systematic conceptual analysis. Like a growing number of authors, Amundsen has explicitly used the concept and term *institutional sexism* to refer both to intentional and unintentional discrimination against women, with a particular emphasis on intentional discrimination.[32] Her analysis relies heavily on, and is thus limited by, earlier interpretations of institutional racism. Moreover, the legal development of the "effects" concept of discrimination in certain federal court cases (noted in the previous paragraph) has covered the situation of women—again, mainly in regard to employment. Nonetheless, the basic ideas of discriminatory effects and mechanisms suggested by the institutional racism arguments seem relevant to the situation of women, as our subsequent chapters will make clear.

These, then, are the three most important streams of thought suggesting the need to move beyond the traditional emphasis on individuals and on a prejudice → discrimination perspective to a more adequate conceptualization of discrimination. This we will attempt to do in the next chapter.

1. Gunnar Myrdal, *An American Dilemma* (New York: McGraw-Hill Paperback, 1964), 1: lxxi, 24, 52n, 78, 101.

2. Robert K. Merton, "Discrimination and the American Creed," in *The Study of Society,* edited by Peter I. Rose, 2nd ed. (New York: Random House, 1970), pp. 449–57.

3. See Melvin L. DeFleur and Frank R. Westie, "Verbal Attitudes and Overt Acts," *American Sociological Review* 23 (December 1958): 667–73; Gordon H. DeFriese and W. Scott Ford, "Verbal Attitudes, Overt Acts, and the Influence of Social Constraint in Interracial Behavior," *Social Problems* 16 (1969): 493–505; John C. Brigham, "Racial Stereotypes, Attitudes, and Evaluations," *Sociometry* 34 (1971), 360–80.

4. Alan C. Acock and Melvin L. DeFleur, "A Configurational Approach to Contingent Consistency in the Attitude-Behavior Relationship," *American Sociological Review* 37 (December 1972): 715–18; William L. Ewens and Howard J. Ehrlich, "Reference-Other Support and Ethnic Attitudes as Predictors of Intergroup Behavior," *Sociological Quarterly* 13 (Summer 1972): 348–60; Lyle G. Warner and Rutledge M. Dennis, "Prejudice Versus Discrimination: An Empirical Example and Theoretical Extension," *Social Forces* 48 (1970): 473–84.

5. Gordon Allport, *The Nature of Prejudice,* abridged ed. (New York: Doubleday Anchor Books, 1958), p. 14; George E. Simpson and J. Milton Yinger, *Racial and Cultural Minorities* (New York: Harper & Row, 1970), p. 28; Melvin M. Tumin, *Patterns of Society* (Boston: Little, Brown, 1973), p. 418; Graham Kinloch, *The Dynamics of Race Relations* (New York: McGraw-Hill, 1974), p. 54; John S. Butler, "Institutional Racism: Viable Perspective or Conservative Bogey?" paper presented at the American Sociological Association meetings, August 1975.

6. Robert Blauner, *Racial Oppression in America* (New York: Harper & Row, 1972), p. 7.

7. See Gary S. Becker, *The Economics of Discrimination,* 2nd ed. (Chicago: University of Chicago Press, 1971); Lester Thurow, *Poverty and Discrimination* (Washington, D.C.: Brookings Institution, 1969).

8. See Milton M. Gordon, *Assimilation in American Life* (New York: Oxford University Press, 1964); Nathan Glazer, "Blacks and Ethnic Groups: The Difference, and the Political Difference It Makes," *Social Problems* 18 (Spring 1971): 444-61; Talcott Parsons, "Full Citizenship for the Negro American? A Sociological Problem," in *The Negro American,* edited by Talcott Parsons and Kenneth B. Clark (Boston: Houghton Mifflin, 1965), pp. 709-754; Talcott Parsons, "Revised Analytical Approach to the Theory of Social Stratification," in *Class, Status, and Power,* edited by R. Bendix and S. M. Lipset (Glencoe, Ill.: Free Press, 1953), p. 118; Nathan Glazer, *Affirmative Discrimination* (New York: Basic Books, 1975), pp. 3-76. For a useful critique of economic and sociological perspectives, see Jeffrey Prager, "White Racial Privilege and Social Change: An Examination of Theories of Racism," *Berkeley Journal of Sociology* 17 (1972-1973): 117-50.

9. Myrdal, *An American Dilemma,* 2: 1077; Helen M. Hacker, "Women as a Minority Group," *Social Forces* 30 (October 1951): 66; Allport, *The Nature of Prejudice,* p. 32.

10. See Paul B. Sheatsley, "White Attitudes Toward the Negro," in Parsons and Clark, *The Negro American,* pp. 303-324; Herbert H. Hyman and Paul Be. Sheatsley, "Attitudes Toward Desegregation," *Scientific American* 211 (July 1964): 16-23; Andrew Greeley and Paul B. Sheatsley, "Attitudes Toward Racial Integration," *Scientific American* 225 (December 1971): pp. 14 ff.

11. See Arnold Rose, "Intergroup Relations vs. Prejudice," *Social Problems* (October 1956): 173-76; A. Antonovsky, "The Social Meaning of Discrimination," *Phylon* 21 (Spring 1960): 81.

12. Herbert Blumer, "Race Prejudice as a Sense of Group Position," *Pacific Sociological Review* 1 (Spring 1960): 3-5.

13. Robin M. Williams, Jr., "Prejudice and Society," in *The American Negro Reference Book,* edited by J. P. Davis (Englewood Cliffs, N.J.: Prentice-Hall, 1966), pp. 727-30. Others emphasizing a structural perspective include: Pierre L. van den Berghe, *Race and Racism* (New York: Wiley, 1967), and R. A. Schermerhorn, *Comparative Ethnic Relations* (New York: Random House, 1970).

14. David M. Wellman, *Portraits of White Racism* (Cambridge: Cambridge University Press, 1977).

15. Personal correspondence to senior author, 1975.

16. Michael Hechter, *Internal Colonialism* (Berkeley: University of California Press, 1975), p. 39.

17. Blauner, *Racial Oppression in America*, pp. 9–10. On Mexican Americans and colonialism, see Joan W. Moore, "Colonialism: The Case of the Mexican Americans," *Social Problems* 17 (Spring 1970): 436–72.

18. Kate Millett, *Sexual Politics* (New York: Avon Books, 1969), p. 25; also see pp. 40–42.

19. See Friedrich Engels, *The Origins of the Family, Private Property, and the State* (Chicago: Charles H. Kerr, 1902).

20. Karen Sacks, "Engels Revisited: Women, the Organization of Production, and Private Property," in *Woman, Culture, and Society*, edited by Michelle Zimbalist Rosaldo and Louise Lamphere (Stanford, Calif.: Stanford University Press, 1974), pp. 209, 220–21.

21. Heidi Hartmann, "Historical Perspectives on Job Segregation by Sex; or, the Fruits of Patriarchy," paper presented at Conference on Occupational Segregation, Wellesley College, May 1975, p. 3. I am drawing on Hartmann throughout this paragraph.

22. Ibid., pp. 1–10; see the similar paper by Hartmann, "Capitalism, Patriarchy, and Job Segregation," in *Signs* 1 (Spring 1976): 137–69.

23. Millett, *Sexual Politics*, pp. 24, 40–42.

24. Friedrich Engels, "The Origin of the Status of Women," in *Woman in a Man-made World*, edited by Nona Glaser and Helen Youngelson Waehrer (Chicago: Rand McNally, 1977), p. 151.

25. Charles Hamilton and Stokeley Carmichael, *Black Power* (New York: Random House, 1967), p. 4.

26. Ibid., p. 6.

27. Louis L. Knowles and Kenneth Prewitt (eds.), *Institutional Racism in America* (Englewood Cliffs, N.J.: Prentice-Hall, 1969), p. 5.

28. Peter G. Nordlie, *Measuring Changes in Institutional Racial Discrimination in the Army* (McLean, Va.: Human Sciences Research, 1974). John S. Butler played a major role in this report.

29. Anthony Downs, *Racism in America and How to Combat It* (Washington, D.C.: U.S. Commission on Civil Rights, 1970), pp. 5, 7.

30. Thomas F. Pettigrew, "Racism and the Mental Health of White Americans: A Social Psychological View," in *Racism in Mental Health*, edited by Charles V. Willie, Bernard M. Kramer, and Betram S. Brown (Pittsburgh: University of Pittsburgh Press, 1973), p. 271.

31. Blumrosen distinguishes three stages in the evolution of the concept. See Alfred W. Blumrosen, "Strangers in Paradise: *Griggs* v. *Duke Power Co.* and the Concept of Employment Discrimination," *Michigan Law Review* 71 (November 1972): 67–71; see also Alfred W. Blumrosen, *Black Employment and the Law* (New Brunswick, N.J.: Rutgers University Press, 1971), p. 232.

32. Kirsten Amundsen, *The Silenced Majority* (Englewood Cliffs, N.J.: Prentice-Hall, 1971), pp. 42–61.

Institutionalized Discrimination

chapter two

Before examining discriminatory practices in specific areas such as education or housing, we need to establish our own conceptual framework. Previous discussion of race and sex discrimination, as we have seen, has been hampered by a number of conceptual problems. One is the tendency to distinguish a concept of individual discrimination from a fuzzy concept of institutional discrimination, implying that individuals are somehow not relevant to the operation of the latter type. This has confused supporters and critics of the institutional-discrimination model alike. Some writers, moreover, have been tempted to include prejudiced attitudes as an essential part of institutional discrimination. Another problem in many specific analyses is the failure to spell out in detail the concept of discrimination being used, or even to provide a definition. Perhaps a more serious problem is the tendency to blend together direct and indirect types of institutionalized discrimination, a problem which will become

19

clearer as we proceed. The purpose of this chapter is to suggest a better set of types and definitions of discrimination and to offer a few clear illustrations. Subsequent chapters will systematically present specific examples of institutionalized discriminatory mechanisms.

First let us reconsider briefly the ideas of prejudice and discrimination. The term *prejudice* has a generally accepted meaning which will be adopted here: an irrational and negative attitude directed at an outgroup because of real or alleged physical or cultural characteristics; or put more simply, "thinking ill of others without sufficient warrant."[1] The critical notions here are that (1) the attitude is not well founded in fact and (2) it has a negative cast. Yet prejudice is not the only motivation for intentional discrimination; in the first chapter we saw how important can be the prejudices of "relevant others" (family, friends, etc.) in shaping one's actions, whether one is prejudiced or not. We have also seen that intent to harm can involve protection of one's vested economic or political interests, with no necessary relation to prejudice. We must keep in view these different types of motivation behind acts of discrimination.

As we have seen in Chapter 1, the term *discrimination* usually remains undefined, and variously conceptualized, in public and scholarly discussions. *Discrimination* is an old word in English, dating back at least to the mid-seventeenth century; its oldest meaning was the simple one of distinguishing between one thing and another because of their different qualities. Only later did its meaning include differential treatment of a group because of its physical or cultural characteristics.

As we discussed in Chapter 1, the traditional understanding of the word *discrimination* in the social sciences has been in terms of acts with harmful effects and precipitated by prejudice or concern for the prejudice of others. This traditional view will not be accepted as adequate here, for the emerging literature on institutionalized racism and sexism we just reviewed suggests that neither prejudice, nor concern for the prejudiced views of others, is absolutely necessary to a sociological definition of discrimination. The working definition used hereafter is as follows: *Discrimination here refers to actions or practices carried out by members of dominant groups, or their* *representatives, which have a differential and negative impact on members of subordinate groups.**

Discriminatory behavior has both effects and mechanisms. *Effects* refer to the negative impact of behavior; *mechanisms* refer to the modes of operation, the behavior leading to the harmful effects. In the past and present, many writers have focused heavily on the effects of discrimination. This is not surprising, for the impact is more directly observable, while the practices leading to that impact often are subtle and difficult to document. We will make an effort in this book to distinguish impact or effects from mechanisms and to identify the actual practices which are the "guts" of discrimination. In the interest of brevity, the subordinate groups under consideration in this book are limited to a few nonwhite minority groups —particularly black Americans—and nonminority women, those groups with considerably less group power and resources than dominant white male groups.** In addition, our discussion assumes that race and sex discrimination are *unjust* and should be remedied, a point to which we will return in the final chapter.

Dimensions of Discrimination

One way to highlight important dimensions of discrimination and to illustrate the similarities and differences between the traditional prejudice→discrimination approach and the type of institutionalized discrimination approach we are accenting in this book is to compare briefly these two approaches. Here one should think of the two approaches' *tendencies* rather than of their radical either/or

*"Representative" could include subordinate group members carrying out the directives of dominant group members, co-opted persons who are not fully "in" the dominant group but are used by it. Note that it is possible to be a member of a subordinate group in some situations, and thus be on the "receiving end" of discriminatory actions, and also to be a member of a group with greater power than another in other situations, and thus be on the "giving end" of discriminatory actions. Some white women, to take just one example, can be found in both situations. A more extensive analysis than this might develop a perspective envisioning a *hierarchy* of several groups, with white males as a group occupying the top position.

**It should be clear that in this book we are not considering so-called "reverse discrimination" as falling within our conceptual framework. See Chapter 6.

differences. The portrait in Table 1 is idealized for purpose of discussion.

TABLE 1   SOME DIFFERENCES IN EMPHASIS

Dimension (Typical)	Emphasis of Traditional View	Emphasis of Institutionalized Discrimination View
1. Discriminator(s)	Single or multiple discriminators	Multiple discriminators
2. Action(s)	Single, multiple acts	Multiple acts
3. Victim(s)	Single or multiple victims	Single or multiple victims
4. Time dimension	Episodic, sporadic	Continual, routinized
5. Overt/covert	Overt	Both
6. Size of discriminating group	One person, small group	Institutions, organizations
7. Intentional/ unintentional	Intentional (especially prejudice)	Both

Looking at the first three dimensions, we see that both approaches recognize the importance of a discriminator, an act having a differential and harmful effect, and a victim, although in each case the institutionalized discrimination approach tends to accent the larger scale. It is in regard to the last four dimensions that the differences between the two perspectives become more evident. The traditional perspective often tends to view discrimination as more individualistic, sporadic, and episodic than the institutional perspective, which accents the routine, continual character of discrimination. In addition, the traditional perspective tends to view discrimination as an overt, blatant, door-slamming phenomenon with the discriminators identifiable, while the institutional perspective we are accenting sees discrimination as being overt or covert, as obvious or as hidden from public view.

The last two dimensions seem particularly important, for they summarize and capture differences in emphasis between the two perspectives. The sixth dimension, size of discriminatory group, implies differences in the scale and degree of imbeddedness" of discrimination. While both approaches include recognition of variation in the number of discriminators, the traditional approach tends to focus on individuals or smaller groups of individuals, while the institutionalized discrimination approach emphasizes the plural, institutional, organizational character of the actions. The critical emphasis in the institutionalized discrimination approach is on the social patterning of discriminatory actions, especially their "imbeddedness" in large-scale bureaucratic organizations.

Clearly, we are speaking here of differences in *emphasis*. The distinction between different sizes of discriminatory groups applies to many, but by no means all, discussions of those holding to what we term the traditional perspective. For example, one important exception to this idealized scheme in regard to scale is the emphasis some holding to the traditional perspective have placed on legalized (and thus institutionalized) patterns of racial segregation across large areas of the South.

Moreover, related to the scale of the discriminatory group is a different view of the sources of the standards affecting discriminatory behavior. A traditional view highlights the importance of prejudiced personalities generated by faulty socialization at home or in peer groups, while the institutional perspective suggests that the beliefs guiding discriminatory behavior are "normal" and can come not only from informal group sources but also from secondary group sources such as organizational rules and regulations. In addition, in terms of the critical last dimension, the traditional perspective views discrimination in terms of intent, typically as applied prejudice; or intent to harm lies behind the actions. From the institutional discrimination perspective discrimination can be viewed either as intentional, involving a conscious intent to harm, or unintentional, involving a real lack of awareness of the discriminatory effects.

Scale

The last two dimensions in the above tabulation (Table 1) can be seen as encompassing most of the others and deserve a broader discussion, one not tied to distinctions between traditional and institutional discrimination models. Thus discriminatory actions can vary in their degree of social *imbeddedness,* a term that refers essentially to the organizational environment of actions, to the size and complexity of the groups carrying out the discriminatory practices. The size can vary from individual action on one's own to very large numbers of individuals engaged in routine practices in a large organization such as the personnel division of a corporation. Individual and small-group actions may not be imbedded in large organizations, but rather in small-scale family or friendship groups; in some cases such actions may not be immediately tied into a normative context, as in the action of an isolated individual. Discrimination in the larger-scale setting often involves sets of interrelated actions prescribed by well-institutionalized organization rules. Both actions and organizational regulations or policies directing actions can be taken as examples of institutionalized discrimination.

In popular usage, the word *bureaucracy* often conjures up negative images of mountains of red tape, paperwork, inefficiency, and suppression of individuality. But modern bureaucracy is much more than this. Its essential features include specific positions and roles and a clear division of labor, a hierarchy of positions with increasing control as one moves up, sets of rules or norms defining the roles and their attached duties, employment on the basis of "merit," and the organization of activities in a way that is presumably more systematic and rationalized than other alternatives.[2] While all bureaucracies vary from this ideal description, in general terms it seems accurate. Organizations have formal norms enshrined in written documents, including their public statements and internal memoranda, as well as informal norms remaining in an unwritten state. Where do these goals and norms come from? In many cases the individuals who founded the organizations shaped the initial goals and norms; subsequent occupants of the roles in the organizations may have modified the original norms. Norms can range from those dictating discriminatory treatment of minorities and women, to those spelling out the goals of the organization, to those formal and informal rules establishing authority relations in the organization. People therein can say that the rules dictate this, the regulations prohibit that. Rules in large-scale organizations can block, restrict, and limit the efforts and mobility of individuals.[3]

Within large-scale organizations *informal* operations exist in intimate relationship with the formal rules. Some formal, written rules can be violated by powerful figures in an organization; strict "merit" criteria for hiring are manipulated by those "in the know" in every bureaucracy, simply because those in powerful positions— usually white males—can bend the rules. Thus an important caveat should be entered here. Many analysts of bureaucracies write as though individuals in organizations were passive robots concerned only with conforming and securing an economic payoff for themselves. But although most people in organizations do conform to the rules, formal and informal, most of the time, individuals in organizations can be active as well as passive. Some prefer excitement and challenge to higher salaries; and some can and do play a role in changing the rules and regulations in the organizational environment.

Note too that whatever the scale of the organizational context all discrimination involves individual actors. The "bottom line" in all types of discrimination is someone actually doing something to someone else. However impersonal an action may appear—as in a firm's letter to a potential employee reporting the unfavorable results of a personnel test—some person administered the test, some person scored it, and some person wrote the rejection letter. One must be careful to avoid the reification fallacy in assessing organizational practices. Large corporations and bureaucracies *do not act* except in some metaphorical sense; the people in them do act, even though they may be routinely carrying out required regulations inherited from some dusty past. While large bureaucracies may not act, smaller groups can sometimes act. Loose groups of dominant-group members may jointly create new norms and jointly act to carry them out, whether they be in large organizations or rebel groups acting in defiance of their environments. For nearly a century southern blacks found out just how lynch mobs could act. But even here the practices, however much they may have been spurred on by new beliefs generated in the heat of passion, were carried out jointly by individuals. In this critical sense, all acts of discrimination, even those routine, institutionalized practices carried out by a large number of employees in bureaucracies, are personalized. Having noted the importance of individuals, however, let us also underscore the point that the critically important organizational environment can add *legitimacy* to discriminatory actions which individuals might not otherwise engage in or can sometimes provide an organizational "screen" which enables individual discriminators to hide their actions.

Intent and Lack of Intent

Where does the notion of prejudice fit into a discussion of behavior and of group contexts? The problem here is that the usual definition of *prejudice* as an attitude has no spelled-out action component. What we have termed the traditional view of prejudice➡️ discrimination often omits a systematic discussion of how a biased, stereotyped, or hostile view of an outgroup gets translated into actual behavior. Prejudiced or bigoted attitudes about the inferior qualities of the outgroup can certainly be related to treatment of an outgroup, but it may be that such attitudes are, as it were, put through a personality screen of other intent-to-harm beliefs or obedience norms more intimately linked to actual behavior. Then it may be more meaningful to speak of actions as intentionally discriminatory, in that the individual(s) involved intended to bring harm to the victims.

Individual actions are frequently guided by norms in the community or organizational context. *Norms* are rules or standards of expectation about behavior. How do these norms, these expectations about behavior, get translated into individual actions? By the internalization of norms, by the acceptance of the standards pressed by others as guides for one's own action. From one perspective this internalization is part of the socialization process in which the norms of the family or of small peer groups are handed down. Prejudices are learned from these others. As we have previously noted, more sophisticated analysts have recognized the importance of the prejudices of others in shaping actions even on the part of an unprejudiced individual.

In recent years a few analysts have underscored the further point that the intent to harm (or to differentiate) lying behind discriminatory acts may have no relation to prejudice, but rather can be tied to protection of one's own political and economic interests. This is particularly relevant to institutionalized discrimination, since the conscious intent behind the patterns of discrimination there often has less to do with hostility toward minorities than with protecting the privileges of the white (or white male) group.

This leads to the further point that the internalization of norms and beliefs can come in large-scale social contexts, in large organizations as well as in smaller social groups. The norms of bureaucracies also become guides for individual behavior. Conformity to relevant norms, be they those of one's family or one's boss, is the critical feature. Fear of punishment and desire for rewards—physical, psychological, or monetary—usually channel the conforming process.

We will add a word here on *congruence,* the extent to which an individual's or a group of individuals' actions are in accord with the expectations or standards in a specific community or organizational context, such as a local white community. In one situation the implementation of the norms learned from the relevant social environment is routine for an individual. Yet in another case departure from the norms of that relevant social environment may be reflected in a given individual's actions. We can have conformity to the norms of the social context or departure from the norms in the social context. In the latter case there is typically a situation of normative conflict. A small group of white Ku Klux Klan members may bomb several homes of black community leaders, following the informal beliefs of their small group about what ought to be done, even though the majority of whites in that local community hold to norms abhorring violence. There is a question as to what is the reference group for a given individual's actions. The internalization-of-norms process can be short-circuited so that individuals reject certain expectations in their relevant social contexts. This sort of deviation usually occurs because of acceptance of the norms of yet another social context; such deviation probably is much less often the result of a uniquely individual psychopathic condition than of tuning into the expectations of another social group. Some persons simply are listening to the beat of a different group of drummers.

While intent to harm (or to differentiate) can be viewed more broadly than the traditional perspective suggests, even this does not go far enough in reconceptualizing discrimination. We must also seriously consider the possibility that much contemporary discrimination—defined as practices which have a differential and harmful effect on minorities or women—is not motivated by an intent to harm the victims. Here the idea is that acts having a harmful effect may have that effect because of their linkage to intent-to-harm practices in other areas or in the past. Unintentional discrimination can be extensive in a modern society.

Scale × Intent

The two variables of scale and intent can, for the sake of argument, be cross-tabulated as in Figure 1.

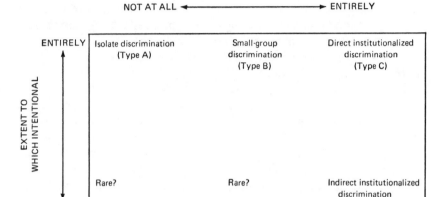

EXTENT OF IMBEDDEDNESS IN LARGER ORGANIZATIONS

NOT AT ALL ◄───────────────► ENTIRELY

Isolate discrimination (Type A)	Small-group discrimination (Type B)	Direct institutionalized discrimination (Type C)
Rare?	Rare?	Indirect institutionalized discrimination (Type D)

ENTIRELY

NOT AT ALL

EXTENT TO WHICH INTENTIONAL

Figure 1 Types of discriminatory behavior.

It seems to us that development of a typology of discrimination is a useful step in moving toward a more adequate theory of discrimination. Four important types of discrimination are indicated in Figure 1, what we will term isolate discrimination (Type A), small-group discrimination (Type B), direct institutionalized discrimination (Type C), and indirect institutionalized discrimination (Type D). Before defining and examining each of these types, we should note three points. First, the two types indicated by "rare" in the chart can probably be subsumed under the indirect discrimination rubric, since practices having an unintentionally harmful effect and carried out by individuals and smaller-scale groups on a repetitive basis seem to us to be typically linked to the norms and environments of larger-scale organizations. Because of their apparent rarity we will sidestep a further analysis of this issue, although further thought along these lines may be fruitful. Secondly, these four named types are abstract categories which only *roughly* correspond to examples in the real world. The types interact and overlap in real-life situations. Thirdly, a few other important dimensions of discrimination seem to be correlated with these dimensions. For example, the variable of time (episodic to routine) tends to be correlated with the degree of imbeddedness, with Types A and B often toward the episodic end of that continuum and Types C and D often toward the continual end. The types of discrimination also vary on a source-of-norms variable, with family and peer groups appearing most important in the case of Types A and B and the norms of large-scale organizations becoming more important in the case of Types C and D.

Some Basic Types

Let us now look at our working definitions of each type and illustrate them with some concrete examples.

1. The Type A category, *isolate discrimination*, refers to intentionally injurious action taken by an individual against members of subordinate groups—minorities and women—without being immediately imbedded in a large-scale organizational context. An example of this type of discrimination is a white male police officer who implements his antiblack hostility by beating black prisoners at every opportunity, even though police department regulations specifically prohibit such actions. (If the majority of officers in that department behaved in this fashion, these beatings would no longer fall in this category, for they would be imbedded in the informal normative consensus of a large-scale organization.) Another example would be the male personnel officer in an industrial firm who expresses his personal prejudice against women by defying his peer group's expectations and his company's personnel regulations by repeatedly hiring less-qualified men over better-qualified women. Type A covers prejudice-motivated as well as other types of intent-to-harm-motivated discrimination. Note too that isolate discrimination can include both flamboyant acts of discrimination as well as less visible acts, and that the intensity of the intent-to-harm feelings behind the acts can vary from white-hot, irrational bigotry to cooler feelings of protecting one's self-interest. The term *isolate* should *not* be taken to

mean that Type A discrimination is not common in the United States, for it is indeed commonplace; rather, the term is used to indicate an individual's action taken without the immediate support of norms in a large-scale organizational context.

2. The Type B category, *small-group discrimination,* refers to intentionally injurious actions taken by a small group of individuals acting against members of subordinate groups without the support of the norms prevailing in a larger organizational or community context. This is a somewhat larger-scale version of Type A. The singling out for racially motivated bombings of several black churches in a southern city or of the homes of a few black families in a northern city by small Ku Klux Klan–type groups are examples of this type. Thousands of lynchings of black men in the recent and distant past are also examples. The assumption here is that in many cases of small-group discrimination the majority in the larger organization or community do not support such action. Historically, small-group discrimination has posed a serious threat to the lives and property of minorities, for it has periodically taken the form of violence. Where such practices attain the level of majority support, they fall into the Type C category below. Also included under this type are small-scale conspiracies by male personnel officers to subvert company regulations requiring promotion on a merit basis, simply because the disliked persons are women or minority employees. As in the Type A case, acts of discrimination here can vary from the flamboyant to the less visible, and the intensity of the motivation can range from white-hot to cool.

3. The Type C category, *direct institutionalized discrimination,* refers to organizationally-prescribed or community-prescribed actions which have an intentionally differential and negative impact on members of subordinate groups. Typically these actions are not carried out on an episodic or sporadic basis, but continually or routinely by a large number of individuals guided by the rules of a large-scale organization. With Type C we come to the institutionalization and bureaucratization of discrimination. Examples of this type include the legally required or informally prescribed practices resulting in the segregation of minority persons in inferior facilities in such areas as public schools and public accommodations in the South and in the North. The original and present intention of the formal

regulations requiring such practices is to differentiate and subordinate, to maintain what some call internal colonialism. Today this direct institutionalized discrimination can be shaped by informal, unwritten rules as well as by more formal laws; both types of rules have often been imbedded in a bureaucratic system. Additional examples would include the legal regulations and informal norms, still very much alive, guiding those real estate practices that result in segregated housing patterns for minorities. Similar practices have made much housing inaccessible to single white women. The patterns of practices can be imbedded in larger-scale organizations such as public school systems, private bus lines, and real estate networks; and the norms guiding patterned discrimination can also be institutionalized in the form of pervasive local community norms about what is appropriate treatment for minorities or women. Examples here include such practices in southern communities as requiring all black persons to enter by the back door.

These discriminatory actions can be blatant, door-slamming actions or subtle and covert practices. The motivation for such discrimination can also vary. Some such practices are creatures of prejudice and intolerance, while others reflect economic or political self-interest. We will, in the chapters which follow, see examples of blatant, door-slamming and covert discrimination. Moreover, in acting upon norms requiring discriminatory practices, some individuals may enjoy expressing their own prejudices, while unprejudiced individuals may regret their actions. This is not to say that individuals cannot or should not be held accountable for their actions. Rather, the point is that organizational or community sanctions against non-conforming members who refuse to discriminate can often be overwhelming. Direct institutionalized discrimination requires only substantial, not unanimous, support for its persistence.

4. The Type D category, *indirect institutionalized discrimination*, refers to practices having a negative and differential impact on minorities and women even though the organizationally prescribed or community-prescribed norms or regulations guiding those actions were established, and are carried out, with no prejudice or no intent to harm lying immediately behind them. On their face and in their intent, the norms and resulting practices appear fair or at least neutral. One can perhaps distinguish two forms of indirect institution-

alized discrimination: (1) side-effect discrimination and (2) past-in-present discrimination.

Side-effect discrimination refers to practices in one institutional (organizational) area which have a negative impact usually because they are linked to direct discriminatory practices in another institutional (organizational) area. Intentional discrimination by persons in one sphere can result in unintentional discrimination by those in another sphere, because most societal spheres (the economy, the polity, etc.) are intimately linked to one another. Discrimination has an inter-institutional character.

For example, direct institutionalized discrimination in the education and training of minorities or women often handicaps them when they attempt to compete with white males for jobs in the employment sphere, since hiring and promotion standards in the employment sphere often incorporate educational requirements. Such education credential requirements often have a negative impact, yet they were frequently not established as expressions of prejudice or intent to have a negative impact. A number of the usual substitutes for ability used by employers as criteria to screen out potential employees can often be seen as examples of side-effect discrimination. It is also possible for indirect discrimination in one area (e.g., in employment) to shape indirect discrimination in yet another area (e.g., in medical assistance).

Past-in-present discrimination refers to apparently neutral practices in an institutional (organizational) area which systematically reflect or perpetuate the effects of intentional discriminatory practices in the past in that same institutional (organizational) area. One kind of past-in-present discrimination involves organizational penalizing of women or minorities in the present because they lack some ability or qualification intentionally denied them in the past. One can think here in terms of specific organizations or of sets of organizational sectors. For example, many minority persons and women have suffered in recent years because of established seniority or tenure practices, practices which usually were established with no prejudice or intent to harm or differentiate behind them. Since businesses or plants were intentionally segregated in the past, however, members of subordinate groups could not accumulate the experience or tenure necessary for weathering recessions.

A second kind of past-in-present discrimination has a negative impact not because minorities or women lack some ability or skill denied them in the past, but because current rules and practices reflect the physical characteristics possessed by those dominant group members who always have in the past routinely filled the positions in an organization. This results in a built-in physical or appearance bias which might not have been there if early, nondiscriminatory access has been provided to minorities or women. An example may make this clearer: the height and weight requirements for positions in police or fire departments, positions traditionally filled by white males. Such requirements screen out disproportionate numbers of women and of certain non-European minorities, such as Mexican Americans and Asian Americans. Various screening regulations of business organizations which assume that workers must have the physical traits most characteristic of white males come under this category.

Note that in these examples of unintentional discrimination imbedded in organizations the criteria guiding the practices may be functionally relevant to the practices—for example, the ability to read and write might be necessary for a given type of job. As we will show later, the criteria *assumed* to be functionally relevant are often poor substitutes for ability and competence. But leaving this issue aside for the moment, it is demonstrable that some screening criteria are relevant to job performance. Still, from the viewpoint adopted here, the implementation of such normative criteria can have a systematically negative and differential effect on minorities and women. They can be discriminatory, even though unintentionally so.

The Interaction of Types

We have just seen how Type D discrimination is closely tied to Type C discrimination and, to some extent, to Types A and B. For the sake of argument, the linkages might be diagrammed as in Figure 2. All four types are interrelated, but the main thrust is from Types A, B, and C to Type D. We would have to make this diagram three-dimensional and put feedback loops into it to suggest the true

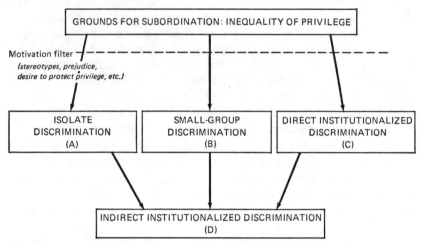

Figure 2

complexity of the relations here. We can go beyond this simple way of viewing interaction by noting (1) the overlap of discrimination which can occur in a given setting, (2) the complex web of discrimination in this society, and (3) the ways in which the character of the same discriminatory behavior can change.

First, various combinations of the types of discrimination can coexist in a given organizational or community setting. It is quite possible for minorities or women to suffer from regulations, both those intended to have a harmful effect and those not so intended, as well as to suffer from the flamboyant acts of prejudiced individuals who focus their hostility on minority or female targets within their reach even though those actions are not guided by the immediate organizational context. Moreover, a given action, such as turning away a minority applicant because of company regulations, might be carried out more vigorously, and thus more oppressively, by a bigot. The intensity of the motivation can affect the harm inflicted in the implementation of organizational or community norms.

Secondly, the interactive character of discriminatory mechanisms can be seen in another way. We have already noted the extensive

34

shaping effect of direct discrimination on indirect discrimination. But, particularly in recent years, the situation has become more complex. It is also important to note the way in which mechanisms typically exemplifying indirect discrimination can be used intentionally by more sophisticated discriminators. In recent years a few discriminators, realizing that the traditional mechanisms of direct oppression are now illegal, have sometimes resorted to the use of mechanisms which are not intentionally subordinating in most other contexts. Blumrosen notes, for example, that recently in the South some business organizations instituted screening tests, specifically with the intent of excluding minority applicants, at the same time that they removed formal discriminatory barriers.[4] In a similar fashion, it is likely that some organizations have instituted new requirements, with regard to height or hours worked, which discourage the employment of women.

Thirdly, from a broader, total-society point of view, sets of patterns of discrimination interlocking several political, economic, and social organizations might be termed "systemic discrimination" or a "web of discrimination." For a given victim, group oppression can be interlocking and cumulative, involving many institutional sectors. Several decades ago Myrdal, analyzing white prejudice and blatant, legal discrimination in the Deep South, touched on the interlocking character of white actions, a phenomenon he termed the "principle of cumulation."[5] More recently, the idea of cumulative impact lies behind the pioneering analysis of institutional racism by Carmichael and Hamilton. They underscore the cumulative impact of institutionalized racism in the areas of food, housing, and medicine on the higher death rate of black children in the South.[6] Baron has discussed similar issues using the phrase the "web of racism." Focusing on the urban scene, he notes that discrimination in the basic sectors of housing, employment, and education are intricately interrelated and mutually reinforcing.[7] No one organizational complex stands alone, and the interlocking phenomenon insures that the negative impact of the web of racism or sexism is much greater than it would be if discrimination were limited to one organizational sector. The cumulative and systemic character of subordination warrants the term *internal colonialism.*

The Cultural Underpinning of Discrimination

One important issue not explicitly dealt with so far is the broader cultural context within which discrimination occurs. Social psychologist James Jones has suggested that the racial bias in the North American cultural context can be termed "cultural racism," by which he means those basic cultural "values, traditions, and assumptions upon which institutions are formed and within which individuals are socialized to maturity."[8] One can expand this idea to include cultural sexism. Since the term *culture* usually has a very broad meaning, the "total of the mental and physical attainments of a people," it is difficult to distinguish just where cultural racism and sexism begin and institutionalized racism and sexism leave off. More specifically, Jones pays particular attention in his own analysis to white European-American (Anglo-Saxon) dominance in shaping fundamental and original American values and arrangements—such as law, language, and religion—in the formative historical period, a dominance which continues in these and other areas. At base, all organizations and communities embody these fundamental values and transmit them to individuals. Such values are accompanied by an ethnocentrism in which other cultural or subcultural traditions, such as that of Africa, are devalued.[9] The intensity of the cultural problem is particularly clear in the cases of non-European minorities, such as Chicanos and Native Americans, whose distinctive cultural traditions and languages have been the target of practices intentionally designed to suppress them.

Other empirical studies have touched on this broader cultural dimension. In his study of institutional racism in social work organizations Sanders found respondents who noted the serious bias in the underlying American value system. According to minority respondents the social work organizations were not recognizing the dignity of minority people, but were implementing rigorously the "middle-class, white way."[10] Using different terminology, Barndt has probed this same issue in terms of "foundational assumptions." While he sees foundational assumptions as the foundation level of institutional racism, he has in mind the guiding white middle-class values which provide the basis for operations in all institutional areas.[11] The main example he gives of these foundational assumptions is in connection

with police departments and minority communities; police organizations are grounded in a basic white world view which is oriented,
consciously and unconsciously, toward preserving the status quo.

There is a critical issue here which goes beyond the immediate
practices of discrimination aimed at subordinate groups—the
dominance of basic Anglo-Saxon or white middle-class values in the
basic institutions of the society. Non-European minorities, and to a
lesser extent white women, find themselves in organizational settings
where not only various types of discrimination are prevalent but
the deep underpinning of that discrimination lies in the underlying
white (male) cultural perspective. Needed today is a systematic
analysis of the masculine bias, the cultural sexism, in the basic
values of this society. Some analysts have pointed up the sometimes
subtle patriarchal bias in basic foundational assumptions, but no
one has yet developed the concept of "cultural sexism" even as far
as Jones and others have taken the concept "cultural racism." Additional analytical work is obviously needed on this "fuzzy" issue,
work which should flesh out the broader cultural context within
which the various types of discrimination operate.

A Note on Comparing Racism and Sexism:
Similarities and Differences

Why are we treating racial discrimination and sex discrimination within the same framework? Although some may see this as
natural, we need to be more explicit on this point here. There are
some who would argue, with some legitimacy, that the contemporary
situation of white women in the United States is not nearly so bad
as that of nonwhites, that the two groups should be treated in separate
analyses. From this perspective the double burden of white women,
the family and market colonialism, is partially offset by the closeness many of these women enjoy to white male power. For example,
in the labor force, until quite recently, there were significant differences in occupation and income between white and nonwhite
women, with an advantage for white women. Moreover, a typical
married white woman who encounters one type of discriminatory
hurdle may have greater economic resources than a nonwhite woman,

because of her husband's higher-income background, to move on up in her job or career. In addition, white males do not force white females to live in segregated neighborhoods, nor do they resist dating or marrying white females—three of the intimate types of social relations whites generally refuse to have with nonwhites. And many (married) white women do gain some social prestige from their ties to white men, a social elevator to which nonwhites far less frequently have access.[12] The separateness of nonwhite Americans makes it easier to practice some types of discrimination on them than on white women. Nonwhites spatially isolated in a separate community are easier to oppress than are wives in men's homes.

While there is substantial truth to these arguments, the differences between nonwhites, men and women, and white women can be exaggerated.* If one focuses on them as groups, as social categories, then both general and specific similarities appear. Take the segregation issue. While white women are usually not physically segregated in separate neighborhoods like other colonized peoples, there are even here some similarities. Female homosexuals and prostitutes are physically segregated; and women who work often find themselves physically segregated from male workers, such as secretaries in different rooms. Segregation of work and leisure-time activities—women at home and men at the factory or office, or women in women's groups and men "with the boys,"—also suggests a different picture. A careful time and spatial study of men's and women's activities might find more aspects of physical colonization, at least by day, than one might initially expect. Clearly, however, the frequently temporal colonization is *by no means* as complete as the physical colonization of nonwhite Americans into their more ghettoized worlds.

One can also exaggerate the closeness of white women to the centers of power in the United States. One problem is the character of that closeness. As Hacker has noted, marriage can mean nothing more than physical intimacy and a division of labor; it need not entail

*One must also keep in mind that perhaps 20 percent of all women in the United States are nonwhite. They are in a kind of "double jeopardy."

equality of power or even communication.[13] Marriage, dating, and physically living together can easily be, and often are, coupled with subordination of the female, ranging from severe to mild in degree. Internal colonization analysts might carry this even further. Although their land is not taken, the labor of women is appropriated by men in that women become unpaid house slaves freeing men from household and childrearing work. Their lives and fortunes often become dependent upon the male of the species. Black slaves serving in the slaveowner's house typically had more privileges than field slaves, but they were part of a colonial system nonetheless. White women may on the average enjoy more privileges than nonwhites, but as a group they are "house slaves" nonetheless. Women, like slaves, often come to accept their position as a means of survival. A typical paternalistic system—literally, one might note—characterizes the relations of white men and white women. Men rationalize the position of their spouses as the weaker group, appropriate their labor at no or low pay, but also provide for the material needs of their spouses. And in the job market the economic rewards of both single and married women signal sex subordination. The dominant individualistic perspective of the United States forestalls the collective organization of an oppressed group, be it female or minority. White males have control of ideas as well as of wealth and power.

Conclusion

In the analysis which follows we will move away from these broad differences and similarities to more specific issues. For example, we will examine such matters as employment and housing. It is true that in the past white women did much better in employment than nonwhite women. Yet job opportunities for white women were, and still are, sharply different from those for white males, with women heavily overrepresented in clerical, teaching, and nursing jobs. Here is an important difference in circumstances by race within the same sex. However, the recent job mobility of *nonwhite* women has brought them "up" only so far as the subordinate level of *white* women. Although the impact of discrimination clearly has been greater on nonwhite than white women, the mechanisms of discrimination often seem quite similar.

Our central focus in this book is on the effects and mechanisms of direct and indirect *institutionalized* discrimination, with a particularly heavy emphasis on the more neglected type—indirect institutionalized discrimination. Whether the mechanisms of discrimination operate differently for nonwhites and white women is an issue which should become clearer in the analysis which follows. In this volume we do not presume to equate the two groups; there is no desire here of equating their situations across the board. Yet with numerous other analysts we here regard the problems of discrimination faced by nonwhites and by white women as sufficiently similar to warrant a comparative analysis. Insight into the discrimination faced by one group frequently, if not usually, leads to insight into the discrimination faced by the other group.

1. Gordon Allport, *The Nature of Prejudice* (Doubleday Anchor Books, 1958), p. 7.

2. See Samuel Krislov, *Representative Bureaucracy* (Englewood Cliffs, N.J.: Prentice-Hall, 1974), pp. 25–27; Michel Crozier, *The Bureaucratic Phenomenon* (Chicago: University of Chicago Press, 1964), pp. 1–9.

3. Peter Blau, *Bureaucracy in Modern Society* (New York: Random House, 1956), pp. 28–29; Charles Perrow, *Complex Organizations* (Glenview, Ill.: Scott, Foresman, 1972), p. 32.

4. Alfred Blumrosen, *Black Employment and the Law* (Princeton: Princeton University Press), p. 32.

5. Gunnar Myrdal, *An American Dilemma* (New York: McGraw-Hill Paperback, 1964), 1: 75–77.

6. Charles Hamilton and Stokeley Carmichael, *Black Power* (New York: Vintage Books, 1967), pp. 3–9.

7. Harold M. Baron, "The Web of Urban Racism," in *Institutional Racism in America*, edited by Louis L. Knowles and Kenneth Prewitt (Englewood Cliffs, N.J.: Prentice-Hall, 1969), pp. 143–44.

8. James M. Jones, *Prejudice and Racism* (Reading, Mass. Addison-Wesley, 1972), p. 116.

9. Ibid., pp. 148–59.

10. Quoted in Charles L. Sanders, *Black Professionals' Perceptions of Institutional Racism* (Fair Lawn, N.J.: R. E. Burdick, 1972), p. 68.

11. Joseph Barndt, *Liberating Our White Ghetto* (Minneapolis: Augsburg Publishing House, 1970), pp. 71–73.

12. Helen Mayer Hacker, "Women as a Minority Group," in *Woman in a Man-Made World,* edited by Nona Glazer and Helen Youngelson Waehrer (Chicago: Rand McNally, 1977), pp. 138–42.

13. Ibid.

Discrimination in the Economy: A Focus on Employment

chapter three

Until the mid- to late- 1960s overt, often blatant, direct discrimination in employment practices was the rule in many government agencies and private businesses. Employers routinely turned away women and minorities for many categories of jobs. With the protest movements and civil rights legislation of the mid-1960s came changes in the type of discrimination, with a decline in direct institutionalized discrimination of the most overt, door-slamming type and the appearance of subtle forms of direct discrimination and of indirect institutionalized discrimination, as well as an increase in isolate and small-group discrimination among those whites (especially males) resisting new pressures to change employment patterns. In this chapter we will focus primarily on the less blatant types of direct discrimination and on indirect discrimination, particularly in employment practices.

Before looking at discriminatory mechanisms, it will be useful to look at some broad demographic data on the probable effects of discrimination on employment and income patterns. Recent statistics on the employment of nonwhite minorities and white women in the United States highlight these effects. For example, from 1968 to 1973 women held about one-third of all federal government white-collar jobs, but their percent in higher-level white-collar positions (a rating of GS 13 or higher) stayed around 4 percent, growing slightly from 3.7 percent in 1968 to 4.5 percent in 1973.[1] In the 1972–1974 period minorities (black, Native American, Asian, Spanish-surnamed) comprised approximately 16–17 percent of the white-collar (GS) grades, but the proportion in higher-level grades was much lower. The proportion of minorities in Grade 13 was 5.0 percent in 1972 and 5.8 percent in 1974; the proportions in the highest grade (GS 18) were only 3.1 percent in 1972 and 3.6 percent in 1974. The proportions of blacks in higher grades reflected even greater underrepresentation.[2] Higher-level minority employees, moreover, have been particularly concentrated in certain civil rights bureaucracies such as the U.S. Commission on Civil Rights and the Equal Employment Opportunity Commission (EEOC) and in such agencies and departments as the Office of Economic Opportunity and the Department of Housing and Urban Development. In addition, a 1973 EEOC survey of state and local government employees also found blacks to be lower paid on the average than whites (medians of $7,361 versus $8,844) and white women to be lower than white men (medians of $7,069 versus $9,873). Occupational distributions showed blacks to be disproportionately and heavily concentrated in lower-paying blue-collar and paraprofessional jobs and women to be concentrated in clerical and paraprofessional jobs in state and local governments.[3]

The probable effects of discrimination can also be seen in business and industry. According to government reports employment patterns in 1966 showed that 85 percent of black males in private industry were in service jobs and unskilled or semiskilled blue-collar work; in 1973 the proportion was still high, 73 percent. The comparable white male figures were 39 percent in 1966 and 35 percent in 1973, with most in the higher-level jobs in these categories. For black women the proportions in these lower-paying blue-collar positions was also high, with a figure of 69 percent in 1966 and 58 percent in 1973, compared to 37 percent and 33 percent in the same years for white females. Many black women have moved into lower-paying white-collar work (e.g., as secretaries) since the 1960s. These more recent figures show both improvements for blacks and persisting concentration, even in the peak year of 1973, in lower-paying positions. (This position tends to be similar for other nonwhite minorities, with the exception of some Asian groups.) Over this same period, 1966 to 1973, the proportion of white women in lower-paying blue-collar positions and in lower-paying white-collar categories (clerical and sales) in the private sector went from 87 to 83 percent.[4]

Clearly, some modest employment gains were made by women and minorities in the late 1960s and early 1970s, but the 1974–1975 recession slowed that progress or, in some cases, rolled it back. In December 1976 the unemployment rate of minority workers was still twice that of white workers, following the historical pattern. By 1977 it was the highest it had been for decades. The unemployment figures for adult women remained higher than for adult men. The occupational gap continued to exist; in 1976 minorities and women "remained more likely to hold relatively low-paying, low-skilled jobs, and their gains in the expanding white-collar job category remained generally limited to clerical rather than managerial and administrative positions."[5] The income gap remained substantial in 1976, with median minority family income still only 62 percent of that of white families. And in 1975 women working full time had median incomes only 58 percent of that of men working full time, a figure down from 60 percent in 1965.[6] Women and minority persons are also much more likely than white males to have part-time rather than full-time employment and to be employed less than the full year.[7]

Such data showing minorities and women in the lower-paying, lower-status jobs in the United States confirm one's suspicions about continuing discrimination.* But showing the probable effects of discrimination is not sufficient. We also need to understand the dynamics of discriminatory mechanisms underlying these effects. Discrimination in employment may be seen in (1) recruitment and

---

*The issue of other factors entering into occupational and income differences between whites and nonwhites, or between men and women, will not be addressed here. Our basic assumption here is that discrimination is a major, if not the major, reason for these differences. Productivity explanations have been examined in the literature and found to be of little utility, since in most cases it is difficult to find large numbers of dominant and subordinate persons doing the same jobs under the same conditions.

soliciting practices; (2) employment screening practices; (3) tracking systems; (4) promotion practices; (5) terms and conditions of employment; and (6) layoff, discharge, and seniority practices. In the discussion which follows the discriminatory barriers to both women and minorities will be examined, although it should be noted that not all barriers affect each group to the same extent.

Recruitment Practices

A number of important discriminatory barriers face nonwhites and women in the recruitment aspect of employment. Take, for example, job advertising. Although job advertising with explicit racial designations has generally disappeared in the period since the 1960s, media advertising still reflects in subtle and not-so-subtle ways the segregation of the job markets. Selectively placing ads for unskilled or semiskilled jobs (only) in the minority press is one example of this phenomenon. The persistence of sex-segregated job advertising into the 1970s—a format with columns of female jobs and columns of male jobs—has resulted in a number of court cases in which judges have equivocated on the illegality of this ingrained practice because of ostensible conflict with the First Amendment's guarantee of freedom of the press were such a format to be prohibited. Whatever the legal status of such practices, they are clear-cut examples of intentional institutionalized discrimination.[8] The negative impact of such recruiting practices has been documented. One study clearly showed that sex-segregated ads discouraged female applicants from inquiring about "male jobs." And while many newspapers have desegregated their ads in recent years, sometimes even the language used ("girl Friday") still reflects job market segregation.[9]

An important example of indirect institutionalized discrimination can be seen in many word-of-mouth recruitment networks used by employers with a predominantly or exclusively white (male) employee population. Such recruitment practices are at least partly shaped by direct discrimination in housing and by past discrimination in employment and thus exemplify both side-effect and past-in-present indirect discrimination. For example, suburbanization of many industries and retail trade operations has had a sharp effect on minority employment. With new jobs opening up in the suburbs, far away from most minority housing areas, it becomes increasingly difficult for minority persons to enter the appropriate word-of-mouth recruitment networks. Using present white (male) employees for new referrals perpetuates the existing makeup of the labor force because potential minority or female employees will be outside the major web of recruitment information. Even without prejudice or intent to discriminate underlying them, such conventional recruitment practices can have an exclusionary effect, thus severely limiting employment opportunities.

Traditionally, word-of-mouth recruiting has served a positive function for employers, providing inexpensive advertising; indeed, it is probably the most widely used method of recruitment in most areas of employment. Many studies have found that from 60 to 90 percent of blue-collar workers found their jobs through informal social networks of friends or relatives. Studies of white-collar workers have found a similar pattern. Granovetter concluded from his study of professional, technical, and managerial workers that these higher-level jobs were obtained more often through the use of personal networks than through any other method.[10] Bloom and his associates found heavy reliance on employee friendship and kinship networks for recruiting in retail trade industries, including drug stores, supermarkets, and department stores.[11]

The W. T. Grant Company's reliance on word-of-mouth recruitment networks as its primary method for obtaining over-the-road drivers resulted in an all-white work force in this job category in one community that was 25 percent black.[12] Preference given to friends and relatives of present (white) employees in the Akron, Ohio, police department resulted in a police force that was only 3 percent black in a city with a 17.5 percent black population.[13] In an examination of the relative employment rates of blacks and whites in white-collar positions in major urban firms in fifteen cities, Eidson found that the best predictor of the rate at which blacks applied and were hired for white-collar positions was the rate at which blacks were currently employed. This factor was found to be more important even than the attitudes of personnel officers. Eidson concluded that a "reasonable inference is that the distribution of white collar jobs to Negroes depends heavily upon informal networks of information, radiating outward from persons currently employed in upper rank slots."[14] In a general review of sex discrimination, Chaftez underscored the widespread presence of a "protégé" system for higher-status, higher-income jobs, particularly in the professions. "Top positions in many fields are filled by an informal process in which the potential employer calls around to his (male) friends and asks whom they recommend."[15] The use of such informal recruitment networks is not limited to industrial or business employment. Similar "old boy" recruitment networks can also be found in education; college departments commonly solicit candidates for professional positions through feeder channels built up between (typically white male) professors.[16]

In many business and industrial situations reliance on informal recruitment networks is coupled with the practice of relying on local-area recruitment or "walk-ins." When a company located in a predominantly white community depends on walk-ins from the local area, it often ends up with a predominantly white work force. The recent trend in suburbanization of business operations has accentuated this source of the side-effect type of indirect discrimination, since residential segregation has changed little in recent years, with minority families still largely confined to central cities or segregated suburbs. Thus a 1973 Civil Rights Commission study of housing found that "despite a variety of laws against job discrimination, lack of access to housing in close proximity to available jobs is an effective barrier to equal employment."[17] Interestingly, some business and industrial firms near minority areas do not rely (perhaps intentionally) on walk-ins; or they may vary their position on walk-ins depending on the race of the applicant. For example, one study suggests that employers in areas with minority walk-in applicants can discriminate against them by refusing to accept their applications, asserting that walk-in applications are "too much trouble" or "likely to get misplaced."[18]

The business practice of recruiting through government or private employment agencies, which often directly discriminate against women and minority persons, is an example of unintentional side-effect discrimination. Business recruitment practices which depend heavily on unions for supplying new employees can have a similarly negative impact. Formal and informal segregation in unions, including exclusive-membership unions and segregated referral systems, typically signals an entrenched form of direct institutionalized discrimination.[19] Some employers who might otherwise be receptive to minority or women employees are forced by contracts with skilled-worker unions to hire only white males who are referred by or are members of a discriminatory union. Mandatory use of this union system by an employer who has no intent to discriminate is an example of indirect discrimination, even though the employer may simply be the victim of the union's prescreening recruitment procedures. Race- and sex-segregated (formally and informally) union locals, which have persisted into the 1970s, reflect intentional discrimination. For example, a 1972 court case revealed that separate locals for waiters and waitresses maintained by the Hotel and Restaurant Employees and Bartenders International Union have resulted in discriminatory work assignments and pay for women.[20]

Some unions' influence on employers' hiring policies is informal; that of others is more formal and systematic. The unions with the most influence on hiring policies are referral unions, so-called because of the practice of referring their members directly to employers for hiring. The degree of control which referral unions have in a specific labor market depends on a number of factors. In general, the more workers a referral union can control, especially in a highly skilled trade, the more influence it can wield in hiring policies and wage negotiations. Referral unions operate in most of the best-paying industries, including the building trades, the transportation industry, and printing and publishing.[21] Discrimination there, thus, can have widespread spillover effects.

Attaining union membership can mean a sizeable increase in pay for minority and female workers. Data for 1970 show that minority men in unions earned 31 percent more than those not in unions. For minority women the differential was 19 percent; for white women, 8 percent. But even with the benefit of union membership, minority and female union members nationwide still earn less than white male union members. A 1976 study of discrimination in referral practices by the U.S. Commission on Civil Rights revealed that "in trades where minority membership is especially low, earnings are especially high."[22] The percentages of minorities and females in the highest-paid categories of referral unions are substantially below their percentages of all union members. In the early 1970s key unions such as electrical workers, iron workers, plumbers, asbestos workers, carpenters, and the like had very small proportions (1-3 percent) of black workers. Until quite recently virtually no women were members of these unions.[23] The obvious corollary of this finding is the fact that women and minorities are disproportionately overrepresented in unions representing less-skilled, lower-paying positions.

In order to maintain members' high wages and job security, unions seek to limit the number of "journeymen" entering a trade, a practice with an ostensibly legitimate goal, but one which has had discriminatory effects. Some unions admit members primarily through an apprenticeship program with age limits. This "fair-in-form" practice, however, continues to bar from membership an older minority or female "journeyman" who could not apply for apprenticeship at the beginning of his or her career because of past direct discrimination. A union's policy of intentional discrimination in the past may not have ended until many an applicant passed the rather young age limit for admission to the apprenticeship program. Female applicants are at a particular disadvantage because of age limitations, since many either (1) are not informed of apprenticeship programs in high school, as male students are; or (2) are less likely to enter military service, a primary source of information on apprenticeship and careers for young men; or (3) enter the labor force at a somewhat later age than young men because of childrearing duties.[24]

Other union admission policies present further obstacles to minority and female applicants. The same informal word-of-mouth and nepotistic policies which predominate in other areas of employment recruiting are common in bringing members into referral unions as well. For example, membership in the New York City area Newspaper and Mail Deliverers' Union was found to be open almost exclusively to the family and friends of union members. And this union was found to be "the exclusive bargaining agent for the collective bargaining unit which embraces all workers in the delivery departments of newspaper publishers and of publications distributors in the general vicinity of New York City. . . . Of 4200 current Union members, 99% are white."[25] Similarly, trade unions in the skilled construction trades have been described as "quite secretive, byzantine in some cases in the recruitment and selection processes." According to Dubinsky, few outside the close circles of acquaintances hear about apprenticeship openings.[26]

Frequently used criteria for admission into the building trades unions include "proof of experience or competence in the trade; passage of an examination; approval by the local membership, good moral character, and nomination or endorsement by present members."[27] These criteria allow a great deal of room for subjective, and intentionally discriminatory, decisions. The practice of requiring a new apprentice to be nominated or sponsored for union membership by an existing member has been invalidated in a few specific instances by the courts not only because of the subjective nature of this criterion, but because it limits the willingness of those previously discriminated against even to apply. A similar adverse effect on the willingness of minorities and women to apply has been seen in the discriminatory reputation of a union. A few courts have also held to be discriminatory the oral interview for union membership and the subjective evaluation of the quality of past experience in the trade.[28] Since the most frequent source of past experience in a trade is working for a friend or relative already in the trade, even this criterion for admission to apprenticeship can be viewed as an example of indirect discrimination.

In recent years pressure has been placed on unions to change in the direction of bringing in more women and minorities. Some have grown optimistic as the number of federal court cases has grown. Yet the patterns of discrimination linger on. For example, in spite of a great deal of litigation over discrimination charges in the construction industry and some court victories ordering affirmative action plans,* direct discrimination remains. In a 1977 analysis of the construction industry Gould concludes that "despite the multitude of plans and programs, not a great deal has been done to alter the institutional rigidity which limits black access to construction jobs."[29] Increases in female and minority membership in many major building and trade unions were still low in the early- and mid-1970s.

Affirmative action plans spelled out by courts typically require more than passive nondiscrimination by employers found to be guilty of discrimination. They require active, affirmative plans to overcome the impact of discrimination, such as by developing new and more accessible recruitment networks or by setting specific hiring goals.

Screening Practices

Discrimination is particularly well institutionalized in conventional screening practices in both public and private employment. Prejudice and intent to discriminate still play a role in hiring standards and procedures, indicating the persistence of direct discrimination, particularly the more covert variants. At the same time, indirect discrimination built into credentials requirements and testing procedures plays a major role in screening minorities and women out of jobs.

Blatant, door-slamming discrimination against blacks and other minority males seems to have declined significantly since the 1950s, although into the 1970s court cases such as *Griggs* v. *Duke Power Co.* (1971) were still documenting the formally different hiring standards for blacks and whites.[30] Today, however, much intentional discrimination seems to be built into the informal norms, the unwritten rules, of personnel and hiring procedures. Subtle manipulation of standards has occurred. In a number of areas where minorities have never been hired before, qualifications have been increased, with *leniency* in the hiring process itself practiced only in the case of white applicants. One study found that minority truck drivers were turned down even though they had greater experience than whites who were hired. Another study suggested that banks were interested in hiring only "superqualified" minority group members, rejecting ordinary minority applicants on a variety of apparently plausible grounds.[31]

Employment interviews have become particularly important as part of the job screening process. One study of Bell System hiring data found that some of their companies eliminated 30–40 percent of job applicants by means of a screening interview.[32] Informal hiring standards applied in such interviews make possible direct institutionalized or isolate discrimination. Since screening criteria can be vague or subjective—such as an evaluator's impressions of "intelligence," "appearance," "self-confidence," "vigor," and so on—the evaluator's stereotyped notions about minorities ("They can't get to work on time," They are sloppy and lazy") may lead to rejection in the screening process simply because a nontraditional applicant does not conform to a middle-class image. In such cases, discrimination is intentional, guided by a widely accepted stereotyped image of minorities. Similar widely-accepted stereotyping can operate against women. Notions that "they lie about their age" or "have a high absenteeism rate" may lead to informal norms dictating the rejection of a woman who "doesn't look quite right."[33] Stereotyped views of a woman's family responsibilities have routinely disqualified women from employment in certain settings. For example, the Equal Employment Opportunity Commission found one employer guilty of sex-based discrimination in refusing to hire a woman on the grounds that her husband's long-term illness involved family responsibilities that would interfere with her job performance. In *Phillips* v. *Martin Marietta Corporation* (1971) the Supreme Court held to be discriminatory under the law employment restrictions against women with pre–school-age children; denial of employment to unwed mothers has likewise been ruled discriminatory.[34] The point here is that these women were differentially excluded because of employers' views of their family or marital responsibilities even though men with *similar* family or marital situations were hired. Such stereotypical attitudes are particularly likely to lead to subtle discriminatory actions when held by personnel interviewers in situations where the interview plays an important role in hiring.

Some businesses and industries have attempted to justify intentional discrimination in screening out nonwhite minorities as an alleged business necessity. Several recent studies have documented intentional discrimination in refusing to hire blacks as sales clerks because of the anticipated negative reactions of white customers. Such market concerns in the highly competitive retail trade industries can shape the intentionally discriminatory hiring and promotion practices of store managers. Bloom found employers in the department store, drug store, and supermarket industries reluctant to advance "too quickly in terms of employment of Negroes for fear of offending important segments of the buying public."[35] Bloom also found that fear of consumer attitudes has to some degree shaped discrimination in other industries as well, including the oil and automobile industries.

Women continue to be the victims of intentional discrimination in hiring in a variety of areas. For example, in the mid-1970s a number of studies found women employees reporting intentional discrimination and unequal opportunities in college and university departments.[36] In fact, by the late 1970s overt, blatant discrimination against women in employment may have become more common than against minority men because employers and unions are more acutely aware of the illegality of blatant race discrimination than of blatant sex discrimination. Most of the *recent* sex discrimination cases tried in federal courts have concerned overt discrimination, while most race discrimination cases have involved either indirect or covert direct discrimination. Babcock and her associates have argued that this is because employers have taken the prohibitions against racial and ethnic discrimination in civil rights laws more seriously. Ironically, the inclusion of the prohibition on sex discrimination in the 1964 Civil Rights Act was a ploy by Southern representatives in Congress to prevent its passage. For those male legislators, and for many male employers, prohibitions on sex discrimination were (and are) seen as a joke. In any event, Title VII of the 1964 Civil Rights Act permits exceptions to the prohibition on sex discrimination in cases where sex is a "bonafide occupational qualification." Employers, when challenged, have defended sex discrimination in these terms. Jobs like commercial representative and railroad telegrapher, for example, have been defended by at least one company as "male jobs," while airlines have defended their position that women are best qualified to serve as "stewardesses."[37] Stereotyped notions of female "liabilities" and male "virtues" underlie such patterns of direct discrimination, however informal and subtle they may be. Note that in the case of race discrimination employers cannot argue for exceptions on the basis of Title VII's "bonafide occupational qualification" section. "Whiteness," unlike "womanness," is simply not a *legally* permissible occupational qualification in any setting.

Indirect discrimination is also well institutionalized in conventional employment screening practices. Reliance on educational credentials and diplomas of various kinds in employment screening decisions is widespread among public and private employers. A number of analysts have noted the accelerating trend toward a "guild system" of credentials and diplomas in the United States.[38] If the routine use of a credential requirement in hiring has a differential and adverse effect on the employment opportunities of women or minority persons, and if the credential requirement is not used intentionally to differentiate by race or sex, this practice can be seen as an example of side-effect discrimination. Because of grossly inadequate and discriminatory ghetto school systems or blatant job discrimination against parents and consequent low family incomes, minority persons are less likely than whites to have many formal credentials required by employers. Direct discrimination against minorities in one area, as in education or training programs, can lead to indirect discrimination in another, as in employment testing. White females face somewhat similar problems, particularly at the post-primary educational levels.

More specifically, lack of a high school diploma, college degree, graduate degree, or similar educational "union card" has been a barrier to employment. Evidence of the negative impact of a high school diploma regulation has been presented in a number of important federal court cases. In *Griggs* v. *Duke Power Co.* (1971), a major employment decision, the Supreme Court examined the high school diploma criterion in screening job applicants. The Court found that the diploma requirement disqualified more black than white applicants and took the position that, whether or not such requirements were intentionally used to discriminate, they constituted unlawful discrimination if they had not been shown to predict successful job performance. The Court underscored the importance of examining employment practices that are "fair in form, but discriminatory in operation."* Several other federal court cases, including *U.S.* v. *Georgia Power Co.* (1973) and *Johnson* v. *Goodyear Tire and Rubber Company* (1974), have also presented data on the discriminatory effects of using a high school credential as a screening device.[39]

More recently, court decisions have vacillated on the question of whether the use of unvalidated credentials—credentials not shown to relate to job performance—is unlawful discrimination. Some courts have required substantial empirical validation, while others have allowed superficial validation. In *Payne* v. *Treveno Laboratories, Inc.* (1976) the federal district court in Mississippi held that a requirement that employees be able to read and write and add and subtract was unlawful discrimination when it could be shown to

---

*Although the position of a number of federal courts on the use of such credential requirements has been that their application can be discriminatory even if the differential and adverse consequences are not intentional, it should be noted that the courts do not regard the use of such screening devices as *unlawful* discrimination if they have been validated—that is, if they can be empirically related to job performance. From our theoretical perspective this "unlawfulness" qualification is unnecessary for such mechanisms to be regarded as examples of indirect institutionalized discrimination.

relate to job performance in only the most remote sense. In *Arnold v. Ballard* (1975), however, the requirement of a high school diploma or the equivalent General Educational Development certificate was allowed as "substantially job related and a valid requisite for employment as policeman" even though it resulted in the exclusion of a large percentage of black applicants.[40] From our perspective, such an exclusion can be viewed as (indirectly) discriminatory, whether or not the federal courts view it as unlawful.

Since the proportion of the population with a high school degree has grown dramatically in the last few decades, it is not surprising that an increased emphasis on college work and degrees has characterized personnel practices. A college degree is now sold as the "union card" for access to the material good life. The use of the college degree requirement was given a boost in the Depression of the 1930s when college experience was apparently used as an easy screening criterion for many employers faced with long lines of educated (white) applicants. Now the use of a college credential requirement is routine for many jobs, guided by the widespread but debatable assumption that such a screening device routinely produces more able, productive, or meritorious employees. In practice, in the past and in the present, college degrees have been available to only a limited segment of the population. The use of a college degree screening requirement for jobs or job-training programs often has a disproportionately negative effect on minority persons, since they are less likely because of educational and other direct discrimination to have had the opportunity to acquire a college degree and are thus more likely to be disqualified by such a requirement. In the case of women the situation is somewhat different, since they are more likely to be disqualified by the type of degree (e.g., education, home economics) which they have acquired, particularly in the case of screening for certain categories of technical positions. In such cases, indirect discrimination is felt particularly hard by those minority persons or women, with the ability to do certain jobs, who are denied either jobs or training opportunities because they lack the requisite college work.[41]

In a similar way, the routine requirement of a graduate degree has been an employment barrier for members of minority groups as well as, in numerous fields, for women. Many technical and professional jobs require graduate work or a graduate degree, a requirement which is again more difficult for minorities to meet because of discrimination in education. Women have been victims of traditional family influences as well as discriminatory counseling at the high school and college levels and have thus been channeled away from securing certain types of graduate degrees, particularly in technical and engineering fields. Because of this they are disproportionately negatively affected by the routine imposition of a certain type of graduate credential standard. The requirement of a graduate degree—increasingly a doctoral degree—is typical of current hiring practices in higher education. The discriminatory nature of this requirement can especially be seen in cases where *veteran* minority social work professionals have been refused employment on the faculty of schools of social work primarily because they lack graduate degrees.[42]

An emphasis in higher education hiring on an applicant's publications can have an effect similar to that of a degree requirement. Many minority and female candidates have labored, because of direct institutionalized discrimination, in teaching positions which provide little time for research and, thus, for publication. Women in this position typically find themselves filling instructorships in many colleges, positions with low pay and heavy teaching loads. Minority faculty until quite recently were typically confined to certain colleges, such as the predominantly black and Chicano colleges in the South and Southwest. Mizio has pointed up the absence of Puerto Rican faculty and staff in schools of social work. Because of direct discrimination, Puerto Rican professionals often had not had the opportunity to publish enough of their work to qualify for appointment to major social work facilities. "The Puerto Rican community is being asked to provide a candidate who is not just a Puerto Rican, but an unusual Puerto Rican."[43] The currently widespread practice of using publication as a filtering device for employment in higher education had no sexist or racist motivation in its development; such faculty credentials were by and large adopted for positive reasons in the belief that the quality of faculty is most easily measured by the quantity and quality of their publications. What Pettigrew has noted about black faculty at Harvard applies more broadly to the situation of women and minority persons in most traditionally white major universities:

> Harvard University in the 1930s set up a variety of meaningful criteria, including publication of scholarly works, to select their tenured faculty. The aim was praiseworthy—namely, to ensure a faculty of high quality. Yet the publishing requirement effectively acted to restrict the recruitment of Black professors, for most of them carried heavy teaching loads in predominantly Black colleges, which limited their time to write.[44]

It comes as no surprise, then, that Harvard and most other public and private universities have had few minority and female professors and have had difficulty recruiting minority and female professionals, however able and experienced they may be, who meet their publication qualifications. Here is yet another example of discriminatory effects resulting from social arrangements established for ostensibly positive reasons.

Another screening device which has acted to bar disproportionate numbers of minority applicants from employment is the aptitude or intelligence test. Documentation of the negative impact of such tests has been provided in many Equal Employment Opportunity Commission cases: "In many cases, the use of intelligence, aptitude and other tests developed to provide 'objective' evaluation of applicants has had major disproportionate effect in rejection of minorities, without having any proven relation to predicting successful job performance."[45] The first major Supreme Court decision in this area, *Griggs* v. *Duke Power Co.* (1971), examined the use of standard aptitude and intelligence tests as devices for rejecting applicants who achieved less-than-satisfactory scores, finding that their use had a negative effect on minority workers. The justices also noted that "evil intent" in the use of the tests was not necessary for discrimination to exist: "Good intent or absence of discriminatory intent does not redeem employment procedures or testing mechanisms that operate as 'built-in' headwinds for minority groups and are unrelated to measuring job capability."[46] As in the case of credential requirements, it was the use of *unvalidated* tests—that is, tests which had not been shown to predict employment success—which has been found to constitute unlawful discrimination. A number of other federal court cases concerning public and private employment, such as *Albermarle Paper Co.* v. *Moody* (1975), have provided further evidence of such negative impact and resulted in similar decisions.[47] The documentation in these cases has made clear the linkage between discrimination in one area and the resultant handicaps in another area. Because of discriminatory practices in educational institutions, minority persons are not as likely to do well on screening tests as whites. Moreover, differences in subcultural background between the (usually white-middle-class) test designers and minority persons are also reflected in the negative impact of various testing procedures.

Although numerous recent federal court decisions have maintained the position that apparently neutral practices which have a discriminatory effect or which perpetuate the effects of past discrimination are unlawful, the 1976 Supreme Court decision in *Washington* v. *Davis* appears to constitute a retreat from these earlier opinions.[48] In its decision the Nixon-shaped Supreme Court held that a screening test for Washington, D.C. Metropolitan Police Department recruits, which screened out substantially more black than white recruits, was not unlawful when no intent to discriminate was found and when the test was weakly validated in terms of predicting training school performance of recruits—even though, as Justices Brennan and Marshall pointed out in their dissenting opinion on this decision, the training school performance of recruits had not been validated in terms of subsequent job performance. This more conservative Court seems to have taken the view that only demonstrably and blatantly intentional discrimination is unlawful, a movement away from the earlier, pivotal *Griggs* decision.

The common use of conventional aptitude tests by employers to screen applicants and the tendency for disproportionate numbers of minorities to do poorly on them indicate the need for much careful examination and research on how these testing mechanisms come to have their negative impact. In one important study of testing in higher education admissions practices, Flaugher has begun the kind of detailed examination of unfairness in testing procedures that should be extended by future researchers to employment testing. He suggests that three different aspects of tests need to be examined: (1) test design and content; (2) testing procedures; (3) use of tests. The discriminatory effects of testing can stem from practices in any

or all of these areas. Sometimes the *design* of test items is unintentionally biased against minority groups in that it fails to account for
the verbal facility, experience, and knowledge characteristic of these
groups. Actual testing *procedures* can also have unequal effects.
"For example, information essential to registering for and taking
the test may not be disseminated in a form that makes it available
to minority groups, or conditions may be allowed to exist in the
test administration itself which are intimidating."[49] A third source
of the negative effects from testing is in the *use* of test scores. Conventional wisdom among employers has led to procedures "such as
requiring high verbal test scores to qualify for a job which in fact
does not depend upon verbal skills."[50] Whether test content is biased
against a certain group or not, tests administered or assessed in a
certain way can have a differential adverse impact on minority job
applicants. Indeed, it is the use of tests specifically to screen out
nonwhites that has been the major problem in some of the employment situations we have just reviewed. (A number of critics have
noted that if the tests were used in a diagnostic way, to aid applicants
or employees in gaining necessary skills, that might be a different
matter from the more typical practice of using a specific test score
as a [poor?] substitute measure of ability to do a job.)

While credential and testing requirements are perhaps the most
important examples of side-effect discrimination in employment
screening practices, other procedures have been identified, including
refusal to employ because of arrest records or bad credit records. The
routine implementation of such requirements by personnel directors
exemplifies the institutionalizing of this discrimination. Because
of experience with discrimination in other areas, such as discriminatory
police practices leading to differential arrest rates or discriminatory
business credit practices, minority persons are often more likely to
be screened out of the employment line than whites who did not
grow up in ghetto areas. For example, *Green* v. *Missouri Pacific
R.R. Co.* (1975), a federal court case, documented the discriminatory
impact of an employer's refusal to hire applicants because of prior
arrest or conviction records, and the decision held this practice to
be unlawful because it could not be justified by "business necessity"
in this employment setting. A similar screening procedure disqual-
ifying from police work persons convicted of serious crimes was

found to be job-related and upheld as lawful in *U.S.* v. *City of Chicago* (1976).[51]

Still other screening practices, such as the use of age restrictions or reliance on cumulative employment records, may exemplify past-in-present indirect discrimination. This occurs when employers, in a fashion similar to the unions noted earlier, intentionally discriminated against women or minority men in the past but no longer do so. In the present employment world the routine enforcement by employers of a relatively low maximum-age limitation for entering certain jobs or training programs can disproportionately screen out women and minority persons who are now too old, even by a year or two, but who could not have been hired when they were younger because of door-slamming discrimination. Another example can be seen in the widespread use of past employment records in hiring decisions. In the case of minorities and women, cumulative employment records are particularly likely to reflect the effects of blatant and subtle direct discrimination in the past by employers in regard to such things as initial hiring, type of position held, and promotion rates. To a subsequent employer (including the same employer who discriminated in the past!) such records may well seem "abnormal" because of an irregular job profile or a series of relatively minor blemishes which add up to an overall negative impression, thus handicapping a minority person or woman competing with white males who have more "normal" cumulative records. Reasonably objective decisions on the basis of data in such cumulative records can thus have severely adverse effects on minority or female applicants. Background investigations of job applicants may similarly become a source of discrimination when they include subjective, vague, and arbitrary assessments and when such background reports are used in the screening process.

Exclusion of minorities and women from employment in the past has also meant that current hiring standards are sometimes routinely shaped to meet the distinctive physical or subcultural characteristics of dominant-group (usually white male) employees in many business and industrial organizations. Hiring standards stipulating weight, height, and other physical requirements have been found to have a discriminatory effect on women and minority persons, especially, among the latter, Mexican Americans and Asian

Americans.[52] In the past the enforced absence of women and minorities from those employment areas which use such physical criteria has resulted in standards based on only one subgroup of the population, the "normal" white male group, even though the precise levels of such requirements are often arbitrary. In addition, enforcement of employment selection criteria based on a certain physical appearance, such as the hair style or dress characteristic of traditional employees, can also have a discriminatory effect on minority persons and women. These standards exist because of the traditional monoracial and monosexual character of the work force.

In concluding this section on screening we need to assess one issue in a bit more detail. This is the issue of the business necessity, or validity, of screening requirements; as we have noted this has been a central concern in recent court cases. Some readers may have raised in their own minds the question of job-related qualifications which are valid and which can be validated as predicting job performance, but which still have discriminatory effects. Screening requirements having adverse effects on minorities and women can be grouped into two broad categories: (1) those which are actually and empirically related to job performance, and (2) those which are not related to job performance. Thus a major problem with many educational and testing requirements traditionally used by public and private employers is that they have *not* been validated empirically as predictors of successful on-the-job performance. Few employers, including those hiring at both low-level and high-level job ranks, have examined their requirements systematically and empirically to see if those who meet them do better on the job than would those who do not. This is even true in regard to such credential requirements as graduate degrees for college teachers and other professional employees. Doubtless, many credential requirements simply are not, and cannot be shown to be, predictive of on-the-job performance.[53]

In cases where screening requirements have been empirically demonstrated, or could be demonstrated, to be linked to job performance—a task whose difficulty should not be underestimated—the issue of indirect institutionalized discrimination still remains. In some situations valid and necessary credential or skill requirements nevertheless produce adverse rejection rates of minority and female applicants. Yet this, too, can be seen as indirect discrimination stemming from blatant discrimination in other areas or in the past, as in education and job histories. Even though the impact of the practices may be negative in both cases, the policy for change may well be different in the two different cases. Unlike unnecessary or invalid screening requirements, which can simply be terminated, the use of credentials clearly tied to job performance raises very fundamental policy issues to which we will return in the last chapter of this book.

Internal Labor Markets and Tracking Systems

Once hired into an employment setting, the discrimination facing minorities and women does not cease. In the recent past many employers separated certain employees into different job lines or tracks. *Internal labor markets,* to use Piore and Doeringer's term, have often been differentiated into white and nonwhite job tracks, or male and female job tracks. Substantial job segregation of whites and nonwhites has been, without challenge until relatively recently, written into the rules or imbedded in unwritten regulations of organizations. Whites who were hired automatically went into better-paying, higher-status positions, while nonwhites were channeled into low-paying, lower-status jobs, regardless of qualifications. Once into such a track, as we shall see in the next section on promotions, it becomes very difficult to switch to another, even when official, formal discrimination in tracking has been outlawed by new civil rights legislation. Even today, a great deal of informal tracking of nonwhites (and women) into lower-paid positions and whites (and males) into better-paying positions occurs throughout the business world. A minority person who "doesn't look right" may, for example, be strongly encouraged to take an unskilled job such as ditch digger or janitor.

This kind of tracking, for both minorities and women, is documented in a number of studies. For example, one analysis of the many companies in the Bell Telephone System in 1970 found a clear pattern of tracking discrimination: "Black men have been excluded from white-collar and crafts jobs. White and black women have been generally excluded from blue-collar jobs. They have also been grossly underrepresented in most companies in sales jobs, both of the management and nonmanagement categories."[54] Virtually all craft (skilled blue-collar) employees were men; virtually all experienced telephone operators were women. Many other companies have had similarly separate tracks or ladders for different types of employees. Minority men are still channeled, albeit subtly, informally, and less systematically, into unskilled or semiskilled blue-collar positions; women are channeled into clerical work.

Blatant segregation of minority men into different tracks has declined significantly in recent years; overt discrimination against women is still quite common. Even today most employed men are in occupations with small (or no) proportions of women, while most women are in occupations which are predominantly if not exclusively composed of women. And this sex segregation in occupations has begun to change very slowly. In numerous industries jobs requiring physical strength are still automatically labeled "for men only," while secretarial jobs are reserved for women. In the worlds of finance, manufacturing, and the federal government the sharp separation of women into less-well-paying clerical jobs and men into higher-paying white-collar jobs has been documented, even though women in office occupations often have approximately the same median education level as men in the same office. Women office workers become part of a system of institutionalized sexism in which the occupational roles they must take, both because of discriminatory upbringing *and* company discrimination,* are consistently less-well-paying and lower-status, frequently with a personal service component not spelled out in formal job descriptions. Minority women are "doubly damned" in this regard. In the clerical sphere the entrance of black women in the 1960s was typically at the bottom. Young white women dominate the world of private secretaries, while "black clericals are mainly reserved for the keypunch room, the typing pool, or the data-processing center across town—the routine, pressurized, low-paid jobs."[55]

*Channeling is affected not only by discrimination in occupations but also by discrimination in the family and peer-group socialization processes which shape the aspirations of girls and young women. Such socialization processes also operate in the case of minority males.

Promotion Practices

Promotion, job progression, and transfer practices have also had a differential and adverse impact on minority persons and women. In many situations one might speak of "second-generation" discrimination here, since internal employment barriers did not become significant for large numbers until women and minority persons were actually hired. The hiring of women or minority persons in nontraditional positions does not guarantee them equal and open access to higher-level jobs in an organization, be it business, industry, government, or education. Promotion procedures, which often operate relatively secretly, are very difficult to observe or control from the outside. Formal regulations governing promotion may be spelled out in writing by most companies and government agencies for all their evaluators who have a "say" in promotion matters; but unwritten, informal rules or expectations often have a much greater impact.

Direct institutionalized discrimination in some organizational settings can be seen in promotions for minorities and women, particularly for those who have gained a toehold in the form of an entry-level job in a job category once reserved for white males. Butler's 1976 study of enlisted men in the army found a high degree of inequality of grade distribution for blacks; an even greater inequality was noted in the air force, marine corps and navy. Butler further found that in the technical occupation categories, even for white and black personnel groups with comparable scores on the Armed Forces Qualification Test (a test similar to so-called "IQ" tests), black enlisted men were significantly underrepresented.[56] Following basic training, job categories are assigned by an ostensibly racially unbiased computer system. Yet in spite of a supply of qualified blacks, this group remains underrepresented in the more prestigious, powerful, and remunerative technical positions. It is indeed difficult not to conclude that, in spite of the army's advertised policies of equal opportunity, a degree of direct discrimination in the form of (subtle?) racial monitoring of upward mobility exists. Moreover, Butler analyzed the length of time required for promotion to various grades within the army for enlisted men. Comparing groups with *similar* civilian education, Armed Forces Qualification Test scores, and military occupational specialties (technical or nontechnical), he discovered that in all but two subgroups blacks took *longer* to gain promotions than did whites. Butler concludes that such racial inequality cannot be explained "by the failure of blacks to meet universalistic criteria" but rather is the result of direct discrimination by "real-life people."[57]

Overt discrimination in current promotion practices for women has also been documented. As recently as the late 1960s one study found half the employers in large firms surveyed (300 of Fortune's top 750) openly admitted that discrimination against women was institutionalized in business and management; three-quarters of a sample of 300 smaller firms surveyed also admitted such discrimination. The discrimination often cited by these respondents was in both promotions and pay. Also in the late 1960s a survey of 144 women in management positions found 70 percent reporting overt, intentional discrimination, including salary inequalities and differential promotion criteria. There were numerous reports that women had to be "superwomen" or "water walkers" to make it up into higher administrative levels. As one respondent put it, "women are expected to be *extra-ordinary* workers to qualify for management."[58]

Even more recent studies have also found that male executives and managers continue to harbor stereotyped views of women workers which can shape the promotion of women. Bass and his associates found that many men thought male workers would not work under women supervisors and that women workers were supposed to "serve" men. A study of a large industrial supply corporation found numerous examples of overt, intentional discrimination in promotion practices. Rationalizations given for not promoting qualified women included "She's likely to quit and get married" and "She has children and her family responsibilities will interfere with a higher-level job."[59] Interestingly, these two sets of guiding stereotypes appear contradictory. A woman is "damned" if she's married, or "damned" if she's not.

There also exist numerous instances of subtle direct institutionalized discrimination in promotion practices. For example, a minority person might be passed over for promotion for "lack of initiative or aggressiveness" when the real reason for nonpromotion is the employee's racial identity. Ferman found that subjective, and subtle, discriminatory criteria for promotion are sometimes applied to blacks but not to whites, such as the criterion that blacks must get along well with white employees.[60] A subtle form of "cover" for intentional discrimination is to bandy about affirmative action or equal employment opportunity rhetoric and official pronouncements while actually doing the least possible to promote qualified women and minorities within the organization. Studies of several companies have revealed that industry and government tend to move very slowly in making nontraditional employment opportunities available to minorities. Intentional decisions (or "nondecisions") are to "foot-drag" in order to keep most minorities from moving up into non-traditional jobs, particularly those at higher salary levels. Minority persons, as well as white women, brought into nontraditional jobs at the entry level often remain there or, at best, near by.

What specific mechanisms block their ascent? Again, tests and credentials come into play. Whether intentionally used to discriminate or not, psychological test scores and educational credential requirements can be barriers not only in hiring but also in the upward mobility process as well. One conspicuous example has often been noted: there are female secretaries who are actually "administrators" in company divisions, yet the enforcement of formal educational credential rules (e.g., a college degree or graduate business degree) may play a role in preventing them from being promoted into management. Evidence of the negative impact of a high school diploma requirement has been provided in such recent court cases as *Watkins* v. *Scott Paper Co.* (1976).[61] In 1963 Scott opened previously "white" job categories to blacks and at the same time imposed a high school diploma requirement for transfers or promotions to higher-paying job categories. As the federal court observed, there were already white non–high school graduates, hired or promoted before implementation of the diploma requirement, successfully performing the relevant jobs which black non–high school graduates were being denied. Enforcement of various other credential requirements, such as the publication requirements for promotion to senior positions in higher education, also operates to reduce the promotion rates of minorities and women. The problems here are similar to those discussed previously in regard to hiring.

One of the most discussed issues which often arises in promotion as well as in hiring situations is that of the "best-qualified" candidate. To what extent does promoting the "best-qualified" candidate tend to discriminate against minority and female employees who are "qualified" but who are not, in some conventional terms, the "best-qualified"? In many situations the additional on-the-job experience, interpersonal experience, or educational credentials of white males make them "better-qualified," and thus give them an advantage in the promotion process, even though minority or female competitors are qualified. This situation has been documented in a few federal court cases, such as *U.S.* v. *Jacksonville Terminal Company* (1971).[62] An emphasis on promoting the "best-qualified" in terms of certain conventional criteria may serve a positive purpose from the point of view of organizational goals, but may also institutionalize inequality in advancement processes within organizations.

The advantages of "better-qualified" white male employees in the promotion process stem from a number of sources. White male employees tend to have an edge in several areas adding up to a significant advantage in the promotion process. For example, some organizations' internal training programs, particularly technical programs geared to upgrading present employees, may be set at a too advanced level for new female and minority employees hired into entry-level positions and may thus act to screen them out of regular promotion lines. Often such training was originally designed for white male employees with substantially more on-the-job experience or entry-level education. Thus organizations with new minority group or woman employees are often confronted with training needs they find difficult to cope with. The discrimination in promotion rates that follows may be unintentional. However, as Roscoe Brown has cogently noted, "some organizations hire large numbers of minorities to entry level jobs, do very little to upgrade them, and they give the excuse that the minorities just don't have the skills to be promoted."[63]

"Interpersonal training," moreover, may be taken for granted by the employer who makes decisions regarding who will be considered "better-qualified" for promotion. Personal interaction on the job is often critical in providing informally the information needed for successful job performance and thus for job advancement. Informal networks play an important role in information circulation, as well as in bringing employees into the employment setting in the first place. New minority and female workers with weak peer training from their already experienced white male coworkers may be less knowledgeable than the latter, less sure of themselves, less innovative in dealing with on-the-job problems, and thus less likely to be promoted. Brown has termed the cumulative interpersonal interaction necessary for successful or outstanding job performance the "incremental bump."[64] Limitations on critical informal interaction and communication can be intentional or unintentional.

Referring to decision making in higher-status positions, Chafetz has noted that "to a large extent, policy is formed, 'deals' are closed, contracts are made, and information is exchanged in male-only clubs, bars, and such lofty sites as men's rooms and locker rooms."[65] These "normal" informal patterns have built up over the years when white males have been virtually the sole occupants of various positions and have come into being to facilitate decision making. Newcomers, whatever their race or sex, may be assimilated into these critical communication settings slowly if at all. In the many cases where such arrangements make it more difficult for minorities or women to carry out the duties of their jobs, reliance on such informal socialization as grooming for the promotion process might be seen as an instance of indirect discrimination.

The traditional division of employment tracks or lines by race or sex in internal labor markets often continues informally even after formal (legal) desegregation occurs, handicapping minorities and women seeking promotions out of the traditional job lines. For example, the established structure of female/male jobs, with women in clerical work and men in management, makes it very difficult for many women in clerical jobs to get promotions to other types of positions. As Tepperman notes: "Most companies are organized in a way that makes promotion difficult. A clerical worker in a large modern office rarely has the chance to get to know people in management. And typing information on forms all day probably doesn't prepare her for any other job. Besides, most higher-level employees are recruited from outside the firm."[66] While recruitment from outside varies from one company to another, it is generally the case that, once one is locked into certain lines, such as secretarial or other clerical lines, it is very difficult to move into most supervisory and management lines. Furthermore, low-mobility tracks in turn shape workers' attitudes, thus handicapping women and minorities in their willingness to protest treatment in promotions. Some may see the limitations on mobility in the personal characteristics of women and minorities, but Kanter suggests that the real limitations come from blocked opportunity tracks.[67]

Internal transfer and seniority rules can be serious barriers to upward mobility; often such rules are clear-cut examples of past-in-present discrimination. Rules requiring that those transferring from one department to another within a given company forego seniority and other benefits—rules typically instituted for nonracial, business reasons—can have severe adverse effects on minority persons or women attempting to transfer out of low-wage departments to which they had been consigned in the past because of direct discrimination. If personnel or supervisory officials have intentionally discriminated in the past, then the enforcement of such rules perpetuates the subordinate position of minority persons and women in the present. "Loss of seniority and other rights effectively discourages employees from moving to areas with better advancement opportunities."[68]

The routinized, discriminatory operation of internal transfer practices has been documented in a number of recent federal court cases, including *Watkins* v. *Scott Paper Co.* (1976), *U.S.* v. *Bethlehem Steel Corporation* (1971), and *Franks* v. *Bowman Transportation Company* (1976).[69] Reviewing data on employment practices, the courts have found that such seniority and transfer policies perpetuate employers' earlier practices of direct discrimination, whether or not the discriminatory effect on such transfer rules themselves was intentional. In the *Bethlehem* case a steel plant had in the past intentionally forced black employees into less desirable positions solely on the basis of race. More recently, transfers from low-status departments were permitted, but only under the old transfer rules, rules presumably designed for safety and efficiency in the plant. Since the rules required that an employee lose seniority and be reduced to the lowest pay level in the new department, minority employees, obviously not wishing salary and seniority cuts, were effectively locked into their old departments. Similarly, in *Patterson* v. *American Tobacco Company* (1976), the data presented showed that although the company had abolished its departmental seniority system, a minority employee desiring a transfer was required to progress through a series of nine previously white lines of progression in order to advance to the highest-paying jobs for which he or she might already possess the necessary plant seniority.[70]

Indirect institutionalized discrimination can be seen in job posting procedures affecting promotion. In public and private organizations there has often been a failure to publicize widely and routinely all promotion opportunities, relying again on the old-standby informal networks as the primary means of communication. Such practices, although often neutral in intent, can have a negative effect on the opportunities of women and minority employees, particularly where previously excluded employees coming into a desegregated plant have little access to established informal networks.

Routine personnel office decisions on promotions which rely heavily on the subjective recommendations of an immediate supervisor, and which as a result have a disproportionately negative impact on women or minorities, might also be seen as examples of indirect discrimination. In *Rowe* v. *General Motors Corporation* (1972), a federal court examined data on promotion practices in a recently desegregated automobile plant in the South which had in the past directly discriminated against black applicants and employees. It was found that black wage earners were not notified of the qualifications needed for salaried positions and that a disproportionately small percentage of black wage earners were transferred or promoted to salaried positions. Data in the *Rowe* case showed that the recommendation of a (white) supervisor was the most important factor governing promotion, and that supervisors were given no written instructions for making recommendations. The unwritten instructions were found to be vague and subjective. There was a clear implication of a widely shared view among white supervisors not to recommend minority employees, an illustration of intentional discrimination operating in response to informal norms. An appellate federal court ruled that this promotion system constituted unlawful discrimination, underlining the point that it made no difference that management did not necessarily construct these procedures with the intent to harm: "All we do today is recognize that promotion/transfer procedures which depend almost entirely upon the subjective evaluation and favorable recommendation of the immediate foreman are ready mechanisms for discrimination against Blacks, much of which can be covertly concealed and, for that matter, not really known to management."[71] The use of subjective evaluations by supervisors was similarly held to be discriminatory in *Robinson* v. *Union Carbide Corporation* (1976).

Cumulative personnel records can also hamper promotions, particularly for nonwhite minorities. Consider, for example, the military data in the Butler study cited at the beginning of this section. Blacks of equal ability were shown to have been promoted more slowly than whites. In addition to the direct discrimination which persists in military personnel decisions, it seems likely that indirect discrimination also comes into play in retarding promotions. For example, direct discrimination, long the basic pattern of the army, shaped *past* promotion rates as well as the training opportunities available and the types of positions held in the *past.* These experiences go into the cumulative record of each soldier-employee. In other cases, blemishes on the service records of minority personnel have resulted from intentional discrimination by bigoted white officers. The cumulative effect of such past discrimination, currently seen as "facts" in an impersonal personnel folder, often has placed black personnel significantly behind whites in their particular entry cohort in promotion progress. This record may make it difficult for minority persons to be promoted, even in the present, less discriminatory atmosphere. Cumulative personnel records used in other occupational settings can similarly impair the mobility of minorities and in some cases of white women.

Conditions and Terms of Employment

Women and minority persons have traditionally been "second-class citizens" in terms and conditions of employment. This is true in the amount of income which they can expect to receive as well as in the type of jobs held and the extent of their participation in the labor force. In 1974 the income of all black males was 61 percent that of white males; black females received 32 percent and white females 36 percent as much as white males.[72] An analysis by Featherman and Hauser of income data for employed women, controlling for such variables as education, occupation, and time- and age-related factors, concluded that there was an earnings gap between males and females in the experienced civilian labor force in 1973 of $6942, 84 percent of which was attributable to sex-based discrimination.[73] This represents no real change since 1962, when discrimination was found to account for 85 percent of the male-female earnings gap.

Even today, conditions of employment, including job categories and pay levels, are frequently influenced by past and present policies of intentional discrimination. For example, the Scott Paper Company in Mobile, Alabama, maintained racially segregated job opportunities until 1963, with the lower-paying, more physically demanding jobs going to blacks. Even after official racial barriers to the higher-paying jobs were removed, the vague, sometimes irrelevant, and poorly understood criteria for transferring into the formerly white lines of progression represented new barriers which kept black employees out. As a result, in 1972 a substantial wage differential favoring whites remained among long-time black and white workers, those with eighteen or more years seniority.[74]

Women and minority persons continue to suffer intentional discrimination in the form of unequal pay for essentially the same work as white male employees, although the formal use of separate pay scales has been banned by federal legislation. Examples are numerous in the recent women's literature. In one report a legal secretary noted that she drafts many legal documents, such as wills and real estate statements, but makes only one-sixth the salary of attorneys who do basically the same work. She went on to spell out the way in which legal secretaries are systematically degraded: they are often hired for their "legs"; they must serve and defer to their bosses. The same institutionalized pattern of lower pay and degrading conditions is frequently characteristic of women workers in other professional and managerial offices controlled by men.[75]

Discrimination in fringe benefits is not uncommon in this society. Part-time workers, who are usually women or minority persons, receive few fringe benefits. Clerical employees (women) frequently receive less in benefits than professional and managerial employees (men). In some cases, death benefits and health benefits, by intention, vary for male and female workers. Several court cases have documented the widespread policy of lower pension benefits and lower retirement ages for women.[76] Discrimination against women can also be seen in personnel actions providing company fringe benefits conditional on an employee being a "head of household" or "principal wage earner" and in employer practices of denying sick leave benefits for pregnancy and childbirth while allowing such benefits for voluntary sick leaves for men, such as for hair transplants or vasectomies. Interestingly, although a federal district court found this latter type of discrimination to be unlawful in *Gilbert* v. *General Electric* (1974), a more conservative Supreme Court subsequently reversed this decision, holding that employee disability benefits could not legally be required to be all-inclusive.[77]

Conditions of everyday employment also reflect intentional discrimination. Particularly well-institutionalized examples can be found in the data in numerous recent court cases involving the airline industry. Direct discrimination against women has been documented in company regulations that female employees such as stewardesses were expected or pressured to remain single, wear contact lenses rather than eyeglasses, wear sexy attire, maintain low weight, and use certain kinds of luggage, although the same regulations were not applied to male flight attendants.[78]

An unusual example of indirect discrimination can be seen in the operation of state protective laws regarding women since the 1960s. In the first decades of the twentieth century numerous states adopted protective laws—concerning, for example, maximum hours of work—which have been regarded as attempts by progressive reformers to protect women workers from extreme exploitation by unscrupulous employers. Yet others have viewed these laws as intentionally designed, under pressure from male workers, to cut back on competition from female workers. Whatever the original intent, protective laws limiting the hours women can work (or the weight they can lift) have operated in recent years to bar women from many skilled, and frequently better-paying, occupations. Although protective laws still exist, they have been held to constitute unlawful discrimination by numerous federal courts.[79]

Layoff, Discharge, and Seniority Practices

In times of recession or reduction in the labor force one of the most serious types of indirect institutionalized discrimination can be seen in layoffs which systematically and differentially affect women and minority members because of low seniority. Typically, the purpose of a plantwide seniority system is to guarantee that employees with the greatest seniority will receive the greatest protection when cutbacks or layoffs take place.* Such guarantees are often part of collective bargaining agreements with unions. Generally, seniority systems, hard-won in the union-management struggles of the past, have been designed to protect veteran workers from arbitrary termination and to insure experienced workers for management.

Yet seniority systems operating today often exemplify past-in-present discrimination, with effects which become dramatic in times of economic contraction. If women and minority persons have only been hired recently in a particular organizational setting, they will have little seniority to protect them and thus will constitute a disproportionate number of those fired in a recession. The popular phrase for this phenomenon is "last hired, first fired." Evidence of its negative impact has been clear. For example, General Motors laid off all of its women employees at a Linden, New Jersey plant in early 1974 as part of a seniority layoff procedure. Relying on seniority regulations, many other recession-pressured plants have laid off disproportionate numbers of women and minority employees.[80] A critical point here is that in the past many white males, including poorly and marginally qualified white males, benefited by *not* having to compete with minorities and females. Now these white males retain their jobs because seniority rights perpetuate the effects of that past discrimination. While the current implementation of seniority rules is typically "fair in form," nonracist and nonsexist in intent, the effects of its operation are discriminatory. Ironically, seniority practices did not become a serious problem for minority or female workers until the recessions of the 1970s resulted in the firing of disproportionate numbers of persons hired under recent minority protest and federal affirmative action pressures.

Documentation of the negative effects on minorities and women of routinely utilizing existing seniority rules and similar regulations has been provided in several court cases, although the solutions developed by judges for seniority problems have not been consistent with one another. In *Watkins* v. *Steel Workers Local 2369* (1974),

---

*Plantwide seniority refers to the number of years of employment that a person has put in at a specific plant or at a specific company location; *departmental* or *divisional seniority* refers to time employed in a subdivision of a plant.

one federal court found evidence of the negative impact of seniority provisions and ruled that the use of those provisions constituted unlawful discrimination. Decisions of other courts have refused to alter seniority systems when they found proven discriminatory effects on minorities or women in layoffs. In a circuit court opinion, *Waters* v. *Wisconsin Steel Works* (1974), a steel plant's discriminatory seniority system was upheld as lawful in spite of evidence that the system reflected the effects of direct discrimination in the past. In *Jersey Central Power and Light Co.* v. *IBEW Local Unions* (1975), a federal district court ruled that minority employees would be adversely affected and that a conciliation agreement between the Equal Employment Opportunity Commission and Jersey Central would be violated if the employer followed its contractual seniority system. The court ordered layoffs to proceed in such a way that minority persons and females would suffer no more than other employees. However, the Third Circuit Court of Appeals vacated this district court order and upheld the traditional policy of layoffs in reverse order of seniority.[81]

On the related issue of developing a measure of retroactive seniority, as of this writing the most recent Supreme Court ruling on the last-hired, first-fired question has come in the case of *Franks* v. *Bowman Transportation Company* (1976).[82] In this decision the Court awarded retroactive seniority to minority persons who had been denied employment because of their race after such discrimination had become unlawful. But this retroactive seniority status is available *only* to persons who had applied for jobs and is calculated from the time the applicant was refused employment; this ruling offers no protection for those persons who did not apply for work because of the employer's known or reputed discriminatory policies.

In addition to seniority, other mechanisms have had a differential negative impact on the layoff or discharge of minorities. For example, the practice of discharging workers because of garnishment* or other financial problems has a disproportionate effect on minority workers. Here is another example of routine business practice. Problems in one area trigger effects in another sphere. In *John-*

Garnishment refers to a legal order requiring an employer to hold out a specified portion of an employee's wages for a creditor.

son v. *Pike Corporation of America* (1971) a federal court found evidence that a company regulation requiring the discharge of employees with garnisheed wages had a disproportionately negative effect on minorities.[83] Here the court again ruled that such an employment practice could be neutral on its face and objective in its application and yet still be discriminatory. Because of their general economic status and business contacts, minority group individuals are more likely to have their wages garnisheed. When discharge policies are linked to garnishment, they can result in institutionalized actions having a routinely and disproportionately negative effect on minority employees, even preventing them from making a decent living.

While seniority and other regulations shaping the practices we have cited here are generally examples of unintentional discrimination, some seniority systems have been intentionally implemented to give certain male employees greater protection. A number of federal court cases have documented such use of openly discriminatory seniority systems differentiated by sex. In at least one airline case it was shown that men were actually and intentionally favored under an existing seniority system.[84]

A Note on Discrimination in the Marketplace

So far in this chapter we have focused on employment. But economic discrimination can also be seen in the consumer area as well. In particular, minority persons are often at a disadvantage in the marketplace. For example, in a study of merchants in New York's East Harlem ghetto, Caplovitz found that most merchandise for sale was of poor quality but was still offered at high prices. Often price tags were not placed on merchandise, leaving the merchant free to assign a higher price to a (usually black) customer judged by him (or her) to be more naive or a poor risk. An especially poor-risk customer might even be referred to another store with a less conservative risk policy whose manager would pay a commission to the referring salesperson, the amount of which would be added to the selling price of the merchandise. "Bait and switch" sales were found to exist in many ghetto stores. This is a common practice in which the customer is lured into the store by advertisements of extremely low prices and then is told by a salespeson that this poor-quality merchandise is not what he or she really wants and is sold other merchandise at much higher prices.[85]

Although state laws regulate credit terms and information, many merchants were found to give a minority customer only a card noting the weekly payments due, focusing the customer's attention on the relatively small weekly installments rather than the total cost of the purchase. Caplovitz found that ghetto merchants were very much aware that many of their minority customers were unable, or found it difficult, to comparison-shop outside the ghetto and were thus captive to higher markups on low-quality merchandise, markups which ghetto merchants frequently claim are needed as protection against their greater credit risks. The ghetto customer who feels he or she has been cheated or who has difficulty keeping up with installment payments may be coerced into paying by threats of garnishment of wages, a situation which frequently will result in the loss of his or her job or the refusal of credit in all area stores.

In a recent study to determine whether exploitation in the marketplace is a function of racial status or income position, Sturdivant and Wilhelm conducted a survey in Los Angeles in which prospective customers in three major ethnic groups who had *comparable* credit profiles shopped for identical merchandise at stores in Watts (predominantly black), East Los Angeles (predominantly Mexican American), and Culver City (middle-class Anglo-white).[86] Some difficulties were encountered in matching stores in the three areas because of the predominance of low-quality, frequently off-brand merchandise in ghetto area stores. However, they found that in all cases prices for identical merchandise were higher in the ghetto areas. In two out of three Culver City stores minority customers were quoted higher prices or higher credit terms than the white customers, but in most instances the discriminatory prices asked in the white community stores were still substantially less than the prices asked in ghetto stores. The wide variation of credit charges, often at illegal rates, quoted to the various customers caused Sturdivant and Wilhelm to conclude further that "merchants find credit charges an excellent vehicle for exercising economic and racial or ethnic discrimination." Even stores in the same chains have different policies varying from one area of a community to another. Subjection to this direct institutionalized discrimination is forced on a disproportionate number of minority buyers because of their lack of cash, lack of access to shopping outside the ghetto, lack of knowledge of sophisticated shopping methods, and poor credit position. The institutionalization of marketplace practices having a negative impact on minorities, both men and women, is common in American cities and towns, and the more general economic limitations of minority Americans further compound the impact of intentional discrimination.

1. U.S. Civil Service Commission, *Study of Employment of Women in the Federal Government* (Washington, D.C.: Government Printing Office, 1973), p. 12.

2. U.S. Civil Service Commission, *Federal Civilian Employment: Women, 1973 Study* (Washington, D.C.: U.S. Government Printing Office, 1973), p. 15; U.S. Civil Service Commission, *Federal Civilian Manpower Statistics,* December 1975, p. 36, and January 1976, p. 35.

3. 1973 EEOC-4 *Reports,* cited in U.S. Equal Employment Opportunity Commission, *Minorities and Women in State and Local Government, 1973* (Washington, D.C.: U.S. Government Printing Office, 1973), 1: xv.

4. Equal Employment Opportunity Commission, *Equal Employment Opportunity Report* (Washington, D.C.: U.S. Government Printing Office, 1973), 1: 1.

5. U.S. Commission on Civil Rights, *The State of Civil Rights: 1976* (Washington, D.C.: U.S. Government Printing Office, 1977), p. 13.

6. Ibid., pp. 13–16. This analysis draws substantially from recent Department of Labor, Bureau of Labor Statistics data.

7. U.S. Bureau of the Census, *A Statistical Portrait of Women in the U.S.,* Current Population Reports, Special Studies Series P-23, no. 58 (Washington, D.C.: U.S. Government Printing Office, 1976), p. 79.

8. See *Pittsburgh Press Co.* v. *The Pittsburgh Commission on Human Relations,* 413 U.S. 376 (1973); and *Brush* v. *San Francisco Newspaper Printing Co.,* 469 F. 2d 89 (1972).

9. Sandra L. Bein and Daryl L. Bein, "Sex-segregated Want Ads: Do They Discourage Female Job Applicants?" in *Discrimination Against Women,* edited by Catharine R. Stimpson (New York: R.R. Bowker Co., 1973).

10. Mark S. Granovetter, *Getting a Job: A Study of Contact and Careers* (Cambridge: Harvard University Press, 1974), pp. 6–11, 16; see also Alfred W. Blumrosen, *Black Employment and the Law* (New Brunswick, N.J.: Rutgers University Press, 1971), p. 232.

11. Gordon F. Bloom, F. Marion Fletcher, and Charles R. Perry, *Negro Employment in Retail Trade* (Philadelphia: University of Pennsylvania Press, 1972), passim.

12. *Barnett* v. *W. T. Grant Co.,* 518 F. 2d 543, 549 (1975); see also *U.S.* v. *Georgia Power Co.,* 474 F. 2d 906 (1973) and *Parham* v. *Southwestern Bell Telephone Co.,* 433 F. 2d 421 (1970).

13. *Arnold* v. *Ballard,* 390 F. Supp. 723 (1975).

14. Bettye Kirkpatrick Eidson, "Institutional Racism: Minority Group Manpower Policies of Major Urban Employers," Ph.D. dissertation, Johns Hopkins University, 1971, p. 262; these factors were not as important for blue-collar positions.

15. Janet Saltzman Chafetz, *Masculine/Feminine/Human* (Itasca, Ill.: F. E. Peacock, 1974), p. 123.

16. Joan Abramson, *The Invisible Woman* (San Francisco: Jossey-Bass, 1975), pp. 78–79.

17. U.S. Commission on Civil Rights, *Understanding Fair Housing* (Washington, D.C.: U.S. Government Printing Office, 1973), p. 1.

18. Jack E. Nelson, *Equal Employment Opportunity in Trucking: An Industry at the Crossroads* (Washington, D.C.: U.S. Equal Employment Opportunity Commission, 1971).

19. See William B. Gould, "The Seattle Building Traders Order: The First Comprehensive Relief Against Employment Discrimination in the Construction Industry," *Stanford Law Review* 26 (April 1974): 775–76.

20. *Evans* v. *Sheraton Park Hotel,* 5 FEP Cases 393 (D. D.C. 1972).

21. U.S. Commission on Civil Rights, *The Challenge Ahead: Equal Opportunity in Referral Unions* (Washington, D.C.: U.S. Government Printing Office, 1976), pp. 15–26.

22. Ibid., p. 26.

23. Herbert Hammerman, "Minority Workers in Construction Referral Unions—Revisited," *Monthly Labor Review* 96 (May 1973): 43–46.

24. See U.S. Commission on Civil Rights, *The Challenge Ahead: Equal Opportunity in Referral Unions,* pp. 104–113; *U.S.* v. *Local 638 Steamfitters,* 360 F. Supp. 979 (1973).

25. *Patterson* v. *Newspaper and Mail Deliverers' Union of New York and Vicinity,* 514 F. 2d 767, 769 (1975); see also *U.S.* v. *Local 73, Plumbers,* 314 F. Supp. 160 (1969).

26. Irwin Dubinsky, *Reform in Trade Union Discrimination in the Construction Industry* (New York: Praeger, 1973), p. 26.

27. U.S. Commission on Civil Rights, *The Challenge Ahead: Equal Opportunity in Referral Unions*, p. 62.

28. See *Vogel* v. *McCarthy, Inc.*, 294 F. Supp. 368 (1967); *U.S.* v. *Local 357, IBEW*, 356 F. Supp. 104 (1972); *U.S.* v. *Local 10, Sheet Metal Workers*, 6 FEP Cases 1036 (1973); *U.S.* v. *Local 24, Plumbers*, 364 F. Supp. 808 (1973).

29. William B. Gould, *Black Workers in White Unions* (Ithaca, N.Y.: Cornell University Press, 1977), p. 281.

30. *Griggs* v. *Duke Power Co.*, 401 U.S. 424 (1971).

31. Jack E. Nelson, *Equal Employment Opportunity in Trucking: An Industry at the Crossroads;* Rodney Alexander and Elisabeth Sapery, *The Shortchanged: Women and Minorities in Banking* (New York: Dunellen, 1973).

32. Felix Lopez, "The Bell System's Non-Management Personnel Selection Strategy," in *Equal Employment Opportunity and the AT&T Case*, edited by Phyllis A. Wallace (Cambridge: MIT Press, 1976), pp. 226–27.

33. Edgar S. Ellman, *Managing Women in Business* (Waterford, Conn.: Prentice-Hall, 1967).

34. EEOC Decision No. 71-2613, 4 FEP Cases 22 (1971); *Philips* v. *Martin Marietta Corp.*, 400 U.S. 542 (1971); EEOC Decision No. 71-332, 2 FEP Cases 1016 (1970).

35. Gordon F. Bloom, F. Marion Fletcher, and Charles R. Perry, *Negro Employment in Retail Trade*, p. 20.

36. Marianne Ferber and Jane Loeb, "Performance, Rewards, and Perceptions of Sex Discrimination Among Male and Female Faculty," *American Journal of Sociology* 78 (January 1973): 995–1002.

37. Barbara Babcock, Ann Freedman, Eleanor Norton, and Susan Ross, *Sex Discrimination and the Law: Causes and Remedies* (Boston: Little, Brown, 1975), pp. 300–330.

38. See Thomas F. Green and Emily Haynes, "Notes Toward a General Theory of Educational Systems," unpublished paper, Syracuse University Research Corporation, 1972.

39. *Griggs* v. *Duke Power Co.*, 401 U.S. 424 (1971); *U.S.* v. *Georgia Power Co.*, 474 F. 2d 906 (1973); *Johnson* v. *Goodyear Tire and Rubber Co.*, 491 F. 2d 1364 (1974).

40. *Payne* v. *Travenol Laboratories, Inc.*, 416 F. Supp. 248 (1976); *Arnold* v. *Ballard*, 390 F. Supp. 723 (1975).

41. Blanche D. Blank, "Degrees: Who Needs Them?" *AAUP Bulletin* (Autumn 1972): 261–66.

42. Emelicia Mizio, "Puerto Rican Social Workers and Racism," *Social Casework* 3 (May 1972): 270.

43. Ibid.; see also Joan Abramson, *The Invisible Woman*, pp. 1–91.

44. Thomas F. Pettigrew, "Racism and the Mental Health of White Americans: A Social Psychological View," in *Racism in Mental Health*, edited by Charles V. Willie, Bernard M. Kramer, and Betram S. Brown (Pittsburgh: University of Pittsburgh Press, 1973), p. 275.

45. U.S. Equal Employment Opportunity Commission, *Affirmative Action and Equal Employment: A Guidebook for Employers* (Washington, D.C.: U.S. Government Printing Office, 1974), p. 44.

46. *Griggs* v. *Duke Power Co.*, 401 U.S. 424 (1971)

47. *Albermarle Paper Co.* v. *Moody*, 95 S. Ct. 2362 (1975); see also *Baker* v. *Columbus Municipal Separate School District*, 329 F. Supp. 706 (1971), aff'd 462 F. 2d 1112 (1972); *Carter* v. *Gallagher*, 452 F. 2d 315 (1972), cert. denied, 406 U.S. 950 (1972).

48. *Washington* v. *Davis*, 96 S. Ct. 2040 (1976); see also *EEOC* v. *Local 14 International Union of Operating Engineers*, 415 F. Supp. 1155 (1976); *EEOC* v. *Local 638 . . . Local 28 of Sheet Metal Workers International Assn.*, 532 F. 2d 821 (1976); *League of United Latin American Citizens* v. *City of Santa Ana*, 410 F. Supp. 873 (1976).

49. Ronald L. Flaugher, *Testing Practices, Minority Groups, and Higher Education: A Review and Discussion of Research* (Princeton, N.J.: Educational Testing Service, 1970), p. 6.

50. Ibid.

51. *Green* v. *Missouri Pacific R.R. Co.*, 523 F. 2d 1290 (1975); *U.S.* v. *City of Chicago*, 411 F. Supp. 218 (1976).

52. See *Meadows* v. *Ford Motor Co.*, 5 FEP Cases 665 (1973); see also Equal Employment Opportunity Commission, *Affirmative Action and Equal Employment*, p. 43.

53. A useful discussion of the validation issues can be found in George Cooper and Richard B. Sobol, "Seniority and Testing under Fair Employment Laws: A General Approach to Objective Criteria of Hiring and Promotion," *Harvard Law Review* 82 (1969): 1598–679. On college teachers and the Ph.D. see Sheila Huff, "Credentialling by Tests or by Degrees: Title VII of the Civil Rights Act and Griggs v. Duke Power Company," *Harvard Educational Review* 44 (May 1974): 259.

54. Barbara Bergmann and Jill Gordon King, "Diagnosing Discrimina-

tion," in Wallace, *Equal Employment Opportunity and the AT&T Case,"* p. 61.

55. Jean Tepperman, *Not Servants, Not Machines* (Boston: Beacon Press, 1976), p. 49; see also Adele Simmons et al., *Exploitation from 9 to 5* (New York: Lexington Books, 1975).

56. John Sibley Butler, "Assessing Black Enlisted Participation in the Army," *Social Problems* (June 1976): 560–64.

57. John Sibley Butler, "Inequality in the Military: An Examination of Promotion Time for Black and White Enlisted Men," *American Sociological Review* 41 (October 1976): 817.

58. Robert Tsuchigane and Norton Dodge, *Economic Discrimination Against Women in the United States* (Lexington, Mass.: Lexington Books, 1974), p. 54.

59. Bernard M. Bass, Judith Krussel, and Ralph Alexander, "Male Managers' Attitudes Toward Working Women," *American Behavioral Scientist* (November 1971): 228–29; Rosabeth Moss Kanter, *Men and Women of the Corporation* (New York: Basic Books, 1977), p. 67.

60. Louis A. Ferman, *The Negro and Equal Employment Opportunities: A Review of Management Experiences in Twenty Companies* (New York: Praeger, 1968).

61. *Watkins* v. *Scott Paper Co.*, 530 F. 2d 1159 (1976).

62. *U.S.* v. *Jacksonville Terminal Co.*, 451 F. 2d 418 (1971).

63. Roscoe C. Brown, Jr., "Sources of Bias in the Prediction of Job Performance: Implications for Blacks," in *An Investigation of Bias in the Prediction of Job Performance: A Six-year Study* (Princeton, N.J.: Educational Testing Service, 1972), p. 104.

64. Ibid., p. 102.

65. Chafetz, *Masculine/Feminine/Human*, p. 123.

66. Tepperman, *Not Servants, Not Machines*, p. 42.

67. Kanter, *Men and Women of the Corporation*, p. 158.

68. Equal Employment Opportunity Commission, *Affirmative Action and Equal Employment*, p. 49.

69. *Watkins* v. *Scott Paper Co.*, 530 F. 2d 1159 (1976); *U.S.* v. *Bethlehem Steel*, 446 F. 2d 652 (1971); *Franks* v. *Bowman Transportation Co.*, 96 S. Ct. 1251 (1976).

70. *Patterson* v. *American Tobacco Co.*, 535 F. 2d 257 (1976).

71. *Rowe* v. *General Motors Corp.* 457 F. 2d 348 (1972); see also *Robinson* v. *Union Carbide Corp.*, 538 F. 2d 652 (1976).

72. U.S. Bureau of the Census, *The Social and Economic Status of the Black Population in the United States, 1974,* Current Population Reports, Special Studies Series P-23, no. 54 (Washington, D.C.: Government Printing Office, 1975), p. 28.

73. David Featherman and Robert Hauser, "Sexual Inequalities and Socioeconomic Achievement in the U.S., 1962-1973," *American Sociological Review* 41 (June 1976): 480.

74. See *Watkins* v. *Scott Paper Co.,* 530 F. 2d 1159, 1165 (1976).

75. Tepperman, *Not Servants, Not Machines,* pp. 1-19. For laws prohibiting separate pay scales see Equal Pay Act of 1963; Civil Rights Act of 1964; Equal Employment Opportunity Act of 1972.

76. *Rosen* v. *Public Service Electric and Gas Co.,* 477 F. 2d 90 (1973); *Bartmess* v. *Drewrys U.S.A., Inc.,* 444 F. 2d 1186 (1971).

77. *Gilbert* v. *General Electric,* 375 F. Supp. 367 (1974); *General Electric Co.* v. *Gilbert,* 97 S. Ct. 401 (1976). See also Simmons et al., *Exploitation from 9 to 5,* pp. 76-80.

78. *Sprogis* v. *United Airlines, Inc.,* 444 F. 2d 1194 (1971); *Laffey* v. *Northwest Airlines, Inc.,* 6 FEP Cases 902 (1973).

79. *Richards* v. *Griffith Rubber Mills,* 330 F. Supp. 338 (1969). See Equal Employment Opportunity Commission, *Affirmative Action and Equal Employment,* p. 53.

80. *New York Times,* November 10, 1974, pp. 1, 5; *Wall Street Journal,* November 5, 1974, p. 1. A good discussion of the negative impact of seniority systems can be found in Blumrosen, *Black Employment and the Law,* pp. 167-72. See also "Last Hired, First Fired, Layoffs, and Title VII," *Harvard Law Review* 88 (1972): 1544-70.

81. *Watkins* v. *Steel Workers Local 2369,* 369 F. Supp. 1221 (1974); *Waters* v. *Wisconsin Steel Works,* 502 F. 2d 1309 (1974); *Jersey Central Power and Light Co.* v. *IBEW Local Unions,* Lab. Rel. Rep. 9 FEPC 117 (1975).

82. *Franks* v. *Bowman Transportation Co.,* 96 S. Ct. 1251 (1976).

83. *Johnson* v. *Pike Corporation of America,* 322 F. Supp. 490 (1971).

84. *Laffey* v. *Northwest Airlines, Inc.,* 6 FEP Cases 902 (1973).

85. David Caplovitz, "The Merchant and the Low-Income Consumer," in *The Ghetto Marketplace,* edited by Frederick D. Sturdivant (New York: Free Press, 1969), pp. 61-75.

86. Frederick D. Sturdivant and Walter T. Wilhelm, "Poverty, Minorities, and Consumer Exploitation," in Sturdivant, *The Ghetto Marketplace,* pp. 108-17. See also the section "Position Papers: Merchant Behavior in the Ghetto Marketplace," *Social Science Quarterly,* vol. 54 (September, 1973): 374-82.

Discrimination in Housing

chapter four

For the average American family the choice of where to live is based on a number of factors, including cost of housing, personal taste, suitability of dwelling to family needs, desirability of location, and proximity to place of employment and other facilities. In general, as the family's ability to pay increases so do their options in the remaining categoreis—that is, if the family is white. The astounding degree of residential segregation along racial lines to be found in the United States, even into the late 1970s, is evidence that this formula does not apply equally to nonwhite Americans. For nonwhite families numerous direct and indirect institutionalized discriminatory restrictions intervene to limit housing options regardless of the ability to pay.

The limited variety of housing choices of nonwhite minority groups is evidenced by their concentration and segregation in the nation's cities, usually in the most troubled areas of those cities. For example, using the Taeuber scale for measuring residential segregation (0 = random distribution of all racial and ethnic groups; 100 = total segregation), one important study of thirty American cities based on 1970 Census data revealed rather high white/nonwhite segregation scores ranging from 55 (San Francisco) to 93 (Dallas).* This means that in Dallas 93 percent of the nonwhite population would have to change their residence and redistribute themselves throughout the city in order to achieve a situation of no residential segregation. Data for black Americans typically show an even greater degree of housing segregation. Nationwide, three-quarters of all blacks live in metropolitan areas and over half of the black population is to be found in central cities. Within the cities blacks are further confined to limited areas. Thus the black/white segregation scores for the same thirty cities noted above were even higher, ranging from 75 (San Francisco) to 96 (Dallas).[1]

Moreover, data on most cities show little or no change in the segregation indices since the 1950s or 1960s; indeed, some cities have even been found to be more segregated in the 1970s than they were a few years back. Suburban areas, often booming growth areas, typically have small minority populations. Thus in 1970 only one suburban resident in twenty was black, and even then was likely to reside in a disproportionately black suburb next to a central city ghetto; in city after city black suburbanization has occurred primarily in areas adjacent to existing city ghettos.[2] This overwhelming degree of segregation seems unlikely to have occurred merely by chance. It is equally unlikely that it can all be explained by personal preferences or the lower incomes of nonwhites resulting from job and educational discrimination and their resultant lower housing purchasing power. Although the rising incomes of blacks during the late 1960s and early 1970s have narrowed the gap between their incomes and the incomes of whites a bit, a smaller proportion of blacks presently reside in truly integrated neighborhoods than did in the 1940s. Clearly, the "dead hand of discrimination" has had its impact on housing patterns in the United States. Housing discrimination, in its turn, affects the life chances of nonwhite Americans in many ways.

The housing discrimination confronting women has until recently received much less attention in the literature than that fac-

---

*"Nonwhites" here included Asian Americans, Native Americans ("Indians"), and black Americans.

ing nonwhites in general, but, particularly for single women, it is nonetheless real. Perhaps one reason for the neglect in the available literature is the fact that married women usually do not operate alone in the housing market, as they often do in employment; they become involved in the housing market with their husbands, typically operating in a "couple" situation. Thus in this chapter on housing discrimination we will bring in a discussion, primarily of single women, wherever the data provide such an opportunity. There are both similarities and differences in the patterns of housing discrimination facing minorities and women.

THE REAL ESTATE INDUSTRY

Housing discrimination has often been blamed on the prejudices of individual homeowners, and frequently on a kind of isolate or small-group discrimination. Yet the publicly expressed attitudes of whites toward integrated housing have changed sharply in recent years, with at least two-thirds of whites in recent opinion surveys saying, to an anonymous interviewer at least, that they would accept a minority family in their neighborhood. During this same period, as we have noted, residential segregation has slightly increased; the dual housing market still exists.[3] These facts point up the importance of looking at those white-dominated *organizations* which play the major role in the housing market, particularly the real estate and lending industries.

The Historical Background of Discrimination

American housing policy is largely controlled by the real estate industry, more specifically by the National Association of Real Estate Boards (NAREB) through its local member real estate boards. This organization was created in 1908 to standardize "ethical practices" among brokers and to bring respectability and a professional image to its members. Members consider the board to be the central authority in the real estate business. A basic priority of local boards is to protect the livelihood of members (called Realtors) and their sales staffs by maintaining or increasing property values and by maintaining public confidence in member brokers as cooperative members of the community.*

One of the major methods of protecting property values is the assurance of stable and compatible neighborhoods, traditionally interpreted as maintaining homogeneity of race, color, or nationality. It has also been the position of NAREB that brokers not interfere with local preferences in regard to neighborhood homogeneity and continuity. Local real estate operations are over-whelmingly white-dominated, and the vast bulk of their business is conducted with white homeseekers. In her analysis of interview data from real estate brokers in Chicago, Rose Helper found that the economic gain to be realized from "the primary control of land and property" was fundamental to both real estate ideology and operations. Thus real estate brokers were convinced that once property passed into minority control there was no future possibility of profit for whites from the property.[4] On this premise, and related stereotypes about property values, has been based a well-institutionalized structure of intentional racial discrimination. We can now look briefly at the historical roots of this discrimination.

It is not surprising then that when minorities, especially blacks, in large numbers began to move into previously predominantly white central cities, NAREB and its local members felt a need to deal with the situation on an industrywide level. By 1914 members of the Board of Real Estate of New York were engaging in attempts to reclaim previously white housing areas from black migrants. Nationwide, intentional discrimination motivated by racial fears was the order of the day. Legal reinforcement of residential segregation was sought by real estate organizations and local governments in the form of police power ordinances; formal regulations were passed by real estate boards in numerous cities prohibiting members from selling or renting properties in white areas to blacks. In California and Oregon such restrictions were broadened to include Asian Americans, especially the Japanese. Adherence to the rules was virtually unanimous among members of local boards, since members could be expelled for failure to comply.[5] Discrimination was of the blatant, door-slamming variety.

*Capitalized, the term *Realtor* is one only members of the NAREB can officially use. However, *realtor* is often used for any real estate broker or agent.

Deprived of the police power ordinance in 1917, when the Supreme Court declared it unconstitutional, brokers began urging white property owners to organize in order to prevent the uncontrolled movement of blacks into white areas. A committee of the Chicago Real Estate Board in 1917 stated that it was "dealing with a financial business proposition and not with racial prejudice" and that its recommendations were made in an "unprejudiced spirit" when it requested influential blacks to cooperate with the white real estate establishment in confining the settlement of black families to contiguous blocks and requiring that a block be completely filled with blacks before another block was begun. The committee report on house sales to blacks continued:

> Promiscuous sales and leases here and there mean an unwarranted and unjustifiable destruction of values and the loss in the majority of instances is borne by the small owner whose property represents his life savings; the loss is not only individual, but public, inasmuch as reduced values means reduced taxes.[6]

In 1924 the following passage, Article 34, was written into the official *Code of Ethics* of NAREB:

> A Realtor should never be instrumental in introducing into a neighborhood a character of property or occupancy, members of any race or nationality, or any individuals whose presence will clearly be detrimental to property values in that neighborhood.[7]

To this organizationally imbedded discrimination was added the widespread use of realtor-fostered and privately-contracted deed and covenant restrictions (prohibiting the sale of property to blacks, Jews, etc.) as a legal means of maintaining neighborhood segregation. In the interest (or under the guise) of maintaining economic stability, the thoroughgoing institutionalization of segregated housing emerged. The preservation of segregated neighborhoods was thus not left to depend on the isolate discrimination of a prejudiced white owner here and there who refused to sell or rent property to a minority homeseeker solely out of personal hostility, although such instances did, and do, commonly occur. Nor did it depend on the sporadic development of homeowner organizations designed to perpetuate neighborhood homogeneity by use of pressure, threats, or purchase of properties when sale to a minority person seemed likely, although instances of these also are common. Direct institutional discrimination was woven into the basic structure of the real estate industry from the early decades of this century.

In 1948 the Supreme Court officially declared that the Fourteenth Amendment prohibited states, including state courts, from enforcing race-restrictive deeds and covenants. However, the policy of exclusion was by this time so imbedded in real estate ideology and practice that an official of NAREB stated, "I doubt whether these opinions [in the Supreme Court decision] militate in any way against the efficacy of Article 34."[8] In 1950 Article 34 was revised to read:

> A Realtor should not be instrumental in introducing into a neighborhood a character of property or use which will clearly be detrimental to property values in that neighborhood.[9]

Yet this was still clearly understood by the real estate industry to signify, however covertly, the exclusion of racial and cultural minorities.

Housing discrimination, perpetuated with an intent to segregate minorities in inferior housing, and practiced as a means of protecting the dominant white real estate industry from stereotyped notions of property value declines, has had far-reaching and continuing effects in shaping residential patterns in American cities. Thus a Baltimore Urban League survey reported in June 1950 stated that Baltimore brokers' policy not to sell homes in white areas to black customers "contributes substantially to the fact that this 20 percent of the population [i.e., blacks] occupied not more than 8 percent of the city's residential area." William Price's 1955 Detroit research documented that housing mobility of blacks in that city was similarly affected by the local real estate board's policy of residential segregation. In recent decades punishment of deviant brokers by expulsion from the local real estate board assured the compliance of the vast majority of members. As recently as 1956 a real estate broker was *expelled* from a local board in South Gate, California for selling a house in a white neighborhood to a Mexican couple.[10]

Direct Institutionalized Discrimination: The Present

The recent invalidation of many direct discrimination practices, resulting from court cases and fair housing laws at the local, state, and national level, has not meant radical change in housing patterns or practices, for the straitjacket of the past constrains contemporary practices. "All these consciously made decisions have been invalidated. But the mold has been cast; the prison door has already been locked, and no one has yet been able to find a key that will open it."[11]

Blatant, door-slamming discrimination against minority homeseekers seems to have given way to more covert or subtle forms of discrimination in recent years, but overt, even blatant, discrimination is still evident in the treatment of minority real estate agents, treatment which in turn affects minority homeseekers. Paralleling the dual housing market has developed a dual real estate industry. The discrimination which occurs when minority brokers are denied membership or full participation in white firms and in local white boards (and thus in NAREB) prevents them from having full access to real estate listings in white areas, a measure which white realtors consider necessary in order to preserve markets for themselves. Because minority real estate brokers are denied, or limited in, the possibility of sales in these restricted areas, minority customers are denied the possibility of obtaining housing in restricted areas both because white brokers are reluctant to sell (or rent) to them and because minority brokers cannot.

The exclusion of a qualified black real estate broker from the dominant multiple-listing organization in Pittsburgh was found to constitute illegal discrimination and characterized as "an unlawful combination and conspiracy in the restriction of the interstate trade and commerce" by the District Court of Western Pennsylvania in 1967.[12] However, even today such devices as requiring sponsors to nominate a member, membership approval by the local board, waiting periods, and large membership fees (typically $500–1000, sometimes annually) act to eliminate most nonwhite brokers from local multiple-listing boards and thus from competition.

91

In testimony before the U.S. Civil Rights Commission a black member of a white California real estate board reported that white brokers developed separate listings which were not available to black brokers. He further documented the use of "Caucasians only" designations on multiple listings which were covered by state fair housing laws. He stated that when he had protested this practice to the Oakland Real Estate Board he was informed that it was the "ethical duty" of a member to make known to fellow realtors the color of prospective buyers.[13] Today, informal manipulation of listings for the purpose of restricting the access of minority real estate brokers remains common in numerous cities.

Subtle, but still intentional, discrimination in real estate practices with regard to minority homeseekers seeks to circumvent the law and often relies on the difficulty of proving intent to discriminate to stave off remedial action by victims. Such subtle discrimination can be seen in the persisting practice of "steering" minority customers to segregated or mixed areas and discouraging them in a variety of ways from considering white areas, while steering white customers to those white areas. Steering was the major device cited when white and black residents of northwest Detroit brought suit against real estate agents and agencies on the grounds of alleged violations of the federal Fair Housing Act of 1968, Section 3604 of which makes it unlawful to deny access to housing on the basis of race. A black client testified that a real estate agent had refused to show him housing in a white suburb, saying that anything he could afford was substandard and that he would be uncomfortable in an area with no black neighbors. He was steered to an area which was 43 percent black. (A few white homeseekers testified that realtors steered them away from integrated areas which blacks had entered, giving such reasons as "coloreds have moved in pretty good there" and "housing values are down and will continue to drop." They were cautioned regarding the schools with statements such as, "you know what will happen eventually.") Steering was backed up by other practices insuring that blacks could not settle easily in white areas. When blacks did make inquiries regarding properties for sale in all-white areas, realtors advised property owners to temporarily take the property off the market and to refrain from using "for sale" signs.[14] Moreover, steering practices by one firm often lead to the opening up of a limited number, one or two at a time, of previously all-white areas for predominant minority settlement, triggering the channeling of minority customers to those areas by other real estate firms.

In the mid-1970s a major research study in the Detroit metropolitan area by Pearce found considerable persistence and increased subtlety in the character of housing discrimination directed against blacks. As part of a systematic field study, one black and one white couple, with similar economic (income, credit, etc.) backgrounds, were sent to the same 97 real estate brokers. Consistent differences along racial lines were found in financial advice, personal treatment, houses shown, and time devoted to the couples. Even though roughly the same as the whites, the economic resources of black couples were evaluated as "lower" in terms of the house prices and financing white real estate agents suggested they could consider. But in general, the quality of the financial advice given to black and white couples was similar. Discrimination in personal treatment was also found, but the racial differences in such matters as courtesy were small. Nevertheless, black couples were much *less* likely to be shown houses than white couples on the first visit. And those black couples who were shown houses were more likely than whites to be shown houses in or near already black areas. Interestingly, and as one might expect, brokers often suggested that black couples look in some other area than where the real estate firm was located. On the whole, brokers spent much more time with white couples than with blacks. Pearce illustrates the subtler nature of current discrimination with this example: Although treated courteously, one black homeseeker (with spouse) who went to a suburban real estate firm was told that his income and savings were insufficient to buy housing in that suburb. The man came back and asked if the researcher had made a mistake, not recognizing that a discriminatory act had occurred. "The white couple, however, was sent out with the same income and savings; in their interview, in contrast, no mention was made to them of inadequate resources for the community, and they were both urged to buy and were shown houses in the same community as the firm in question was located in."[15]

The results of this research in Detroit did not support the idea that discrimination would be more likely in smaller real estate firms headed by prejudiced owners. Indeed, Pearce found a tendency for the more discriminatory real estate brokers to be in larger and more profitable firms. This may be because larger organizations are more resistant to pressures for change. Once race-related discriminatory practices are built into regulations, routines of behavior, and training programs, they are not likely to be altered by weak outside pressures for change or even by a few court suits. Analysis of broker attitudes and prejudices led Pearce to the conclusion that "the organizational situation that salespersons find themselves in overwhelms whatever personal predilections they may have had to either discriminate or not."[16] Apparently more important than a broker's own racial attitudes are the attitudes of the owners of real estate firms, particularly about "relevant others." As we saw in Chapter 3, sometimes white employers will hire few or no minority persons out of fear of white clients' reactions. This concern also motivates white brokers who fear the reactions of other real estate brokers or of the (white) public, since they are involved in a service industry sensitive to client behavior. As one broker recently argued, "Selling to blacks is bad business for us; we have to consider our reputation."[17]

Less subtle manipulation of white fears by white brokers further complicates the housing picture. Once a residential neighborhood develops some natural integration—that is, once a few black families have moved in—brokers can act to destroy that natural integration, at the same time often significantly increasing the price of available housing for blacks, using the technique of "block busting." Brokers have exploited the racial fears of whites in neighborhoods which have begun to experience racial change. Telephone, mail, and face-to-face solicitations for property listings have been made. In one litigated case a mail solicitation stated "We think you may want a friend for a neighbor. . . . know your neighbors," while another informed owners that the real estate firm had paid cash for a certain property in the neighborhood and would "do the same for you." Owners were urged to place their property on the market "before it was too late" or "before the value drops further."[18] In this manner, real estate agents fuel the property value decline and other stereotypes which help to sustain direct discrimination in housing throughout the nation.

Direct discrimination by real estate brokers against white women is less common than in the case of minority persons because women frequently seek for housing with their husbands, either present or in the immediate background. However, when it comes to the growing number of single women, white and nonwhite, with or without children, seeking to buy housing, discrimination again rears its ugly head. A mythology exists in the real estate industry with regard to the effect of single female homeowners on property values similar to that which we previously noted regarding the alleged minority effect. However, only a limited number of single women progress far enough in the house-buying process to be "steered" away from a particular forbidden neighborhood. Single women are believed to be poor credit risks by many if not most males in the housing industry. Women are commonly stereotyped as having less business sense than men; their incomes are thought to be unstable, and there is a pervasive fear that they will become pregnant and lose their jobs. A female real estate broker in San Francisco w as told by the Equal Rights Committee of the California Real Estate Board, "Let's face it, you know women cannot take care of property like men can and they are more flighty and we have to understand that and that is a good basis for prudent lending practices."[19] For the prospective female home buyer, the initial screening for a mortgage loan is frequently done by a male real estate broker. Wishing to remain in favor with the lending institutions whose cooperation is necessary for the continuation of his business, he is reluctant to present a client whose eligibility for a loan appears to be "questionable" in conventional terms. Thus potential female buyers are discouraged from pursuing the possible purchase of a home by the real estate agent and indeed may never proceed any further in the home-buying process. It is apparent that this procedure implements widely-accepted stereotypical attitudes. Of course, screening discrimination of this sort is often faced by minority males as well as by women.

Discrimination in Rental Housing

Real estate brokers are not the only factor in segregated housing patterns or in housing discrimination. The cast of characters in the discrimination arena also includes landlords and the credit (mortgage) institutions upon whom they depend. In the rental housing situation, the practices of all three of these white-dominated groups shape minority experiences.

Both employment discrimination and real estate discrimination, including denial of mortgage loans, have forced blacks into rental housing to a greater extent than whites. Nationwide, only 43 percent of black households, compared with 67 percent of white households, live in houses they own. Analyzing 1970 Census data, Struyk found that this lower rate of homeownership held true for blacks for every family composition type and at every income level.[20] Comparing black and white households with equivalent socioeconomic status and at the same place in the life cycle, Kain and Quigley found that the probability of homeownership for blacks in St. Louis was 9 percent less than for whites in that city.[21]

Many inner city areas have relatively few single-family units available for purchase, and those units which are available are less likely to meet the requirements of mortgage institutions. Analyzing eighteen different metropolitan areas, Kain and Quigley found that black homeownership was lower where blacks were denied access to suburbs and where the ghetto contained mostly multifamily units. On the other hand, black homeownership was greater in cities such as Houston and Los Angeles where the ghetto contained more single-family dwellings and/or where blacks had greater access to the suburban market. Only 5 percent of black-occupied dwellings in such northeastern cities as Boston and Buffalo were owner-occupied.[22] By being excluded from homeownership and forced to rent, minority persons are denied such economic benefits as lower monthly payments for housing, accumulation of equity and the eventual amortization of their mortgage, property appreciation, and tax shelter benefits. Kain and Quigley conclude that "limitations on home-ownership over several generations may be an important part of the explanation of the smaller quantity of assets owned by Negro households at each income level."[23]

Blacks and other nonwhites face substantial direct discrimination in the rental housing market. Considerable discussion of the role of exploitative landlords has appeared in the mass media from time to time. Indeed, numerous white "slumlords" have made unreasonable profits off black Americans locked into ghetto areas. Yet recent research has indicated that the small businessperson who has little capital to improve or repair his (or her) rental housing, rather than the exploitative slumlord, may be the more typical landlord in many ghetto areas. Both the landlord and the minority tenants are dependent on credit and lending institutions for funds for capital improvements. This becomes a critical factor, since the investment community generally avoids minority—especially low-income—areas, which usually mean fewer infusions of money for housing repairs on or additions to exisiting rental housing. Bartelt has called this "a racist system of the distribution of capital." Lenders argue that their housing money flows outside the central cities because of more profitable investment opportunities elsewhere, not because of any intention to discriminate against minorities. However, since this policy ultimately shapes the quality of housing available to minority renters, it constitutes a well-institutionalized pattern of discrimination in lending operations, a topic to which we will turn in more detail in the next section of this chapter.[24]

Rental housing in all-white, or virtually all-white, areas is often off-limits to minority persons. In many areas landlords in small apartment complexes discriminate against nonwhites, using old-fashioned door-slamming techniques. In larger complexes subtler types of discrimination are common, practices which sharply restrict, but do not completely exclude, minority renters. Cases coming before fair housing committees indicate clearly the dodges and ruses used to circumvent fair housing laws. Potential nonwhite renters may be told a vacant unit "has just been rented," or that the rent is 50 percent higher than the figure set for whites, or that the apartment must be repainted and will not be available for a while. A nonwhite couple may be told that they will be called when a vacancy appears, but the call never comes. The wall of discriminatory exclusion has been cracked, but the subtle strategies aimed at minimizing nonwhite tenants are difficult to combat.

Women, particularly single women, also suffer discrimination in the rental housing market. Single women, including those separated or divorced, often must depend on rental property because of their lower incomes and the difficulties they experience in obtaining mortgage loans. Within the rental market women face a variety of blatant and subtle discriminatory practices, all rationalized as protecting the economic interests of the landlords. Many such practices were documented by the testimony of hundreds of women in public hearings in five cities in 1974-1975.[25] Sometimes women are simply told that a unit is not for rent to a single woman; a man is needed to "keep up the property." Some are quoted a higher price than a single male or married couple. A San Antonio woman found an apartment which would have rented for $90 to a couple or $120 to a single man; for her the price was $160. A common practice of landlords is to require a male cosigner for a lease, regardless of the individual woman's financial circumstances. Landlords may refuse to consider income from alimony, child care, or welfare payments when assessing a woman's ability to pay for an apartment. One New York witness reported that in some apartment complexes a single female parent with a female child is rented a one-bedroom apartment regardless of the age of the child, whereas a single parent of either sex with a male child is rented a two-bedroom apartment.

Other practices of landlords appear to fall into the "fair-in-form" category of indirect discrimination. Some landlords exclude all separated or divorced persons, a practice which has a greater impact on women, since there are more women than men in this category. And women are disproportionately affected when landlords exclude single parents with custody of their children, since women also outnumber men in this category.

LENDING AND INSURING ORGANIZATIONS

The official policies and practices of mortgage-granting institutions have paralleled those of the real estate industry in establishing a pattern of institutional discrimination which affects both minorities and women. The U.S. Commission on Civil Rights underscored this in its 1974 *Hartford Report:* "For minorities and women, the mortgage finance system is a stacked deck—stacked sometimes inadvertently, often unthinkingly, but stacked nevertheless."[26] The governing policies of lending organizations, as with real estate brokers, are often rationalized in terms of sound business principles, such as the desire to make profitable investments and to protect those investments against loss. In applying these policies, however, lending organizations make certain requirments favoring white males. Since women and minorities are virtually nonexistent among the local and national decision makers of the nation's major housing, lending, and insuring institutions and are represented in only minute percentages in major governmental housing agencies, it is not surprising that the rules, being written by white males, tend to favor white males.[27] Women and racial minorities are automatically assumed to occupy a less economically stable position.

A mortgage applicant's first contact with a lending institution is usually with a loan officer. It is this official's function to assess the creditworthiness of the prospective borrower, as well as the value of the property to be mortgaged, and to make a recommendation to the loan committee of the institution. Like real estate brokers, loan officers see their future career advancement as molded in part by the accuracy of their judgment of potential borrowers.

Overt discrimination motivated by racial or sexual stereotypes is still part of lending procedures. A Federal Home Loan Bank Board survey of seventy-four lending institutions, released in 1972, found some lenders even admitting that they used the race of an applicant as a factor in determining whether he or she would get a loan.[28] This type of overt discrimination may now be on the decline, particularly for minority males. More subtle and covert forms of discrimination increasingly characterize lending practices. Indeed, there is a great deal of formal and informal assessment involved in a loan or credit approval process, where both intentional and unintentional discrimination can enter in.

In determining the creditworthiness of a prospective borrower, loan officers are guided by criteria set forth in standard texts on mortgage credit risks, such as the following:

> In judging a borrower's reasons for requesting a loan, the lender should consider the strength of his attachment to the property and his probable future attitudes toward it. . . . A borrower's relationship to his family and friends is a significant element of risk although it is difficult to rate. Evaluators usually consider whether a borrower has an established reputation, a harmonious home life, associates with good reputations, and if he is active in civic affairs or whether he has been dishonest and untruthful in the past, has a troubled family life, and associates of doubtful reputation.[29]

This broad statement obviously allows much room for the introduction of racially and sexually biased assumptions. When judging women applicants, to take one example, the condition of separation or divorce may be considered to deviate from the "harmonious home life" proviso. Note, too, that even the language of the statement accents the male pronouns ("he," "his").*

Lenders place heavy emphasis on the credit record of applicants and in addition prefer to make new loans to applicants with past mortgage experience. Both of these practices lead to past-in-present indirect discrimination for both women and racial minorities, since both groups have historically had much less opportunity to establish credit, to secure loans, and to have owned property because of blatant discrimination in the past. Nonwhites are likely to be victims of discriminatory actions by credit bureaus, whose credit records go to lenders. Lending organizations do not have uniform standards regarding the length of time covered in a credit history (this can vary between two and seven years) or regarding the consideration of possible mitigating circumstances surrounding an adverse credit report. Women may inherit a bad credit rating from an ex-husband's credit record.[30] Indirect discrimination is also felt by minorities when lenders disqualify applicants on the basis of arrest records, since minorities are more likely to have been arrested for minor infringements, or falsely arrested, than whites living outside the ghetto.

In determining the size mortgage which an applicant may obtain, lenders frequently use some type of ratio of monthly payment to income. To some extent, each lending organization is free to devise its own formula and change it at its discretion. Even what constitutes "income" is subject to debate. Often lenders count only what they subjectively consider to be permanent, reliable, continuing sources of income. Many lenders have traditionally discounted, to some extent, what they consider secondary income, such as that from a second job, overtime, or a wife's job. Since low- and moderate-income families, which include a disproportionate number of minorities, rely heavily on such secondary incomes, this practice amounts to side-effect

*We will not deal further with the issue of rampant sexism in the English language. We disagree with one reviewer of this paragraph who felt that the masculine pronouns in the quote were only generic, referring to both men and women. The repetitive character of such pronouns in real estate and lending manuals suggests otherwise.

discrimination. Census data from the mid-1970s indicate that wives in 54 percent of black husband-wife families were in the labor force, compared with only 42 percent of wives in similar white families. In husband-wife families in which both husband and wife were employed, the earnings of the wife in black families constituted 31 percent of the total family income as compared with 25 percent in similar white families.[31]

A (white or nonwhite) wife's income is counted variously by lenders, from not at all, to some portion, to all, depending on such factors as her age, the number and ages of her children, the type of job she has, and her marital status. This general practice amounts to overt sex discrimination; it is motivated by sexual stereotypes. According to a 1975 HUD report, only 28 percent of more than 400 large savings and loan associations surveyed by the United States Savings and Loan League indicated that they would count a working wife's full income when considering a mortgage application. A young woman with young children is the least likely to have her full salary counted because it is assumed that she will have additional children. One-quarter of the savings and loan associations in another survey said that they would totally discount the full-time income of a twenty-five-year-old mother of two; more than half of these institutions would count 50 percent or less of her income; only 22 percent would give full credit.[32]

Single women, whether never married, separated, divorced, or widowed, have traditionally been less likely to get a mortgage than men. Some lenders simply specify that they loan only to intact families, which obviously means male-headed families. Single women are considered less stable in their jobs than men, and thus greater credit risks. If a mortgage is granted to a single woman, a higher-than-average down payment may be required. A separated woman is considered to have an ambiguous legal status for debt liability. An unmarried woman is assumed likely to have her economic status altered by marriage or pregnancy. A divorced woman receiving "support" income is likely to have this income discounted, and lenders may even require a divorced woman to furnish a complete set of her divorce papers. Single women applying for mortgage loans have been required to pay all outstanding debts before the loan would be approved. Lowering the amount of real income which can be counted toward the monthly payment-to-income ratio may require the prospective female, or minority male, borrower to make a greater-than-usual down payment. This practice has the further effect of steering women and minorities to lower-priced or rental housing, thus limiting their range of housing choices. Not unexpectedly, then, homeownership in 1970 was 20 percent lower among female-headed families than among male-headed families, and 24 percent lower among black families than among white families.[33]

Other practices of lending organizations have a disproportionately negative effect on potential and actual homeowners among minorities. When minority persons seek out the better, repairable housing in ghetto areas of central cities they run up against the profit-oriented regulations of mortgage lenders who often will not grant mortgages or loan money for repairs in what they view as "deteriorating" neighborhoods. Yet these areas are often the only places in which minority persons can find a house to own. Lender decisions based on an overall economic view of a central city rather than on the individual merit of either the prospective borrower or the property to be mortgaged may constitute a particularly restrictive example of indirect institutional discrimination, since because of residential segregation practices proportionately more minority persons than whites will be negatively affected. This practice is sometimes termed "redlining," after the lender's practice of actually or imaginarily circling a financially risky area on a map in red. An area may be characterized as risky based on the age and condition of its properties and the income level of its residents; the racial composition of the neighborhood may also be explicitly considered. Lenders often defend their lack of investment in "declining" areas as a sound business principle, although many critics see racist stereotypes directly involved in many cases.[34] In any event, in light of the vast web of other discriminatory practices both past and present, minorities suffer disproportionately under such a redlining lending system.

Senator William Proxmire, chairman of the U.S. Senate Committee on Banking, Housing and Urban Affairs, made the following opening statement at the hearings on the Home Mortgage Disclosure Act of 1975:

Redlining involves something as basic as the survival of America's great cities. When lenders systematically restrict mortgage credit in a so-called declining neighborhood, their fears can become a self-ful-filling reality. Homeowners move out; new ones can't move in. The community goes into a tailspin, with the ultimate result that sound existing housing prematurely deteriorates and the community dies a premature death. . . .

The individual lender may defend his decision to make loans on newer homes in the suburbs as economically prudent. He may regard the inner-city loan as a marginally poorer risk.

The only problem is that when we add up all of these individual lenders' supposedly rational decisions, they are irrational taken as a whole, and viable neighborhoods die for lack of mortgage credit. That is redlining.[35]

In testimony before the Proxmire hearings George Sternlieb, director of the Center for Urban Policy Research at Rutgers University, documented the decline in availability of mortgage financing for ghetto areas in cities across the country, from New York, Newark, Boston, Hartford, and Washington, D.C., to Milwaukee, St. Louis, and Memphis, to Los Angeles and San Diego, and dating back to the 1920s. The drop in mortgage availability for most cities has been particularly severe in recent years. Sternlieb noted, for example, that for the decade between 1961 and 1971 the yearly number of mortgage loans granted by savings and loan associations, mutual savings banks, and commercial banks within the city of Newark had dropped by almost 90 percent. The total number of mortgages from all sources had declined by approximately 60 percent. Sternlieb pointed to the prevalence of redlining as the primary cause of this decline in available financing.[36]

In an analysis of the residential investment activities of 127 lending institutions in Chicago from 1970 to 1973, the Federal Home Loan Bank of Chicago found that for heavily redlined areas reinvestment by the savings and loan associations in the area averaged 4¢ per dollar deposited by people there, compared with suburban reinvestment of 31¢ per dollar deposited by people in suburban areas. Between 1972 and 1973 investments in redlined areas in Chicago fell as much as 64 percent. What mortgage money is available in urban areas is accompanied by a loan-to-value ratio which is frequently lower than for housing in suburban areas. Sternlieb cited a Milwaukee survey which showed a 60 percent loan-to-property-value ratio in urban areas at the same time that the loan-to-value ratio in suburban areas was 80 percent. Savings and loan associations in Chicago required a 40 percent down payment in redlined areas, and would make no loans on homes over fifteen years old. When the loan-to-property-value ratio is low, or when a property is appraised below its actual selling price, the ghetto buyer must either make a larger-than-usual down payment or take a second loan. Mortgages in ghetto areas often have the additional problem of short terms, ranging from five to twelve years, and higher-than-usual interest rates, ranging up to 30 percent.[37]

The difficulty in obtaining mortgages from conventional lenders on favorable terms, if indeed at all, causes many borrowers in ghetto and central city areas to seek out loans from private speculators. Not only are interest rates usually much higher and terms much shorter for these private "land installment contracts," but frequently the sales price is sharply inflated. Properties examined by the Chicago Commission on Human Relations found markups from 35 to 115 percent over the original cost. Sternlieb calls these additional costs a "black tax." Surveys of New York, Newark, and Chicago revealed that installment contracts accounted for between 50 and 83 percent of mortgages in some ghetto neighborhoods.[38] The Chicago Commission on Human Relations concluded:

> For the black contract buyer, the present state of affairs spells hardship, suffering, exhaustion, and despair. It means that husbands must work two and sometimes three jobs in order to make ends meet. It means that wives must work, that family life is all but destroyed, and that children must be left unsupervised, and then people ask why there is a high crime rate in black areas. ... Couples were faced with the choice of continuing to pay exorbitant rents comparable to their current monthly installments or buying on contract with the hope that someday they might own their own homes. It also means that they must stand under the criticism of the white community for not maintaining their buildings and living in squalor. And it hurts all the more because they are only too well aware that they cannot do much in the line of repairs after having put all their money into the pockets of speculators through their outrageous monthly installments.[39]

A related example of housing discrimination can be seen in the behavior of insurance companies which have different insurance rates for different residential and geographical areas, rates officially set by "good business practices." The rate maps which many agents carry often show rates as much as 30 or 40 percent higher in ghetto areas. The more costly areas tend to be minority residential areas, usually not because insurance companies desire to discriminate directly against minority persons, although in some cases this is doubtless an underlying factor, but because rates must go up as the risk of insurance losses from fire, theft, or vandalism increases. These insurance practices in turn make mortgage loans more difficult to secure. In addition, insurance companies often consider single women homeowners, especially those with children, too great a risk to insure. For example, an Atlanta woman found her homeowner's insurance policy promptly canceled following her divorce, even though the same property had been insured when owned jointly with her husband prior to the divorce.[40]

GOVERNMENTS
AND HOUSING DISCRIMINATION

The various housing-related laws, regulations, and administrative practices of governmental units from the national to the local level have also contributed to the institutionalization and continuance of direct and indirect discrimination in housing markets in the United States.

The Federal Government

At the national level, the Federal Housing Administration (FHA) and other branches of the Department of Housing and Urban Development (HUD) have perhaps been the most influential agencies shaping the nation's housing character and residential patterns. The FHA was organized in 1934 for the purpose of making home mortgages more easily available to home buyers by providing government-backed mortgage insurance. By decreasing the risk of the lender, mortgages could be made at lower interest rates, for longer periods of time, and with lower payments. Guidelines for mortgage risk ratings were set down in the FHA's *Underwriting Manual*, written with the advice and assistance of members of the private (white) National Association of Real Estate Boards. The racial ideology of the FHA expressed in the *Manual* and elsewhere has reinforced the development of the dual housing market and furthered the encapsulation of minorities. In its early editions, the *Underwriting Manual* (1936) emphasized the importance of homogeneous neighborhoods for making favorable appraisals, listing "the presence of incompatible racial elements" as a basis for assigning a low rating to, or rejecting, a dwelling in a racially mixed area. Racially restrictive deeds were recommended to protect an area from "inharmonious racial groups." Subsequent editions of the *Manual*, beginning in 1955, omitted explicit mention of race but still prescribed low ratings for houses in areas undergoing change and for older homes—the housing most often available to minority buyers.[41] Indeed, for many decision makers the phrase "areas undergoing change" refers covertly to "minority areas." These influential federal government regulations have served greatly to restrict the housing choices and homeownership possibilities of minority persons, dictating blatant direct discrimination along racial lines in the real estate and lending sectors and reinforcing real estate brokers' propensity to discriminate.

Actions by other federal agencies have also shaped segregated housing patterns. For example, suburbanization has often been stimulated by government action in the form of federally subsidized circumferential highways which encourage housing developments and job expansion outside central cities where minorities typically live. In addition, inner cities are frequently the sites of urban renewal, a process carried out under the auspices of HUD and its predecessor, the federal Housing and Home Finance Agency, which more often than not has left former residents homeless while replacing their deteriorated dwellings with commercial structures or expensive apartment buildings. Although the rhetoric behind urban renewal speaks of improving housing for the poor, far more reasonably priced housing units have been destroyed by urban renewal than have been rebuilt after clearance. As Scott Greer put it, "at a cost of more than three billion dollars the Urban Renewal Agency (URA) has succeeded in materially reducing the supply of low-cost housing in American cities."[42] Since nonwhite families are disproportionately represented in inner city neighborhoods, they have borne a disproportionate burden of the housing demolition in the urban renewal process. An estimated 60–70 percent of those in ripped-through central city neighborhoods have been minority Americans. The real goal of urban renewal was to expand the profits of private business at the expense of the poor. Minority families also are disproportionately displaced when highway construction connecting expanding white suburbia with the central business district either replaces their central city neighborhoods or cuts through in such a way as to add further scars, noise, and pollution. The middle-class white can usually leave the central city with ease; the middle-class minority person has far fewer options. And displaced low-income families, especially if minority group members, usually find themselves forced into housing situations at least as segregated as those from which they were displaced by such government action.

Local Government

Let us here explore the implications of "local control" as it applies to housing patterns. Local control of residential areas is the rule in American towns and cities; local areas control zoning, building codes, and subdivision regulations in all states but Hawaii.[43] Cities have used these powers to keep many neighborhoods homogeneous, that is, all-poor, all-rich, all-white, etc. Zoning is also used by suburbs to control population density. Many suburban areas ringing the cities are self-governing, which means that most such areas are controlled by whites, with no blacks participating in the establishment of their goals or regulations. The objectives of the suburbs do not include the minority point of view. This in itself is an important effect of past housing discrimination. Suburban governments have shown an intense desire to maintain certain requirements which provide green areas, uncrowded schools, and adequate water facilities. "Exclusionary zoning" in suburbia usually includes such things as prohibition of multifamily units and mobile homes, restrictions on the number of bedrooms per unit, minimum lot size, minimum number of square feet per structure, and restrictions on types of building materials. Large lot size not only serves as a control for density; by making land more scarce, it raises its cost and also the per-lot cost of such improvements as streets, sidewalks, and sewers. Such suburban zoning laws have been successful in excluding not only low-cost housing but also as a result many minority families.[44] Yet in numerous suburbs the zoning for low density was originally established with little thought of keeping nonwhite homebuyers out, since they were at that time kept out by deed restrictions and other types of blatant racial discrimination. Today, however, zoning can operate as an indirect means of discrimination by legally requiring housing types which a disproportionate number of nonwhites cannot afford.

In some towns and cities zoning regulations have been intentionally, if sometimes covertly, established to exclude nonwhite families from certain residential areas. Racial stereotypes are lurking behind these discriminatory actions. Recently in Cleveland, for example, a black mayor's attempt to develop a new residential community was blocked by suburban mayors concerned over the possibility of blacks moving out of the city. In Black Jack, Missouri, a St. Louis suburb, the threat of a nonprofit sponsor building multifamily housing led to that area incorporating itself and banning multifamily housing under new laws. Other suburban areas have incorporated in order to keep minorities out. Although the intent in such cases is clearly racial, it is increasingly masked by publicly expressed concerns over property values, high densities, and overcrowded schools.[45] The use of zoning laws to exclude minorities is usually a more covert type of discrimination; it is very difficult to prove in court that the use of these laws to exclude is racially motivated, a problem to which we will return.

The location of publicly subsidized housing, and especially multifamily housing, in both city and suburban areas has provoked considerable discussion of the use of zoning and related housing laws. Local governments control the sites for public housing and whether public housing gets built or not, while the federal government provides most of the money and, at least officially, supervision of such housing. But HUD and its predecessor agencies have provided no protection for minorities against discrimination by local governments. Instead, federal housing agencies have played an important role in perpetuating the encapsulation of minorities in ghetto areas by allowing federally subsidized housing projects to be concentrated in already segregated areas by local government agencies. Although HUD has the authority to cut off federal funding to local housing agencies which do not comply with fair housing laws, it has long shown a preference for going along with local wishes. The earliest public housing units sometimes took the form of huge, often ugly, high-rise structures built close together in the poorer areas of the inner cities. Soon many became minority-populated. Governments have not only forced minority families needing subsidized housing to live in segregated areas but have created an image of high-rise housing which suburban whites fear, even though today new public housing units are typically two- to three-story and usually indistinguishable from comparable nonsubsidized housing.[46] White fear has even prompted many suburban governments to turn down federal development funds in order to retain local control and exclude public housing, and thereby minority families. Frequently intentional institutionalized discrimination is barely concealed in the use of zoning laws by suburban communities to restrict or exclude federally subsidized housing. In addition to zoning laws, a recently developed device used to keep out federally subsidized housing is the community referendum. By the 1970s numerous suburbs established laws requiring that all proposed subsidized housing be approved in a public referendum. Danielson has concluded that "suburbanites tend to equate subsidized housing with public housing, which in turn is closely identified with blacks."[47]

We can now look at some specific examples of public housing controversies in cities and suburbs. In the mid-1960s the Chicago Housing Authority (CHA) presented a proposal to the Chicago City Council to begin construction of low-rent public housing projects throughout the city. At that time 99.5 percent of public projects already built were located in the ghetto, with 99 percent of the units occupied by nonwhites. Only four units were located in white neighborhoods, and these were listed on CHA forms as "suitable for white families only." The proposal was rejected by the city council; the CHA then made an unsuccessful appeal to HUD officials in Washington, following which the CHA retreated to the segregated public housing policy which the city council desired. In 1966 a group of black tenants in and applicants for public housing filed suit against HUD and the CHA. The CHA was charged with purposefully selecting its public housing sites to keep blacks out of white neighborhoods, with their typically better facilities, and HUD was charged with financially supporting these discriminatory practices. Three years later the federal district court officially found CHA guilty of violating the constitutional rights of the black tenants and applicants by its discriminatory site selections and tenant assignments and ordered the CHA to disperse future public housing in previously all-white neighborhoods, discontinue its discriminatory tenant assignment procedures, and move rapidly to increase the supply of nonsegregated units. In 1970 HUD was also found guilty of helping to perpetuate "a racially discriminatory housing system in Chicago."[48]

The CHA's refusal to comply and HUD's refusal to enforce compliance prompted a maze of further litigation. However, by the late 1970s the public housing situation in Chicago remained unchanged. In 1976 all the family-type public housing units in Chicago were still located in black ghettos, and 95 percent of the tenants black.[49] As of this writing the CHA case is still in the courts.

Moreover, in 1976, the Supreme Court held that HUD must provide low-income housing in the Chicago suburbs in order to relieve the segregated condition which it has long perpetuated. But the Court also allowed local governmental units to retain their zoning powers and their "right to comment on specific assistance proposals."[50] Commenting on this 1976 decision, the white mayor of a predominantly white Chicago suburb said, "I really don't think the federal government will go charging out to the suburbs to put in housing where it's not wanted. If you don't have local cooperation, you'll have a hell of a situation."[51] Alexander Polikoff, an attorney who has been involved with the CHA case since it was first filed in 1966 and who argued on behalf of the plaintiffs before the Supreme Court, also felt that the Court's decision to uphold local zoning powers would limit the effectiveness of the low-income housing dispersal order: "Any community that wants to oppose subsidized housing can use its land-use powers just as it always has."[52]

Arlington Heights, an affluent Chicago suburb, resisted the building of low- and moderate-income multifamily housing units there by using its zoning regulations. The publicly expressed concern did not explicitly touch on race (some of the new families were likely to be minority), but rather on the way in which local property values in a single-family area would be affected by multifamily housing units. After the local zoning board voted nine to two against the necessary rezoning proposition, the case went to the federal courts. Because there was no evidence of racially exclusionary action on intentional grounds, the Supreme Court eventually upheld this type of zoning decision in an important case, *Arlington Heights* v. *Metropolitan Housing Corp.* (1977).[53] The "Nixon Court" again retreated to the position that discrimination must be *proven* by complainants to be intentional in order for it to be ruled illegal; the exclusionary impact of zoning regulations alone is not sufficient to allow federal courts to intervene on behalf of those excluded.

A final note should be added on the role of government in patterns of housing discrimination against women. Virtually no attention has been given to this issue in the literature on housing. Clearly, women, particularly single women, have suffered discrimination at the hands of real estate agents, bankers, and landlords, in trying both to rent and to buy housing. Yet generally speaking, government agencies seem to have taken little active role, at least in the way of a formal policy role, in reinforcing discriminatory real estate and mortgage practices. Substantial informal support, however, has been provided at the federal government level, as can be seen by the slowness with which federal agencies have responded to civil rights legislation, such as the provisions of the 1974 Housing and Community Development Act extending the 1968 Civil Rights Act prohibitions against discrimination to sex discrimination. No government action was taken by the agencies until the mid-1970s to do anything substantial about real estate and mortgage discrimination on the basis of sex.

In addition, local government actions, as in using zoning laws to exclude multifamily housing, have resulted in some housing segregation for single women, including separated and divorced women with families. Since apartment housing is often concentrated in certain areas of cities, single women—often with lower incomes than single men—must seek out that housing. They, too, suffer a degree of housing segregation, with greater separation from certain facilities perhaps being one result. The separation is not nearly as great for single white women as it is for nonwhite men and women, but even the degree of segregation which exists suggests that many single white women with families are also second-class citizens.

THE IMPACT OF DISCRIMINATION

Racial discrimination in the housing market has a severe negative impact on the quality of the housing and neighborhoods that minorities can secure as well as on the jobs that are readily accessible to them. One effect of the dual housing market is that many minority families must live in certain encapsulated areas, which usually amount to older, perhaps decaying, inner city areas of concentrated poverty, or in some instances new developments set apart from white areas and specified for minority occupancy. In central cities minority persons, whatever their incomes, share the same neighborhoods, frequently troubled areas. For example, a social map of the inner city of Washington, D.C., an area which is almost entirely black, shows this area to have also a disproportionately high share of the city's infant mortality and drug addiction.[54] Nationwide, more than two-and-one-half times as many black households in rental units in 1974 lived in crowded conditions, as defined by federal standards, as did similar white households. Substandard housing quality in rental units, the bulk of ghetto housing, has been documented for numerous cities. For example, over eight times as many units were unsound in ghetto areas of San Francisco as in the white areas, and the average age of the dwellings was approximately double. Seventy-seven percent of ghetto rental units were constructed prior to 1940, compared with 25 percent in the white areas.[55]

When minority group members are able to buy property, their housing package is frequently much less attractive than that of whites. In San Francisco, the least segregated of the thirty large American metropolitan areas in the study cited at the beginning of this chapter, 70 percent of blacks live in only 9 percent of the Census tracts. In an interview survey of 28,000 households there in 1965, Straszheim found proportionately less than half as many homeowners in ghetto areas as in white areas. Among owner-occupied units there were more than three times as many physically unsound dwellings in the ghetto areas as in white areas. The average age of owner-occupied units in ghetto areas was almost twice that of those in white areas; a full 64 percent of such ghetto dwellings were built prior to 1940, as compared with 34 percent in the white areas. Smaller lot size in ghetto areas also contributed to much higher population density.[56] In their research study of St. Louis families, Kain and Quigley, after controlling for socioeconomic status and stage in family life cycle, found that blacks received substantially less than whites in dwelling quality as measured by interior and exterior condition of dwellings, age of structure, and presence of hot water and central heating. They also suffered a substantial difference in both neighborhood quality, as evidenced by the condition of adjacent properties and neighborhood prestige, and in the amount of exterior space. Nonwhite families who can afford housing outside central cities suffer the effects of being forced to accept less in their total housing package than they could otherwise expect in an open housing market. Even when blacks are able to own their own homes, properties available to them have been found to be $3000 to $4000 less valuable than those occupied by white owners with equivalent socioeconomic characteristics.[57]

Shopping and community participation are two additional areas in which the nonwhite person suffers the effects of housing discrimination. Residential encapsulation brings with it limited knowledge of and access to other areas of the city, the stigma of separation, and creates an "ours and theirs" atmosphere with regard to community enterprises and organizations.

To be sure, all blacks do not live in central cities. Since the 1950s significant black suburbanization has occurred. However, the lion's share of this movement has been to segregated neighborhoods. Of the thousands of urban blacks who moved to suburban areas between 1950 and 1970, two-thirds entered old industrial suburbs from which whites were moving, and an additional one-fourth went to suburbs built expressly for blacks.[58] Moreover, only a very small proportion of all blacks have found their way even to the segregated areas of suburbia. Census data show that in 1974 only 17 percent of the black population were residing in suburban rings. Incredibly, 1970 data for twenty-nine of the nation's largest metropolitan areas reveal that a greater proportion of white families in the $5,000–6,999 income bracket lived in suburbia than of black families in the much higher $15,000–24,000 bracket.[59] This dramatic difference is the result of the well-institutionalized patterns of direct and indirect discrimination created by private real estate and lending institutions with the collusion of local, state, and federal governments.

Exclusion from suburbia has also had an effect on job opportunities. Polarization in housing contributes to polarization in jobs. "In St. Louis, Boston, Phoenix, Washington, D.C., and New York the pattern is the same: jobs have been accompanying the movement of middle-class housing to the suburbs."[60] Kain has demonstrated that direct discrimination in suburban housing has limited the job opportunities of black Americans, since much economic development has occurred in the suburban rings.[61]

Conclusion

Discrimination, both direct and indirect, persists in the housing sphere. Patterns of housing segregation seem to have changed relatively little since the 1950s. Intentional, if increasingly subtle, discrimination continues as part of the established framework within which real estate agents and bankers and other lenders operate. Past and present discrimination in the sale and rental of housing has created a well-institutionalized dual housing market, one for minorities and one for whites. Civil rights laws seem to have had a limited remedial impact. Even if intentional discrimination were to disappear overnight, it is probable that established patterns of segregated housing would persist for a very long time because of indirect discrimination. Discrimination against women, particularly single women, also remains entrenched in these same real estate and lending institutions, particularly in regard to their renting and buying housing units in their own names. The outlawing of certain discriminatory real estate and lending practices by federal legislation in 1974–1975, such as the Housing and Community Development Act, has only just begun to result in a decrease in the more blatant instances of discrimination.

In the early 1970s numerous observers of government action became relatively optimistic about changes in segregated housing patterns. At the same time, these observers of suburbia ignored or played down the growing political influence of suburbia, influence which keeps state and federal governments from interfering with the control local governments exert over subsidized housing. For example, in 1972 the prominent syndicated columnist Joseph Kraft, citing a few court rulings and other government and private developments favorable to opening up the suburbs, wrote an article titled "The Coming Apart of Fortress Suburbia." Yet as we have noted, the political changes cited by Kraft have not really resulted in significant desegregation of suburbia.[62] Thus, as the National Committee Against Discrimination in Housing concluded:

> Until local governments have been deprived of the power to exclude subsidized housing and to manipulate zoning and other controls to screen out families on the basis of income and, implicitly, of race, there can be no effective progress in halting the trend toward predominantly black cities surrounded by almost entirely white suburbs—the geographic manifestation of "two nations, one black and one white, separate and unequal."[63]

1. John Tepper Marlin, "City Housing," *Municipal Performance Report* 1, no. 2 (November 1973): 17–18. See also U.S. Bureau of the Census, *Social and Economic Characteristics of the Metropolitan and Nonmetropolitan Population, 1974 and 1970*, Current Population Reports, Special Studies Series P-23, no. 55 (Washington, D.C.: U.S. Government Printing Office, 1975), table F, p. 6.

2. Michael N. Danielson, *The Politics of Exclusion* (New York: Columbia University Press, 1976), p. 8. See also Social Science Panel of the Advisory Committee to the Department of Housing and Urban Development, *Freedom of Choice in Housing* (Washington, D.C.: National Academy of Sciences, 1972), p. 5.

3. Thomas F. Pettigrew, "Attitudes on Race and Housing: A Socio-Psychological View," in *Segregation in Residential Areas: Papers on Socioeconomic and Racial Factors in the Choice of Housing*, edited by Amos H. Hawley and Vincent Rock (Washington D.C.: National Academy of Sciences,

1973). See also Reynolds Farley, "The Changing Distribution of Negroes in Metropolitan Areas: The Emergence of Black Suburbs," *American Journal of Sociology* 73 (1970): 15–31; Leo F. Schnore, Carolyn D. Andre, and Harry Sharp, "Black Suburbanization, 1930–1970," in *The Changing Face of the Suburbs*, edited by Barry Schwartz (Chicago: University of Chicago Press, 1976).

4. Rose Helper, *Racial Policies and Practices of Real Estate Brokers* (Minneapolis: University of Minnesota Press, 1969), p. 25.

5. Ibid., pp. 224 ff. See *Buchanan* v. *Warley*, 38 S. Ct. 16 (1917).

6. *Chicago Real Estate Bulletin* 25, no. 4 (April 1917): 313, quoted in Helper, *Racial Policies and Practices of Real Estate Brokers*, p. 225.

7. Quoted in Helper, *Racial Policies and Practices of Real Estate Brokers*, p. 201.

8. Letter from an official of the NAREB, quoted in Helper, *Racial Policies and Practices of Real Estate Brokers*, p. 233. See *Shelley* v. *Kraemer*, 68 S. Ct. 836 (1948).

9. Part I, Article 5, cited in Harry G. Atkinson and Percy E. Wagner, *Modern Real Estate Practice* (Homewood, Ill.: Dow Jones–Irwin, 1974), p. 236.

10. Baltimore Urban League, *Civil Rights in Baltimore: A Community Audit* (Baltimore, 1950), p. 11, quoted in Helper, *Racial Policies and Practices of Real Estate Brokers*, p. 233; William L. Price, *Factors Influencing and Restraining the Housing Mobility of Negroes in Metropolitan Detroit* (Detroit: Detroit Urban League, 1955), cited in Helper, *Racial Policies and Practices of Real Estate Brokers*, p. 234; Southgate, California incident cited in Helper, *Racial Policies and Practices of Real Estate Brokers*, pp. 234–35.

11. Joseph Barndt, *Liberating Our White Ghetto* (Minneapolis: Augsburg Publishing House, 1970), p. 60.

12. Joe T. Darden, *Afro-Americans in Pittsburgh* (Lexington, Mass.: Lexington Books, 1973), p. 49.

13. A. M. Slaughter, testimony before the U.S. Commission on Civil Rights, Oakland, California, May 12, 1964, cited in William H. Brown, Jr., "Access to Housing: The Role of the Real Estate Industry," *Economic Geography* 48 (January 1972): 70.

14. *Zuch* v. *Hussey*, 394 F. Supp. 1028 (1975). See also Foundation for Change, *Fact Sheets on Institutional Racism: White Control and Minority Oppression* (New York, 1974), p. 7; U.S. Commission on Civil Rights, *The Federal Civil Rights Enforcement Effort, 1974*, vol. 2, *To Provide ... for Fair Housing* (Washington, D.C.: U.S. Government Printing Office, 1974).

15. Diana May Pearce, "Black, White, and Many Shades of Gray: Real Estate Brokers and their Racial Practices," Ph.D. thesis, University of Michigan, 1976, pp. 271-72 and *passim.*

16. Ibid., p. 261.

17. Cited in U.S. Commission on Civil Rights, *Equal Opportunity in Suburbia* (Washington, D.C.: U.S. Government Printing Office, 1974), p. 20.

18. *Zuch* v. *Hussey,* 394 F. Supp. 1028, 1045 (1975); for a further discussion and examples of block-busting practices see Joseph G. Bisceglia, "Blockbusting: Judicial and Legislative Response to Real Estate Dealers' Excesses," *De Paul Law Review* 22, no. 3 (Spring 1973): 818-38.

19. U.S. Department of Housing and Urban Development, *Women and Housing: A Report on Sex Discrimination in Five American Cities* (Washington, D.C.: U.S. Government Printing Office, 1975), pp. 53-54.

20. Raymond Struyk, *Urban Home Ownership* (Lexington, Mass.: Lexington Books, 1976), p. 11. See also U.S. Bureau of the Census, *The Social and Economic Status of the Black Population in the United States, 1974* (Washington, D.C.: U.S. Government Printing Office, 1975), p. 134.

21. John F. Kain and John M. Quigley, "Housing Market Discrimination, Home Ownership, and Savings Behavior," *American Economic Review* (June 1972): 265.

22. Marlin, "City Housing," p. 20.

23. Kain and Quigley, "Housing Market Discrimination, Home Ownership, and Savings Behavior," p. 276.

24. David W. Bartelt, "Institutional Racism in the Rental Housing Market," paper prepared for the 1977 Symposium on Institutional Racism/Sexism, April 28-30, 1977. On the role of lending organizations in central cities, see David Harvey, "The Political Economy of Urbanization in Advanced Capitalist Countries," in *The Social Economy of Cities,* edited by Gary Gappert and Harold Rose (Beverly Hills, Calif.: Sage Publications, 1975), pp. 119-64.

25. The hearings were held by the National Council of Negro Women, Inc. in Atlanta, St. Louis, San Antonio, San Francisco, and New York. U.S. Department of Housing and Urban Development, *Women and Housing,* pp. 33-45.

26. U.S. Commission on Civil Rights, *Mortgage Money: Who Gets It?* Clearinghouse Publication 48 (Washington, D.C.: U.S. Government Printing Office, 1974), p. 33 (hereinafter cited as *Hartford Report*).

27. U.S. Department of Housing and Urban Development, *Women and Housing,* pp. 21-22.

28. U.S. Commission on Civil Rights, *Equal Opportunity in Suburbia,* p. 22.

29. Anthony D. Grezzo, *Mortgage Credit Risk Analysis and Servicing of Delinquent Mortgages* (Washington, D.C.: U.S. Department of Housing and Urban Development, 1972), p. 14, quoted in *Hartford Report,* p. 12.

30. See *Hartford Report.*

31. U.S. Bureau of the Census, *The Social and Economic Status of the Black Population in the United States, 1974,* pp. 30, 40.

32. U.S. Department of Housing and Urban Development, *Women and Housing,* pp. 70, 81n.

33. Ibid., pp. 65–68; *Hartford Report,* pp. 3, 27–29.

34. U.S. Senate, *Hearings on S. 1281 Before the Senate Committee on Banking, Housing, and Urban Affairs,* 94th Cong., 1st Sess., pt. 1, pp. 532–33 (hereinafter cited as *Hearings on S. 1281*). See also D.C. Public Interest Research Group, *Redlining: Mortgage Disinvestment in the District of Columbia* (Washington, D.C., 1975), cited in "Legality of Redlining Under the Civil Rights Law," *American University Law Review* 25 (Winter 1976): 463–95.

35. *Hearings on S. 1281,* p. 1.

36. Ibid., pp. 549–51; for numerous examples of redlining for various urban areas see also pp. 167–514.

37. Freddi L. Greenberg, "Redlining: The Fight Against Discrimination in Mortgage Lending," *Loyola University of Chicago Law Journal* 22 (Winter 1975): 71–89; *Hearings on S. 1281,* pp. 533, 551–54.

38. Ibid., pp. 555–56, 560.

39. Chicago Commission on Human Relations, "Mortgage Availability in Racially Transitional Areas," presented at public hearing of the Commission, August 9, 1967, quoted by Sternlieb in *Hearings on S. 1281,* p. 561.

40. U.S Department of Housing and Urban Development, *Women and Housing,* p. 75. See also testimony before the Illinois Legislative Investigating Commission, July 25, 1974, cited in Greenberg, "Redlining," p. 72; Barndt, *Liberating Our White Ghetto,* p. 62; U.S. Commission on Civil Rights, *The Federal Civil Rights Enforcement Effort, 1974,* vol. 2, *To Provide . . . for Fair Housing,* p. 179.

41. U.S. Federal Housing Administration, Housing and Home Finance Agency, *Underwriting Manual,* Form No. 2049, rev. ed. (Washington, D.C.: U.S. Government Printing Office, 1936), part 2, sec. 2, arts. 252, 228, 229; see also U.S. Federal Housing Administration, Housing and Home Finance Agency, *Underwriting Manual,* Form No. 2049, rev. ed. (Washington, D.C.: U.S. Government Printing Office, 1955), part 3, sec. 13, arts. 1301, 1320.

42. Scott Greer, *Urban Renewal and American Cities* (Indianapolis, Ind.: Bobbs Merrill, 1965), p. 3. See also Chester Hartman, *Yerba Buena: Land Grab and Community Resistance in San Francisco* (San Francisco: Glide Publications, 1974).

43. Danielson, *The Politics of Exclusion*, p. 1.

44. U.S. Commission on Civil Rights, *Equal Opportunity in Suburbia*, p. 7.

45. U.S. Commission on Civil Rights, *Above Property Rights*, Clearinghouse Publication no. 38 (Washington, D.C.: U.S. Government Printing Office, 1972), p. 13.

46. Sylvia Lewis, "Supreme Court Orders HUD to Disperse Public Housing," *Planning* 42 (June 1976): 11.

47. Danielson, *The Politics of Exclusion*, pp. 90, 100-101.

48. *Gautreaux* v. *Romney*, 448 F. 2d 731, 739 (1971); *Gautreaux* v. *CHA*, 296 F. Supp. 907 (1969); *Gautreaux* v. *CHA*, 304 F. Supp. 736 (1969); *Hills* v. *Gautreaux*, 96 S. Ct. 1538, 1541 (1976). See also Frederick Lazon, "The Failure of Federal Enforcement of Civil Rights Regulations in Public Housing, 1963-1971: The Cooptation of a Federal Agency by Its Local Constituency," *Policy Sciences* 4 (September 1973): 263-73.

49. Lewis, "Supreme Court Orders HUD to Disperse Public Housing," p. 9.

50. *Hills* v. *Gautreaux*, 96 S. Ct. 1538, 1549 (1976).

51. Lewis, "Supreme Court Orders HUD to Disperse Public Housing," p. 8.

52. Ibid.

53. *Arlington Heights* v. *Metropolitan Housing Corp.*, 429 U.S., 252 (1977).

54. A social map was prepared by Applied Urbanetics, Inc., cited in Tom Wicker, "A Tale of Two Cities," *New York Times*, February 7, 1971.

55. Mahlon R. Straszheim, "Racial Discrimination in the Urban Housing Market and Its Effects on Black Housing Consumption," in *Patterns of Racial Discrimination*, vol. 1, *Housing*, edited by George M. von Furstenberg, Bennett Harrison, and Ann R. Horowitz (Lexington, Mass.: Lexington Books, 1974); U.S. Bureau of the Census, *The Social and Economic Status of the Black Population in the United States, 1974*, pp. 134-37.

56. Straszheim, "Racial Discrimination in the Urban Housing Market and Its Effects on Black Housing Consumption," pp. 139-64.

57. John M. Quigley, "Racial Discrimination and the Housing Consumption of Black Households," in von Furstenberg et al., *Patterns of Racial Discrimination*, vol. 1, *Housing*, pp. 128-30.

58. Karl E. Taeuber, "Racial Segregation: The Persisting Dilemma," *Annals of the American Academy of Political and Social Science* 422 (November 1975): 90.

59. U.S. Bureau of the Census, *Social and Economic Characteristics of the Metropolitan and Nonmetropolitan Population, 1974 and 1970*, table F, p. 6; Albert I. Hermalin and Reynolds Farley, "The Potential for Residential Integration in Cities and Suburbs: Implications for the Busing Controversy," *American Sociological Review* 38 (October 1973): 605.

60. U.S. Commission on Civil Rights, *Equal Opportunity in Suburbia*, p.

61. John F. Kain, "Housing Segregation, Black Employment, and Metropolitan Decentralization: A Retrospective," in von Furstenberg et al., *Patterns of Racial Discrimination*, vol. 1, *Housing*, p. 9.

62. Danielson, *The Politics of Exclusion*, pp. 325-26.

63. Quoted in Joseph P. Fried, *Housing Crisis U.S.A.* (New York: Praeger, 1971), pp. 50-51.

Discrimination in Education, Health and Social Services, Politics, and the Courts

chapter five

Blatant and subtle patterns of discrimination are not limited to the employment and housing spheres, although discrimination in these basic sectors shapes experiences elsewhere. Race and sex discrimination is part of the fabric of life in other institutional spheres as well. In this chapter we will examine in some depth discriminatory mechanisms and effects in education, then conclude with a brief listing of examples of discrimination in health care, politics, and the courts. The interlocking character of discrimination across institutional spheres should become increasingly clear, for the web of racism and the web of sexism become ever more conspicuous as one searches a variety of areas in this society.

EDUCATION

Many would argue that patterns of discrimination in the educational arena are at least as central as discrimination in employment and housing to the life chances of minorities and women. Clearly, the role which educational credentials play in the hiring and promotion practices of employers signals the need for a careful examination of educational practices. We might note here also that both the origins of and benefits from the educational system in the United States have been the focus of intensive controversy in recent years. We can cite two relevant examples. First, a number of political economists have traced the origins of schooling to the desires of businessmen and other capitalists to socialize workers in the habits required for the occupations they are likely to enter. The desire to shape the values, as well as the skills, of workers can be seen in the traditional emphasis of educators on discipline, punctuality, submission to authority, and individual accountability.[1] Over time public school systems developed lower ("vocational") tracks for the poorer and darker classes and higher ("academic") tracks for the more affluent whites. From these tracks, then, nonwhite students go into lower-paying job categories and whites into higher-paying job categories. In this sense, the basic structure of education in the United States is shaped by the economic system. Secondly, a number of recent research studies have questioned the importance of education in affecting the economic opportunity of minority Americans. Bennett Harrison, for example, has shown that increasing levels of education have less of an economic advantage for blacks than for whites. Other research confirms the finding that attaining higher educational levels does not guarantee minorities corresponding advances into higher levels of employment.[2] In a famous book, *Inequality,* Jencks and his associates also seriously question the general economic importance of education.[3] All this research points up the problems in the conventional assumption that education is *the* avenue of upward mobility for nonwhites. Much the same could be said for women as well, for women with high levels of education have routinely had less-well-paying jobs than their male counterparts. Thus even total eradication of discrimination in education would at best only partially alleviate discrimination in other institutional sectors. And as we shall now see, we are a considerable distance from eradicating race and sex discrimination in schooling.

Discrimination in Elementary
and Secondary Education

In recent years the most blatant type of racial segregation of children in schools, legal segregation, has disappeared; today school doors are seldom slammed in the faces of minority parents and their children. Rather, a variety of more subtle techniques are employed to keep nonwhites in an inferior educational position.* In the 1950s and early 1960s educational discrimination of the most blatant sort was considered to be the exclusive property of southern school systems. However, as a result of widespread black protest and various court decisions, substantial progress was made in the dismantling of the South's system of racial (legal) school segregation. For example, between the late 1960s and the early 1970s the percentage of black children in all-black schools in the South decreased from 40 to 12 percent, while the proportion in predominantly white schools increased dramatically. so that by 1972 the South's schools were less segregated along racial lines than those in the North and West.[4] However, when de facto segregated school systems outside the South, from Los Angeles to Boston, began to feel pressures to desegregate in the late 1960s and early 1970s, white resistance increased to the point that both the courts and Congress began to back off from requiring desegregation of all school systems; critical issues became "intent" and de facto segregation. Advocates for northern systems argued that segregation there resulted from housing patterns, that the school systems themselves had not contributed in a substantial or intentional way to the school segregation of minority children. However, the informal, behind-the-scenes role decisionmakers in these school systems have played, and still play, in perpetuating discrimination in education is no less important than the South's former, more blatant role; it is only more difficult to document.

Today the effects of discrimination in education, North and

*Unless otherwise noted, the discussion in this section is based on data on public schools, although much of what is noted about discrimination probably applies to private schools as well.

123

South, seem more conspicuous than the mechanisms underlying them. Elementary and secondary schools remain highly segregated, more so in the North than in the South. Quantitative analyses show very substantial separation of black and white students in elementary schools in large cities from St. Louis to Chicago, Cleveland, and Los Angeles. Nationwide, in the mid-1970s about one in three Hispanic children and four in ten black children were in a 90-percent (or more) minority school.[5] And a large proportion of the remainder of the minority children in this country are in predominantly (50-percent-plus) minority schools. In spite of the elimination of legal segregation in the south and the movement away from rigid exclusion there, segregation remains the obvious pattern in schools.

North and South, direct discrimination can be seen clearly in school attendance and school building decisions. School attendance district lines are gerrymandered to maximize the segregation of racial groups. New schools are purposely built in the centers of segregated neighborhoods, rather than on the fringes where mixed-race school populations would result. Transportation policies favor white students over nonwhites. Recent court cases have documented these patterns. In a 1973 Denver case, *Keyes* v. *School District No. 1,* the plaintiffs demonstrated that although the Denver school board never issued an order legally mandating school segregation, its actions had accentuated segregation "by manipulating attendance zones, by selecting school sites which would separate the races, and by superimposing a neighborhood school policy on existing residential segregation."[6] Similarly, the next year a Supreme Court decision on Detroit cited evidence that, although Detroit also did not have a history of legal (de jure) segregation, school attendance zones, school construction decisions, and other administrative decisions had accelerated and intensified school segregation in that city.[7]

The heavy reliance of school systems on the neighborhood school principle, a principle which can be implemented without a racist motivation, can be an example of indirect discrimination by reflecting intentional discrimination in housing. When incorporated white suburbs have school systems separate from those of the cities they surround, highly segregated schools result. For example, Baltimore's school system is 70 percent minorities, while the surrounding suburban area schools are 92 percent white. A 1977 report of the U.S. Commission on Civil Rights highlights the joint effects of deliberate and unintentional discrimination in housing and education:

> The migration of blacks and other minorities to the cities in search of opportunities and the suburbanization of whites has left the Nation with a new problem of racial separation—not merely segregated schools, but segregated school systems coexisting within the same metropolitan area. The problem is growing worse, not better. Despite increased mobility for some middle-class minority families, the continued and rapid migration of whites from cities to suburbs has resulted in heightened racial and economic separation. Increasingly, the boundaries between cities and suburbs have become not merely political dividing lines but barriers that separate people by race and economic class.[8]

Within schools and school systems other discriminatory patterns and practices can be documented. Inferior education in many segregated schools, in terms of less-than-adequate facilities, less-well-prepared teachers, and lower per capita expenditures continues to damage the educational lives of minority schoolchildren. Even where money spent per child approaches equality, discrimination in money allocation is still frequently present when a portion of that for minority children is "soft money"—federal grant money tied to a specific purpose (not always the greatest need) and with a short-term life. Supervisors who provide curriculum aid for teachers "have been found to provide less time and assistance to schools with large minority student bodies. In one school district, supervisors spent at least 200 percent more time (on a proportional basis) with the white schools."[9] Another common form of discrimination can be seen in the absence or very small number of minority personnel in high-level administrative positions within school systems. There can be little doubt as to the impact on a minority schoolchild of constantly seeing custodial (or lower-level) duties performed by minority personnel and administrative duties performed by whites.

Even in formally desegregated school situations there can be barriers for minority children. Desegregating school systems have often altered little more than the student mix in the schools, typically by busing minority students to white schools, without altering other critical aspects of the school environment. For example, institutionalized discrimination, intentional and unintentional, can be seen in the guise of extracurricular programs oriented to the values and time schedules of white students from the local neighborhood rather than to bused-in minority pupils. Unequal participation in extracurricular activities can result. Minority student participation in student government is sometimes limited, if not by the action of school administrators, then by the blatant discrimination in voting by white students. Yet another institutionalized factor of importance is the structured-in bias in primary and secondary curriculum materials which are typically grounded in the white middle-class culture. Minority students may often find little in their educational materials which fits in with their own realities. In addition, for those teachers seeking to improve the curriculum for minority children, curriculum assistance and relevant expertise are often lacking, resulting in part from the lack of knowledge and preparation of white supervisory teachers when confronted with minority group children.[10] The result of using biased curriculum materials can be very negative, contributing to hostility toward education on the part of minority children.

Important mechanisms of subtle, structured-in discrimination, which operate conspicuously in formerly white but now desegregated schools, can perhaps be seen in a teaching environment in which the exclusive emphasis is on what linguists call "Standard English."* The adverse effects of such language instruction practices on minority students are no less real because they are unintentional. For example, a number of research studies have shown that many, particularly low-income, black children speak and understand best a type of non-Standard English rather than the Standard English which is usually emphasized by middle-class teachers who often mistakenly assume the children have a pathological, disorderly, or "lazy" language system deficient in concepts. Yet linguistic research has revealed that many of these children speak a highly patterned and complex dialect of English, with its own distinctive grammar and its own sophistication in the use of concepts. "There is undoubtedly a certain strangeness for city ghetto children to read of ducklings and moo-cows in the first grade, but can we seriously maintain that ducklings and

---

*"Standard English" is commonly used to refer to the variant of English spoken by Americans in the "Mainstream, white, middle-class culture."

moo-cows are somehow 'richer' concepts than subways and sky-scrapers?"[11] Ignorance of these facts on the part of teachers can lead to faulty assumptions about the abilities and intelligence of minority students, which in turn can have a negative effect on routine teaching practices, and thus on reading and learning processes. "Thus the system is unable to teach the child to read, but very quickly teaches him to regard himself as intellectually inadequate, and therefore, of low self-worth and low social value."[12] Note that the issue here is *not* the desirability of teaching Standard English to all children, but the means of instruction, the conventional procedures and practices for teaching children with non-Standard English backgrounds. The situation in regard to black children has parallels in regard to other minority children, particularly those Spanish-speaking children in areas such as the Southwest, whose teachers sometimes even have punished them for speaking Spanish.

Even within desegregated schools, many classrooms often remain more or less segregated, sometimes because of intent, sometimes because of heavy reliance on conventional test scores. Internal segregation in the form of tracking systems frequently separates many nonwhite and white students, with the latter disproportionately, even predominantly, tracked into "academic" courses. Grouping into "dull" and "bright" tracks stigmatizes students, sometimes for life. No procedures are better institutionalized in education than the use of "IQ" (intelligence) and other psychometric tests. In spite of the recent criticism of conventional tests (see Chapter 3), they are still routinely used in many school systems to segregate children into ability groups, vocational and academic tracks, and classes for the mentally retarded. Relatively little has been done to change these practices, even to rid them of the obviously unnecessary discriminatory effects. Thus, for example, many Spanish-language children are put in classes for the mentally retarded (in some school systems they make up high proportions of such classes) only because they scored low on a conventional English-language test, not because they are functionally retarded in daily life.[13] Most tests given to non-English-speaking students are given in English, or the instructions are explained in English, or the test situation reflects English-oriented assumptions.

Actually, this type of intelligence testing, with its racial and ethnic effects, is not new in the United States, having begun in the early 1900s. Large-scale testing of military recruits in World War I, to take one major example, found that white ethnic immigrant Americans scored quite low on the IQ tests of the day. Even white groups such as Italian, Russian, and Polish Americans then scored much lower than recruits of British descent. The conclusion often drawn from this early psychometric testing, by distinguished psychologists at Ivy League colleges as well as influential congressmen, was that Italian, Polish, and other southern and eastern European Americans were racially inferior groups whose basic intelligence was dangerously low. Continued immigration would only lower the general American intelligence, according to this reasoning, and these inferior white "races" should thus be excluded. (The superior "race," called Nordic, was considered to be those of North European origin by these early racists.) The racist interpretation of IQ tests contributed to the passage of the 1924 Immigration Act, which set relatively low quotas for immigrants from undesirable white "races."[14]*

Tainted by ideological racism in their origins, the current descendants of these early tests continue to be used to stigmatize subordinate racial and ethnic groups, although today these groups are usually nonwhite. The routine use of certain psychometric tests can contribute to persisting within-school segregation of white and nonwhite students, in part because the tests are designed by whites, using whites as the norm, thus not reflecting what nonwhite children have learned in their different learning environments. In addition, the test-taking ability of children greatly influences the test scores, as does the language in which the tests are given. If one assumes that the major goal of education is to measure every minority child only from the viewpoint of a restrictive white Anglo-Saxon core culture, and to segregate them if they do not measure up, such testing practices may indeed seem legitimate. However, if one's view of what constitutes "culture" or "intelligence" is broader, the regular use of paper-and-pencil tests in this way can be seen as illegitimate and discriminatory. Even the tone set for a desegregated school or class-

*The reader should note that southern and eastern Europeans are no longer considered "racially" (biologically or physically) distinct by most other white Americans.

room can affect the learning experiences of minority students. For example, consider the following items from a long checklist in a pamphlet prepared by the Foundation for Change in Chicago:

1. Do teachers expect equal academic effort by minority children?
2. Are minority teachers given positions of authority in the school?
3. Do all parents, regardless of race, feel welcome at the school?

"No" answers to these questions, answers reflecting the reality in a given school system, would suggest some of the subtle ways in which minority students, parents, and teachers receive unequal treatment.

Some of what we have just underlined in regard to racial discrimination has parallels in the situations female students encounter in elementary and secondary schools. The widespread occupational segregation in elementary schools signals informal discrimination. While most teachers are female, most principals and higher-level administrators are male. Discriminatory practices reflecting sex stereotypes can also be seen in the construction of curriculum materials which tend to play down the woman's role or to suggest that women are best suited for homemaking or jobs such as nursing. A number of research studies of children's books have found that boys are typically pictured as physically active and problem solving while girls are passive or conforming.[15] Just as in the case of minorities, discrimination can take the subtle form of lower expectations for female students in the classroom, a type of behavior which can begin in elementary school:

> The lowered expectations that teachers and counselors hold for female students do not even have to be stated to have their effect. In countless nonverbal ways they are transmitted, almost intangibly, and the impact they have on the student is devastating.[16]

Research studies focusing on the treatment of boys and girls in elementary school classrooms have found that boys often receive more attention, both approval and disapproval, from teachers than do girls. Sears and Feldman suggest that subtle differences in teacher interaction can have significant, differential negative effects:

> One consequence might be a cumulative increase in independent, autonomous behavior by boys as they are disapproved, praised, listened

to, and taught more actively by the teacher. Another might be a lowering of self-esteem generally for girls as they receive less attention and are criticized more for their lack of knowledge and skill.[17]

Studies such as one by Pauline Sears have found that among elementary school boys and girls without equivalent IQs, the girls downgrade their mental abilities more than do the boys.[18] They have learned to do so, and their differential behavior can become a self-fulfilling prophecy.

Similarly, at the high school level many vocational tracking and counseling programs have a negative impact on female and minority students by channeling them into certain vocational programs and away from others, thus limiting future occupational choices. Minorities are often directed away from academic courses and into certain vocational lines. Home economics, secretarial, and cosmetology courses may be prescribed for the non-college-bound girls—courses, it may be noted, which will prepare them for lower-paying, sex-segregated jobs. Boys not oriented to college tend to be prepared for skilled trades, typically those with higher wages.[19] Although some changes have begun to occur, often as the result of court cases, a sex-segregated emphasis remains in many schools. This vocational channeling often stems from inadequately trained counselors who have little realistic orientation to female or minority problems. In addition, the rules of schools accenting vocational education, including high schools and community colleges, can provide a context for direct discrimination to operate by opening their physical facilities to discriminatory employers or unions to be used for job interviews or apprenticeship recruitment. Such practices, perhaps not intentionally discriminatory, clearly can have a negative effect on the employment aspirations and placements of subordinate group members.

The occupational tests administered by vocational guidance counselors also frequently reflect sex stereotypes. For example, the Strong Vocational Test labels occupations such as architect and school superintendent as male. The Kuder Occupational Scale suggests jobs such as nurse or dietitian, rather than doctor or dentist, for girls who score high on the health interest survey. It is partly on the basis of such tests that counselors, even female counselors who are themselves victims of discrimination, frequently pressure women students to consider becoming legal secretaries rather than lawyers, or nurses rather than doctors. Similarly, vocational counselors frequently orient minority students toward less-skilled lower-paying jobs.

Higher Education

Discrimination does not stop at the gates of higher education. Aptitude and related tests (similar in structure and character to IQ tests used at lower levels) are routinely used in the admissions decision-making process to screen out students regarded by these traditional standards as incapable of college work, which in effect means a disproportionate number of minority students. Moreover, the routine use in college admissions practices of grade-point averages from prior educational levels can have a similar result. As we noted in connection with employment (Chapter 3), testing can be divided into three components: content, administration, and use.[20] Testing may have a negative impact as the result of practices in any or all of these areas. Test content may reflect a white middle-class bias, intentionally or unintentionally; and the administration and use of the tests may represent barriers or restrictions for minorities because of handicaps, or different experiences, resulting from direct discrimination in other areas.

On the basis of their review of the research literature dealing with test content and use in regard to black students, Sedlacek and Brooks argue that there is "reasonable doubt that commonly employed predictors (e.g., tests and high school or college grades) can be universally applied to all racial groups."[21] They stress that the use of nontraditional predictors, such as measures of a student's motivation, independence, self-assurance, and understanding of how racial discrimination works—factors not presently incorporated in conventional admissions procedures—might have a less discriminatory result in estimating potential for college work. Their field research underscores the background differences which often distinguish minority and nonminority applicants; "the whole sociocultural process involved for a minority student attending college is different from that of a white. For instance, a prospective minority student often has no people in his past or present environment who are closely or at all associated with higher education."[22] Thus there is little help available from the family environment in dealing with screening barriers. Since most existing screening practices were developed by and for dominant white middle-class groups, the heavy reliance on conventional predictors of college success, on past grades and aptitude tests, perpetuates the effects of discrimination in the past and in other institutional sectors. Future research may also reveal a similar problem with heavy reliance on letters of recommendation.

Flaugher has questioned the use of the first-year grade-point average as a standard criterion for predicting college success. A basic problem is that the freshman grade-point average is not an "important gauge of anything very important in life's list of desirable values."[23] While other measures of college and postcollege success are often spoken of as more important, they are difficult to measure and seldom seriously considered. Indicators such as potential for contribution to the community or occupational attainment in the years after college have seldom been researched. The failure even to *attempt* to measure important criteria such as these leaves the traditional screening procedures predominant and probably results in the exclusion of disproportionate numbers of otherwise talented minority applicants whose skills, experiences, and potential remain unmeasured.

Screening procedures in higher education can also have a negative effect on women. Sometimes the discrimination is blatantly intentional, as in the case of informal restrictive quotas set by administrators fearing too many women. In recent years some colleges have screened out women applicants by setting higher standards for women than for men. Walum notes that "higher standards for women are justified by the belief that women are poor risks, despite the fact that women earn higher grades than males."[24] Direct discrimination at the high school level can have a negative impact both on initial admission to college and on admission to major degree programs. Steering female students away from high school math programs is one example. Sells has noted that in the early 1970s the University of California system required two years of mathematics, including a year of algebra, for admission. Students without that background, who were more likely to be female than male, were denied entrance. Moreover, those admitted without a substantial math background—two years of algebra, a year of geometry, and a half-year of trigonometry—could not enter the standard freshman calculus sequence, a critical sequence required for most physical and biological science programs, as well as for other fields. Until very recently there was no way to remedy deficiencies in order to qualify for admission to this sequence. Of those entering the University of California (Berkeley) in fall 1972 over half of the men, but only one in twelve of the women, qualified for this standard calculus sequence. Most women students, therefore, could not be admitted to many major academic programs at the normal point in time. This type of screening process perpetuates past discrimination in the educational system into the present. Sex-role stereotypes at the high school level "constrain the aspirations and motivations of students deciding what courses to take in high school, even as they constrain the kinds of advice counselors give students."[25] Doubtless a similar differential could be found along racial lines, and its existence explained in similar terms. Other college admissions policies, such as requiring recent recommendations from teachers or recent aptitude test scores based on standard high school courses (or college courses in the case of graduate work), can have a disproportionately negative impact on female applicants, who are more likely to be older students, since such requirements are geared to those who have recently been in school.[26]

Once admitted to college, minority and women students often find an institutional environment shaped for and by others, that is, for and by whites or white males. Many of the practices and actions negatively affecting minority and female students are so subtle, routine, or fundamental to the operation of colleges and universities that they seldom provoke comment. For example, the relative lack of women in teaching or administrative roles above the high school level leaves female students without role models. In fact, the predominance of male faculty in most disciplines has consequences which reach beyond the realm of academic employment to influence the broader career aspirations of female students, who might infer, for example, that not only do women not become professors of mathematics, women also do not become mathematicians. Similar conclusions, based on similar observations, are likely to be drawn by minorities as well. In addition, the white male professor's world view consciously and unconsciously shapes and interprets the educational materials and presentations. Few courses seriously take into account minority or female perspectives, and those which do are usually segregated from traditional departments. And many male professors routinely, if almost unconsciously, discourage women from pursuing graduate degrees in traditionally male fields.

The general campus atmosphere can also be problematical. Analyzing the pervasive undercurrent of sexism in higher education, Frazier and Sadker note that the "policies, procedures, and structure" of colleges and universities are frequently "custom tailored to suit the needs of the male student."[27] Other analysts, focusing on the adverse impact of higher education's white bias on minority students, note that "everyone and everything is oriented in another direction as minority students try to fit in. Again the outcome of such a campus atmosphere is negative for minorities."[28] It should not be surprising, then, if minority students have a higher dropout rate than whites. Moreover, in traditionally white (or white male) schools many extracurricular organizations and activities have been traditionally structured to fit the needs of white (or white male) students, often leaving other students in an isolated position; traditional fraternity and sorority organizations and types of musical events might be examples of this pattern.

Other institutionalized factors of importance include the provision of college counselors without experience with minority or female student problems. For example, in one research study Burrell and Rayder found that white college counselors who had been through traditional counselor training programs were not effective in dealing with black students.[29] Indirect discrimination may also be evident in certain full-time study requirements, including the limitation of most scholarships and fellowships to full-time students, practices discriminating particularly against married women and lower-income minorities who often must be part-time students because of home and work responsibilities. The routine imposition of residency and course-credit requirements in a variety of degree programs can also be viewed as exemplifying indirect discrimination in their differential and negative impact on married women who must change colleges in pursuing their college degrees because of the job mobility of their husbands.[30]

DISCRIMINATION IN OTHER SECTORS

So far the major concern in this book has primarily been with discrimination in the fields of employment, housing, and education. However, before we conclude our discussion of specific examples of discrimination we will briefly discuss other institutional sectors, lest the mistaken impression be given that race and sex discrimination are somehow limited to these three sectors. We will now note the patterns of discrimination which can be found in health and social services, the electoral process, and the courts. These are not the only other areas where examples of discrimination could be cited, but they do provide a diversity which may be useful in stimulating readers' thinking. Our examples, drawn primarily from the sphere of racial discrimination, are by no means exhaustive.

Health and Social Services

Discrimination in health care includes certain well-institutionalized practices of the medical establishment—doctors, clinics, hospitals, and the like. Indeed, a major illustration of differential treatment which led Carmichael and Hamilton to trace out their pioneering ideas about "institutional racism" concerned the routine operation of medical facilities:

> When white terrorists bomb a black church and kill five black children, that is an act of individual racism, widely deplored by most segments of the society. But when in that same city—Birmingham, Alabama— five hundred black babies die each year because of the lack of proper food, shelter and medical facilities ... that is a function of institutional racism.[31]

Inequality in medical facilities has a significant impact on the health and well-being of minority persons; the negative result is evident in statistics which show sharply higher death and disease rates for nonwhite Americans, whose life expectancy is six to seven years less than that of white Americans. Thus a recent article by Dr. June Christmas, a New York official, lists the components of the inequality pattern:

> Still, today the infant mortality rate of whites is 14.4 per 100 live births; for nonwhites it is 22.9. The gap between whites and nonwhites is only slightly narrower than in 1950. . . . In 1974-75 the average life expectancy at birth was 72.7 years for whites and 67.0 for nonwhites. During this lifetime, a nonwhite is three times as likely to die of hypertension as is a white of the same age group; twice as likely to die of diabetes; four times as likely to die of kidney disease; and five times as likely to die of tuberculosis.[32]

Some of this negative impact stems from blatant, intentional discrimination of the isolate type; some from the blatant discrimination of segregated hospitals or hospital wards for nonwhites, as was the rule until recently in parts of the South. Today, however, institutionalized discrimination tends to be more covert, subtle, and indirect. Some wards are informally segregated. Discrimination in employment for minority persons and resultant lower incomes account in part for the discriminatory impact of many medical care decisions and practices:

> If the education, labor, and business institutions make it difficult for blacks to earn a decent living, medicine has helped perpetuate institutional racism by rationing health care according to ability to pay, by providing inadequate and inferior health care for poor people, and by failing to establish structures which can meet health needs in ways acceptable to all patients.[33]

Medical practices which in effect ration health care according to income provide another example of side-effect (indirect) discrimination. For example, this rationing is reflected in the geographical distribution of physicians. In recent years the doctor-patient ratio in numerous central cities has been 1 doctor for every 3000-4000 persons, compared to ratios of 1 doctor for every 500-1000 persons in suburban areas.[34] An underlying reason for this discrepancy is monetary. White physicians are trained in an environment which stresses technical specialties which can be practiced only in certain specially equipped settings and also good "management principles ... which lead doctors to establish their practices outside ghetto areas, outside the areas of greatest need but where there is also the least ability to pay, lowest quality physical plants, and the greatest number of cost and efficiency problems."[35] In addition, few ghetto youths have the chance to become physicians because of direct and indirect discrimination in the educational system. For example, an estimated 2 percent of physicians are black, while about 12 percent of the U.S. population is black.* Access to a physician for a ghetto resident, because of income and transportation reasons, can thus be a difficult problem. Indirect discrimination can also be seen in decisions shaping the location of hospitals and the quality of hospital care in ghettos. Decisions on hospital location tend to be based on money-related reasoning and thus lead to nonghetto locations. Furthermore, "hospitals in the ghetto, when they exist, tend to be characterized by shortage of staff, lack of equipment, and antiquated physical structures."[36] Discrimination against minorities and women persists in the hiring for hospital staff and medical school faculty positions.

Discrimination is sometimes manifested in the uneven distribution and practices of public health delivery systems, and in alcohol and drub abuse programs as well. Recently, press revelations on the use of uniformed minority persons (e.g., prisoners) in drug testing experiments and the sterilization of minority women to train medical students indicate how extreme discrimination can still be.[37] Furthermore, higher-level decisionmakers seldom represent all race and sex groups. As one knowledgeable expert recently noted:

> Administration, planning, and financing in health care—at all levels in the private and public sectors—are essentially lily-white. Minorities do not share or participate in making policy or critical decisions. Accountability to these ethnic minorities is virtually lacking, not only on the level of community involvement, but in the newly mandated Health Systems Agencies and in the PSROs as well, and at the national level.[38]

*Among the millions of Mexican Americans there are approximately 250 physicians, while among the million Native Americans (including Hawaiians and Alaskans) there are fewer than 100 physicians.

Nonminority women, it should be added, typically have a minor role in this higher-level planning and decisionmaking.

The routine practice of rationing health care according to income also has a differential and adverse impact on women, minority and nonminority, who are heads of fatherless households, for they too suffer side-effect discrimination which is linked to employment discrimination and the resulting lower incomes. Other medical practices affecting women in a negative way, such as the lack of substantial medical research on menstrual problems and on morning sickness during pregnancy, seem to involve stereotyping or intent to discriminate on the basis of sex by the overwhelmingly male medical professions.

In a research study on institutional racism in the social service profession Sanders found that most of the black social workers he surveyed noted the presence of institutional barriers, some intentional and some inadvertent. Membership policy was seen as one serious problem in major organizations such as the National Association of Social Workers. Echoing the views of others, one respondent noted the adverse effects that enforcing regulations on dues and educational credentials has on participation in the social work profession, as well as the medical profession:

> Both of these criteria have been organized by white people ... the people who earn the most money and get the highest pay automatically. This tends to cut off a lot of people who are, in fact, doing the same service in black communities.[39]

The Electoral Process

The results of discrimination in the electoral process have received some recent attention; indeed, the effects are obvious in the very low percentages of minority group members and women among all major elected official categories at local, state, and federal levels. For example, in 1975–1976 women made up only four percent of the members of Congress and about 8 percent of the members of all state legislatures; in 1974 less than one percent of all local, state, and federal officials were black.[40] Direct discrimination in the selection of candidates and by voters at the polls is still partly responsible for these consequences. Indirect discrimination also comes into play.

For example, there is the candidate screening process. Past-in-present and side-effect discrimination can be seen in the enforcement of experience, educational, or other candidate qualifications which minority persons or women are less likely to possess, either because of discriminatory practices in the past in the government sector or of discrimination in other sectors touching on government. Side-effect discrimination can be seen in such things as the enforcement of property qualifications in some voting and office-holding settings. In these cases, minority people, who on the average have significantly less wealth and property than whites, have a more difficult time voting and running for political office. Unpaid electoral positions are particularly difficult for minority persons to seek and hold.

Explicit or implicit educational or experience criteria are often built into the process of becoming a candidate for or occupant of public offices. Discriminatory limitations on securing educational or experience qualifications affect the ability of minority persons and nonminority women to win or even run for elective office. Pettigrew suggests this point in his comment on political qualifications, using Richard Hatcher, the black mayor of Gary, Indiana, as an example: "If Mayor Hatcher had been *directly* discriminated against and prevented from attending and graduating from the Law School of the University of Indiana—his alma mater—then this would have had the *indirect* effect of causing him to be unqualified to run for mayor."[41] This hypothetical situation assumes the routine importance of a law degree for those seeking such public offices.

Nowhere is the "good old boy" system more important than in the screening process leading to candidacy for numerous public offices. Nominees of the various political parties or organizations are sometimes selected informally—if not in the legendary smoke-filled back rooms, then by certain white males in other informal settings. Recommendation procedures can intentionally screen out minority and female candidates; or such candidates may be screened out by not being tied into the critical preexisting social networks of white male politicians.

A recent report of the U.S. Commission on Civil Rights enumerates additional barriers in the political process which may not be intentionally discriminatory, then continues:

> The barriers described here are generally not the result of an ad hoc attempt to deal with a particular situation. Here the concern is with

the general rules of the political process. The U.S. Department of Justice, and increasingly the courts, look not only at the purpose of these rules but also their effect.[42]

The operation of such barriers can be seen in political arrangements in parts of the South. One major example of an institutionalized barrier can be the at-large election, a practice which usually predated significant minority voting and often had its origins in liberal attempts to reform corrupt ward-type politics. These have an adverse impact where the minority group "can form a majority in some small district but will not have a majority in the large district."[43] At-large or multimember district elections,* in situations where a majority of the voters are white, frequently result in minority candidates being routinely defeated and only whites being elected. One important study pointed to some of the positive reasons for the establishment of such electoral mechanisms: "Where the large district is considered a political or social unit it has seemed inappropriate to divide it; representatives from large districts are said to be less parochial in their concerns; the problem of meeting the mathematical requirements of one man–one vote is eliminated if there are no separate districts to be represented."[44] A federal court decision dealing with multimember districts in South Carolina noted that discriminatory motivation was absent:

> That the employment of multi-member districts in this case is without racial motivation is beyond dispute. As has already been pointed out, multi-member legislative districts have been part of the tradition of this State from its very beginnings as a colony. Indeed, counsel for the plaintiffs practically conceded a want of racial bias in the apportionment.[45]

The discriminatory aspect of these particular electoral practices can be viewed as a side effect of the voting actions of white majorities expressing their negative or stereotyped views of nonwhite minority candidates in the voting booth. This mechanism ampli-

---

*At-large and multimember elections refer to elections for districts (city, county, etc.) where several representatives serve one large district rather than each individual representing a smaller district.

fies the impact of intentional discrimination in the voting actions themselves. Similarly, routine implementation of other electoral regulations can have an adverse effect on minority political participation. These include regulations such as those requiring a majority vote (rather than a simple plurality) to win or prohibitions on single-shot voting (i.e., voters cannot vote for just one candidate out of several running in a multimember district).[46] Such regulations, perhaps to a lesser extent, can affect women candidates as well.

Moreover, once in office, minority and female officials are likely to face new problems again linked to direct opposition to their presence, to the absence of certain credentials, or to their lack of access to preexisting social networks. In many such situations a new public official is dependent on informal interpersonal groups and relations to learn how to carry out the duties of the office. If the resource fund of interpersonal knowledge is more limited for minority or female officials, the role-learning process may be very difficult, even to the point of resulting in failure.[47]

The Judicial System

The operation of direct and indirect discrimination in employment in judicial organizations is doubtless similar to that in business and government organizations we discussed in Chapter 3. In addition to employment practices there are other examples of discrimination in the judicial system deserving further research. For example, side-effect discrimination can be seen in jury selection practices which result in disproportionately or exclusively white (grand or petit) juries. When educational credentials or similar criteria are routinely used as formal or informal screening requirements for serving on juries, they can act to screen out a disproportionate number of minority persons. A number of research studies have shown a link between educational criteria and the absence of minority persons on juries.[48]

Well-institutionalized practices which amount to the exclusion of hourly wage earners and low-income individuals, because they cannot afford to leave their jobs, can also lead to underrepresentation of minorities on juries. These include the routine procedure of providing low or insufficient compensation for days spent in jury service. In addition, in some areas housewives have been routinely excluded from juries because of assumptions about the limitations of the occupation of housewife. The impact of indirect discrimination on minorities can be seen outside the jury sphere as well. Examples of this occur in the private legal sector closely tied to court operations, such as the rationing of legal services according to income. Only the affluent can ordinarily afford adequate legal assistance. Government legal services reaching some minority areas have been insufficient to significantly alter this side-effect problem.

Conclusion

While the examples in areas we have briefly touched on in this chapter clearly illustrate the broad range of discrimination in the United States, these examples by no means provide a thorough or exhaustive list. A basic problem now facing this society is not the total neglect of race and sex discrimination, for indeed one step achieved since the early 1960s has been a recognition by citizens and researchers of discrimination as at least problematical. Yet a new dilemma for those committed to the eradication of discrimination has now arisen: neither whites, in the case of race discrimination, nor white males, in the case of sex discrimination, recognize discrimination as a very serious problem. As one recent commentator phrased it, "many whites have convinced themselves that racism is largely a problem of the past."[49] We will explore the implications of this in the next chapter.

1. Samuel Bowles and Herbert Gintis, *Schooling in Capitalist America* (New York: Basic Books, 1976), p. 240.

2. Bennett Harrison, *Education, Training, and the Urban Ghetto* (Baltimore: Johns Hopkins University Press, 1972).

3. Christopher Jencks et al., *Inequality: A Reassessment of the Effect of Family and Schooling in America* (New York: Harper & Row, 1972).

4. Thomas F. Pettigrew, "Educational Implications," in U.S. Commission on Civil Rights, *Milliken v. Bradley: The Implications for Metro-*

politan Desegregation (Washington, D.C.: U.S. Government Printing Office, 1974), p. 55.

5. Reynolds Farley, "Residential Segregation and Its Implications for School Integration," paper presented to the Duke University Conference on the Courts, Social Science, and School Desegregation, August 20, 1974, cited in Pettigrew, "Educational Implications," in U.S. Commission on Civil Rights, *The State of Civil Rights, 1976* (Washington, D.C.: U.S. Government Printing Office, 1977), p. 19.

6. Frank T. Read, "Judicial Evolution of the Law of School Integration, Since Brown v. Board of Education," *Law and Contemporary Problems* 39 (Winter 1975): 40; see also *Keyes* v. *School District No. 1,* 413 U.S. 189 (1973).

7. *Milliken* v. *Bradley,* 418 U.S. 717 (1974).

8. U.S. Commission on Civil Rights, *Statement on Metropolitan School Desegregation* (Washington, D.C.: U.S. Government Printing Office, 1977), p. 112.

9. William E. Sedlacek and Glenwood C. Brooks, Jr., *Racism in American Education: A Model for Change* (Chicago: Nelson-Hall, 1976), p. 48.

10. Ibid., pp. 46–48.

11. J. L. Dillard, *Black English* (New York: Vintage Books, 1973), p. 288.

12. Joan C. Baratz, "Teaching Reading in an Urban Negro School System," in *Teaching Black Children to Read,* edited by Joan C. Baratz and Roger W. Shuy (Washington, D.C.: Center for Applied Linguistics, 1969), pp. 92–93.

13. See Jane R. Mercer, *Labelling the Mentally Retarded* (Berkeley: University of California Press, 1973).

14. Leon J. Kamin, *The Science and Politics of I.Q.* (New York: Wiley, 1974).

15. Laurel Richardson Walum, *The Dynamics of Sex and Gender: A Sociological Perspective* (Chicago: Rand McNally, 1977), pp. 57–59.

16. Nancy Frazier and Myra Sadker, *Sexism in School and Society* (New York: Harper & Row, 1973), p. 139.

17. Pauline S. Sears and David H. Feldman, "Teacher Interactions with Boys and with Girls," in *And Jill Came Tumbling After: Sexism in American Education,* edited by Judith Stacey et al. (New York: Dell, 1974), p. 150.

18. Pauline Sears, *The Effect of Classroom Conditions on the Strength of Achievement Motive and Work Output of Elementary School Children,*

U.S. Department of Health, Education, and Welfare, Office of Education Cooperative Research Project No. OE-873 (Washington, D.C.: U.S. Government Printing Office, 1963).

19. Walum, *The Dynamics of Sex and Gender,* p. 55; see also Dinah L. Shelton and Dorothy Berndt, "Sex Discrimination in Vocational Education: Title IX and Other Remedies," *California Law Review* 62 (July–September 1974): 1133 ff.

20. Ronald L. Flaugher, *Testing Practices, Minority Groups, and Higher Education: A Review and Discussion of Research* (Princeton, N.J.: Educational Testing Service, 1970).

21. Sedlacek and Brooks, *Racism in American Education,* p. 51.

22. Ibid., p. 52.

.23. Ronald L. Flaugher, "The New Definitions of Test Fairness in Selection: Developments and Implications," *Education Researcher* (October 1974), p. 15.

24. Walum, *The Dynamics of Sex and Gender,* p. 67.

25. Lucy W. Sells, "Constraints on Minorities and Women in Higher Education," mimeographed fact sheet based on research, Berkeley, California, 1975.

26. Pamela Roby, "Structural and Internalized Barriers to Women in Higher Education," in *Women: A Feminist Perspective,* edited by Jo Freeman (Palo Alto, Calif.: Mayfield Publishing Co., 1975), pp. 171–193.

27. Frazier and Sadker, *Sexism in School and Society,* pp. 155–56.

28. Sedlacek and Brooks, *Racism in American Education,* p. 57.

29. L. Burrell and N. F. Rayder, "Black and White Students' Attitudes Toward White Counselors," *Journal of Negro Education* 20 (1971): 48–52.

30. See Roby, "Structural and Internalized Barriers to Women in Higher Education."

31. Charles Hamilton and Stokeley Carmichael, *Black Power* (New York: Random House, 1967), p. 4.

32. June Jackson Christmas, "How Our Health System Fails Minorities," *Civil Rights Digest* 10 (Fall, 1977): 4.

33. Louis L. Knowles and Kenneth Prewitt (eds.), *Institutional Racism in America* (Englewood Cliffs, N.J.: Prentice-Hall, 1969), pp. 104–5.

34. M. Alfred Haynes and Michael M. McGarvey, "Physicians, Hospitals, and Patients in the Inner City," in *Medicine in the Ghetto,* edited by John C. Norman (New York: Appleton-Century-Crofts, 1969), pp. 117–20.

35. Knowles and Prewitt, *Institutional Racism in America*, p. 109.

36. Haynes and McGarvey, "Physicians, Hospitals, and Patients in the Inner City," p. 121.

37. See Christmas, "How Our Health Fails Minorities," p. 11.

38. Ibid.

39. Quoted in Charles L. Sanders, *Black Professionals' Perceptions of Institutional Racism* (Fair Lawn, N.J.: R. E. Burdick, 1973), p. 61.

40. David Campbell and Joe R. Feagin, "Black Politics in the South: A Descriptive Analysis," *Journal of Politics* (Winter 1975): 129–59; Kirsten Amundsen, *A New Look at the Silenced Majority* (Englewood Cliffs, N.J.: Prentice-Hall, 1977).

41. Thomas F. Pettigrew, "Racism and the Mental Health of White Americans: A Social Psychological View," in *Racism in Mental Health*, edited by Charles V. Willie, Bernard M. Kramer, and Betram S. Brown (Pittsburgh: University of Pittsburgh Press, 1973), p. 271.

42. U.S. Commission on Civil Rights, *The Voting Rights Act: Ten Years After* (Washington, D.C.: U.S. Government Printing Office, 1975), p. 248.

43. Washington Research Project, *The Shameful Blight* (Washington, D.C.: U.S. Government Printing Office, 1972), p. 109.

44. Ibid.

45. *Stevenson v. West*, Civil No. 72–45 (D.S.C. April 7, 1972), quoted in ibid., p. 115.

46. Ibid., pp. 115–31. See also U.S. Commission on Civil Rights, *The Voting Rights Act: Ten Years After*, pp. 204 ff.

47. Campbell and Feagin, "Black Politics in the South"; Joe R. Feagin, "Black Elected Officials in the South: An Exploratory Analysis," in *Black Conflict with White America*, edited by Jack R. van den Slik (Columbus, Ohio: Merrill, 1970), pp. 107–22.

48. See Nijole V. Benokraitis, "Institutional Racism: An Empirical Study of Blacks and the Jury Selection System in Ten Southern States," Ph.D. dissertation, University of Texas, 1975, pp. 27–30.

49. Ellis Cose, "A Changing Mood toward Equality," *Focus*, 5 (October 1977): 3.

Remedies for Discrimination

chapter six

In the preceding chapters we have seen the difficulties involved in carefully identifying the effects and mechanisms of discrimination. Yet as difficult as that task is, it is easier than finding solutions to discrimination that are both effective and likely to be implemented in the present society. The major purpose of this book is to make some progress on the former task, that of documenting the mechanisms and effects of discrimination, but our analysis would be deficient if we cut off our discussion at this point. In this concluding chapter we therefore briefly explore a range of solutions for race and sex discrimination.

Of course, many in the dominant groups neither want nor seek remedies for discriminatory practices. For them such practices still seem just. Discrimination is necessary to keep "inferiors" in their place. However, for others, both many liberals in dominant positions and subordinate group persons alike, the goal is to deal with discrimination. Many of these feel frustrated, helpless, or confused even thinking about this task. In discussing patterns of discrimination with various people, including university students, the authors of this book have often found concerned persons persistently raising such questions as: "OK, so what can we do about discrimination?" "How can I as an individual do much?" "How can you fight the system?" "Isn't something being done?" These troubling questions are omnipresent and real. They must be dealt with. The first step in the direction of wisdom in this matter may be to separate out the several different questions implicit here:

1. What have we as a nation attempted to do about discrimination?
2. What could we as a nation do about discrimination?
3. What will we as a nation do about discrimination?

Note that each of these questions can be personalized for individual action by replacing the "we" with "I." It is these questions which we will now address.

WHAT HAVE WE DONE?

What have we as a nation attempted to do about race and sex discrimination? One way to answer this question is to explore government and private policy and remedial actions, including civil rights laws, executive decrees, and court decisions. Let us briefly examine government and private action in a number of relevant areas.

Employment

Consider, for example, action in regard to employment. In the twentieth century relatively little government action was taken to deal with employment discrimination until the 1940s and 1950s, when a few state and local governments in the North adopted fair employment practices laws, usually with weak enforcement powers and relating to minorities but not to women. Before the 1960s little more than token action was taken by any branch of the federal government to desegegrate employment situations. Several presidents did take a few steps in the direction of enforcing passive nondiscrimination, as in Franklin Roosevelt's establishment of a Fair Employment Practices Committee in the early 1940s, but it was not until the 1960s that significant antidiscrimination action could be observed at the federal level. Executive orders issued by President Lyndon Johnson in the 1960s required, at least on paper, government contractors not only to cease discriminating but also to act affirmatively to desegregate their labor forces. In the mid-1960s enforcement of contract compliance functions came under the Department of Labor, the agency which supervises employers holding federal government contracts. According to recent Department of Labor studies, compliance reviews of contractors have had some impact in improving minority and female employment. The Office of Federal Contract Compliance (OFCC), the office within the Department of Labor directly responsible for supervising the implementation of executive orders, has issued regulations which, when built into contracts, explicitly require federal contractors to take *affirmative action** to eliminate discrimination in their employment practices, from use of recruitment networks to hiring practices and promotion procedures. Since the late 1960s federal contractors have been required to submit written affirmative action plans indicating the current representation of nonwhites and women in job categories and providing for affirmative goals and timetables for categories where underutilization of nonwhites and women exists. The OFCC has delegated compliance actions to other agencies such as HEW, which are supposed to review federal contractors in their areas to see if they are taking remedial action.[1]

The effectiveness of the OFCC-fostered affirmative action has been seriously questioned, however. The U.S. Commission on Civil Rights' and other studies of compliance reviews have indicated that little or nothing in the way of penalties have been applied to nonconforming contractor-employers. Grossly deficient antidiscrimination plans have been approved, and only a dozen or so (mostly small) service or supply contractors had ever been barred from ob-

---

Affirmative action refers to remedial practices going beyond passive nondiscrimination to active, positive actions to bring in previously excluded minorities and women.

taining federal contracts as of 1976; the situation for construction contractors has been similar. Here, then, is a federal enforcement agency charged with desegregating federal contractors which has taken little direct action. In fact, as of the mid-1970s most of the federal government's compliance agencies had reviewed less than half of all the contractors under their supervision; thus it seems likely that the actual pressure for desegregating federal contractors' employment has been modest.[2]

The 1964 Civil Rights Act, together with its amendments in the early 1970s, prohibits discrimination in employment by larger employers. The Equal Employment Opportunity Commission (EEOC) was created to enforce Title VII of that act, primarily to deal with complaints of employment discrimination. The EEOC has the responsibility of investigating legitimate complaints, of seeking conciliation and, failing that, since 1972, of going to court to end discrimination. In the fiscal year 1974 nearly 57,000 persons filed complaints of racial or sex discrimination with the EEOC, an increase over previous years; two-thirds of the complaints were by blacks. Because of the EEOC's management problems and lack of staff, a very large backlog of cases had built up in the mid-1970s, to the point where most complainants could find no practical remedy through this procedure; indeed, the average minority or female complaint was taking more than two years to resolve.

There is no systematic evidence available on the impact of this type of government enforcement activity on the economic mobility of members of subordinate groups. What data we do have indicate increased pressure on employers, from small businesses to corporations and universities, to desegregate their work forces. Thousands of work force forms ("red tape") are filled out by large employers and are tabulated by EEOC annually.[3] However, the data on actual changes in the work force reveal a mixed picture. For example, those large firms (100 or more employees) covered by EEOC reporting requirements reported proportionally greater gains in black employment in the 1966–1974 period than did all employers in the U.S. economy, but the gains were limited to certain areas, such as clerical, craft, and service workers. Gains in the professional and managerial areas for the same firms were proportionally *less* than in the U.S. economy taken as a whole. It is also clear from a number of research studies that the modest employment gains for minorities and women in the 1960s began *before* significant EEOC, Labor Department, and federal court actions had been taken in the area of affirmative action, gains probably reflecting the economic prosperity generated by the wartime economy of the early and late 1960s.[4]

The Courts and Employment

The federal courts have, starting in the 1960s, become increasingly involved in finding remedies for employment discrimination, both intentional discrimination of the blatant sort and, less frequently, subtle direct and indirect discrimination. However, court cases have a limited impact, in that the remedies are case-specific and usually affect only one individual or, at the most, one plant or organization. The courts' ability to reshape employment in an entire industry or other sector is thus restricted. A company or organization is first examined for practices which must be demonstrated to be discriminatory, at least in effect, before court remedies can be imposed.

Once discrimination has been conclusively demonstrated in court, however, the remedies provided by federal courts have often been quite specific, remedies attempting "to make whole" the injured parties. For example, when their recruitment practices were found to have a racially discriminatory impact, the Georgia Power Company was required to recruit at predominantly black colleges. A federal district court in North Carolina ordered a motor lines company to redirect its discriminatory recruiting program. This was to be done through advertising in black community media and seeking applicants through civil rights and local job-training organizations. A controversial remedy for demonstrably discriminatory recruitment practices in the past has been the requirement of establishing hiring ratios by some, but by no means all, federal courts. Because of past discrimination, the Milwaukee Board of City Service Commissioners was required by a federal district court to hire one qualified black person for every two vacancies occurring in a skilled craft job classification until the percentage of black workers in that classification equaled the percentage of blacks in the city. Such court remedies have usually been tied to *demonstrated past discrimination*. In a few important consent decrees and court decisions, women have benefited from imposed hiring and promotion requirements. In a famous 1973 consent decree involving American Telephone and Telegraph, that company agreed to provide back pay and to improve recruitment, hiring, and promotion conditions for women and minority employees.[5]

As we noted in Chapter 3, the court-imposed requirement of proving the *valid* business necessity of some practices has come to the forefront in cases involving employers whose screening practices appeared discriminatory. A number of court decisions have held that screening criteria, whether a simple requirement of literacy, a high school diploma, or some type of aptitude or entrance test, must be validated by being shown empirically to predict successful job performance in order to be lawful.[6] The "rightful place" principle has been applied by a few federal courts to remedy the effects of long-standing discriminatory seniority systems and promotion-evaluation procedures. For example, job applicants for over-the-road (OTR) driving positions who in the past experienced overt discrimination in being denied employment because of race were awarded seniority status retroactive to the date of their original job application by the Supreme Court in *Franks* v. *Bowman Transportation Co.* (1976), a step taken to help nullify the continuing effects of past discrimination. The Court stated, "Without an award of seniority dating from the time at which he was discriminatorily refused employment, an individual who applies for and obtains employment as an OTR driver ... will never obtain his rightful place in the hierarchy of seniority according to which these various employment benefits are distributed."[7] Extending this persuasive line of reasoning about retroactive seniority to minorities who did not apply because of fear, however, has been rejected by a number of federal courts.

While there is probably no way in which a minority or female victim can be completely compensated for the loss of status and money occasioned both by discrimination and the consequent delays in obtaining his or her "rightful place," some federal courts have made attempts to provide monetary compensation for injustice. In such cases as *Watkins* v. *Scott Paper Co.* (1976) and *Patterson* v. *American Tobacco Co.* (1974), the courts have used wage "circling," to freeze an employee's wages at the current level so that he or she will suffer no loss of pay while training in lower-paying (entry-level) jobs in preparation for his or her rightful place in new tracks or departments. In *Watkins* the federal court stated that "a remedial program that allows blacks to transfer into formerly white lines [of progression] but forces them to accept a temporary cut in pay is not an effective way of providing the affected class members their rightful place."[8] In a number of cases, such as *Albermarle Paper Co.* v. *Moody* (1975), the victims have been awarded "back pay," calculated as the difference between the pay actually earned and what he or she would have earned without the effects of intentional discrimination.[9] In most cases, however, this remedial compensation has ended with the date of the court's order, even though the victim might still be a long time away from receiving adequate compensation.

As we cited in Chapter 3, in *Washington* v. *Davis* (1976) the Supreme Court departed from the practice of the late 1960s and early 1970s of granting relief for discriminatory impact regardless of intent and from the strict job-specific validation requirement for screening practices such as entrance tests—both principles laid out in the 1971 *Griggs* v. *Duke Power Co.* case. (Remember that the *Griggs* decision stated that fair-in-form practices which nonetheless had a discriminatory impact had to be remedied if valid business necessity could not be proven.) Although the *Washington* decision ultimately hinges on a technicality—the suit was filed on constitutional grounds and not under Title VII of the 1964 Civil Rights Act, the former being considered by the Court to require less ⁻·gorous standards of proof—the significance of the reversal can be seen in the Court's dramatic new statement: "To the extent that those [prior] cases rested on or expressed the view that proof of discriminatory racial purpose is unnecessary in making out an equal protection violation, we are in disagreement."[10] In *Washington* v. *Davis* and certain subsequent decisions it has become clear that the more conservative "Nixon Court" will probably not require remedies for subtle direct discrimination or for indirect discrimination. The minority or female plaintiff now must prove intent to discriminate, prejudice, or ill will on the part of the discriminator. Proving that a certain prejudiced or hostile "state of mind" underlies discriminatory acts and effects is often extraordinarily difficult. Thus in the late 1970s the Supreme Court, the leader among federal courts, retreated to the position on employment it took before the late 1960s. As one legal analysis of the situation has concluded, less antidiscrimination action can now be taken: "Factual problems of proof rendered [civil rights] statutes and other provisions powerless against patterns and practices which grossly limited employment opportunities of blacks, women and other minority groups."[11] The High Court seems to be saying that intentional discrimination against women and minorities is legal, so long as intent is concealed.

Housing

Civil rights action by state and federal governments in regard to housing has been much more limited even than that in regard to employment. Prior to the 1960s a few federal court decisions invalidated some of the more blatant attempts to force nonwhite Americans to reside only in certain residential areas. In a 1917 case, *Buchanan* v. *Warley,* the Supreme Court moved slightly from its segregationist past, ruling that local ordinances openly enforcing segregated housing patterns (racial zoning) were illegal.[12] Some courts subsequently ruled against segregation in public housing. In the 1920s the Supreme Court upheld private property deed restrictions keeping out minorities, but in effect reversed itself in a 1948 case, *Shelly* v. *Kraemer,* which made such deed restrictions unenforceable in state courts.[13] By the late 1950s a small handful of states and cities, primarily in the North, had some type of fair housing ordinances aimed at private housing, but even these were relatively weak and hard to enforce. It was not until the 1950s and 1960s that any significant federal action, including legislation, was aimed at housing discrimination.[14] Presidential executive action in 1962 desegregated government-subsidized housing, such as public housing and housing on military bases. Finally, in the late 1960s Congress passed a rather weak national fair housing act, the 1968 Civil Rights Act, which was modified and expanded in 1974 to include *sex* as well as *race* discrimination. Title VIII of the 1968 Civil Rights Act officially prohibits intentional discrimination in the rental or sale of an estimated 80 percent of the nation's housing. (Single-family units sold without the aid of a broker are, for example, not covered.)

Now let us examine some major examples of contemporary government action. The Department of Housing and Urban Development (HUD) is the federal agency responsible for the administration and enforcement of civil rights legislation in housing, particularly Title VIII of the Civil Rights Act of 1968. However, the civil rights divisions of HUD have been given no powers stronger than the right to seek conciliation and to use informal persuasion in enforcing these laws. As of this writing, HUD still cannot issue "cease and desist" orders, nor can it institute litigation against discriminating parties. Complaints of noncompliance with the law are referred to the Department of Justice, where "it may take years to remedy a problem, if it can be remedied at all."[15] An investigation by the U.S. Commission on Civil Rights in 1974 concluded that HUD had achieved only very limited success. The commission found that only a few of the housing discrimination complaints investigated by HUD actually brought relief to the complainants. Approximately one-fifth of the cases closed between July 1972 and March 1973 went to conciliation, and just over one-half of these were conciliated successfully. Due to insufficient staffing and the length of time required to process complaints, HUD had a complaint backlog "so high as to produce a lack of confidence in the ability of the Department to obtain timely relief." The Civil Rights Commission report further found that "once HUD has negotiated a hard-won agreement, it frequently makes no effort to monitor the agreement to see that it is carried out."[16]

The Department of Housing and Urban Development is also responsible for enforcing Title VI of the Civil Rights Act of 1964, which, together with a 1962 presidential executive order, prohibits discrimination in federally assisted housing programs. The 1974 Civil Rights Commission investigation found that little time of designated HUD personnel was spent on Title VI cases. Two methods of enforcement are open to HUD in dealing with housing discrimination: (1) investigating individual complaints, and (2) conducting general compliance reviews. The second procedure is considered to be "a far more effective and systematic way of assuring the nondiscriminatory operation of the programs," but HUD's regional offices generally do not have sufficient staff to carry out compliance reviews. What reviews HUD did conduct during the period under review were limited to local public housing authorities and omitted the all-important developers, builders, and sponsors of federally subsidized housing projects, even though these latter projects frequently violated the law.[17] These are but a few of the federal administrative and enforcement deficiencies which the Civil Rights Commission considered so extensive as to nullify the impact of the civil rights legislation on housing opportunities for minorities and women.

One significant step was taken in regard to public housing in 1976, in the *Hills* v. *Gautreaux* case which we discussed in Chapter 4. In that case HUD became involved in a public housing location controversy. The final decision by the U.S. Supreme Court ordered HUD and the Chicago Housing Authority to act to remove racial discrimination in the site location process for public housing. In that year, moreover, the first tentative steps were being taken by the Department of Justice in a suit filed against real estate and lending organizations who were accused of undervaluing housing in integrated neighborhoods. Federal legislation (e.g., the Housing and Community Development Act) was passed in the mid-1970s in the first attempt to deal with race and sex discrimination in lending patterns.[18]

In addition to appealing to HUD for assistance, women and minority group members who are the victims of discrimination may file suit in state or federal court, or the U.S. attorney general may bring suit in district court on their behalf. In a pathbreaking 1968 decision, *Jones* v. *Alfred H. Mayer Co.*, the Supreme Court ruled that the 1866 Civil Rights Act prohibiting discrimination in the sale of property could be cited by a complainant, stating that the act "bars all racial discrimination, private as well as public, in the sale or rental of property." This precedent-setting case is available to minorities and women—*if* they have the energy and money to pursue remedies for discrimination by way of private attorneys and court suits. Private lawsuits are expensive and slow, and the correct legal procedure is not known to most lay people. And when a victim of discrimination does sue, the results may not prove to be of great satisfaction. Consider an important Detroit case, for example, in which a landlord was found guilty of discrimination. "The case took several months to process and we had to be in court from 10:00 A.M. to 4:30 P.M. Then the judge doled out the penalty: the landlord had to show the 'renter' the apartment."[19] Laws are of little benefit to those whom they intend to protect when the procedures for legal recourse are not well known to the victims, when enforcement is not pursued aggressively by the government agencies responsible, and when penalties are virtually meaningless. And there are aspects of covert discrimination, such as that of realtors, which are difficult to prosecute under existing law. Enforcement is further complicated because intentional discrimination, a recurring and now increasing focus of the federal courts, is often difficult to prove. As we noted in Chapter 4, housing was at least as racially segregated in the late 1970s as it ever was.

Education

Federal government remedial action in regard to educational discrimination has primarily been aimed at the traditional local government policy of segregating whites from nonwhites in public school systems. Note that relatively little action has been taken to remedy the educational discrimination facing women* or the many subtle and indirect types of discrimination facing minority Americans. We will consider here two main areas of the educational policy debate: school desegregation and affirmative action programs in higher education.

Simplistically labeled "busing" by its opponents, the recent federal government policy of elementary and secondary school desegregation began in a major way with the famous 1954 Supreme Court decision, *Brown* v. *Topeka Board of Education*, which led to the dismantling of rigidly segregated school systems in the South. But the South dug in; progress toward desegregation came slowly as, over the next two decades, a series of court decisions and federal administrative decisions gradually put more teeth into government action. The 1964 Civil Rights Act gave the U.S. attorney general the right to sue segregated school districts, relieving some of the legal burden falling on nonwhite parents. Other remedial legislation provided additional pressure in the form of possible withholding of funds from segregated districts. The transportation of students ("busing") was permitted by federal courts in order to desegregate school systems. With the establishment of tougher enforcement procedures, substantial desegregation came. (In 1966–1968, for

---

*Much recent attention and controversy has been focused on desegregating school athletic programs, so that women students can have equal opportunity in athletics. This seems to be the major exception to our statement.

example, HEW terminated federal funds to 188 school districts.) Large numbers of formerly segregated black children in the South found themselves in predominantly white schools for the first time. By 1974 federal court decisions for a number of border and northern cities ordered the eradication of discrimination, even where there was no legally established dual school system. The main issue was whether some school boards in locating new school buildings had intentionally, if covertly, contributed to school segregation, even in a part of a school system. Evidence of intentional segregation in one area of a school system, as in the 1973 *Keyes* v. *School District No. 1* case in Denver, was considered sufficient to warrant ordering the desegregation of an entire school system. As desegregation policy was expanded to include schools in the North in the 1960s and 1970s, opposition became so widespread that little desegregation actually occurred there. Liberal northern analysts began to take positions once thought the sole property of southerners. From the northern perspective, the desegregation of public schools was viewed as forcing white children to leave "neighborhood schools" in an unwanted attempt to "balance" proportions of white and black children.[20] This northern opposition in effect set serious limits on how far the federal courts, the federal executive branch, and Congress would go in dealing with discrimination against nonwhites in education. The future of efforts here is unclear.

In the 1970s significant affirmative action programs aimed at going beyond nondiscrimination and aggressively eliminating discrimination in employment and in the student selection process in higher education have been undertaken. Affirmative action pressures in higher education have come from a number of sources. Major pressure in employment has come from the Department of Health, Education, and Welfare (HEW), which is delegated the responsibility of supervising those receiving federal contract funds in higher education. All federal contractors, including colleges and universities, are obligated to "take affirmative action to ensure that applicants are employed, without regard to their race, color, religion, sex, or national origin." Enforcement by HEW has been weak, resulting in protracted negotiations with colleges and universities and little in the way of lasting accomplishments.[21] Far more controversy has been generated by programs for students, particularly to *privately-initiated* affirmative action programs aimed at increasing the number of minority students in colleges and universities. Under pressure from civil rights organizations numerous colleges and universities have developed programs attempting to accelerate the admission of minorities (and in a few cases, women) who have been excluded by the processes of intentional discrimination in the past. A number of colleges and universities have implemented programs reserving a certain number of positions in their entering classes for minority or disadvantaged (primarily minority) students. Just how widespread are such affirmative action programs is difficult to ascertain, but the total number of significant programs may be modest. Many programs have been token and/or short-lived because of a lack of community or financial support. However, some programs have become central issues in legal suits charging "reverse discrimination," as in the 1977 *Allan Bakke* v. *Regents of the University of California* case dealing with a "disadvantaged" admissions program at a University of California medical school. An older white student denied admission to the medical school sued the school, arguing that he had been unfairly excluded by the "disadvantaged" admissions program under which minority persons with lower test scores and grade-point averages than his had been admitted. Sixteen places of the one hundred in the first-year medical school class to which Bakke was denied admission were set aside for "disadvantaged students," which can include poor whites but apparently has so far primarily included Asian Americans, blacks, Chicanos, and Native Americans. The California Supreme Court ruled this program unacceptable, a decision the university regents appealed to the Supreme Court, which as of this writing has not yet ruled on the case. Similar programs have operated in other progressive colleges and universities, with sizeable programs probably in less than half of all such institutions in the United States. The impact of these now-endangered programs, it is likely, has so far ranged from token to modest.[22]

Critics of Remedial Action—and Their Critics

The *Bakke* v. *Regents* case illustrates—with its numerous prominent white male supporters of Bakke—the frequently vigorous opposition to recent government and private remedial efforts. Yet opposition and criticism from dominant group members, although given much attention in the mass media, is by no means the only criticism of current remedial programs. While many white males argue that "too much" is being done to combat discrimination, many minority persons and women argue that "too little" is being done.

In the sphere of employment and education numerous critics, predominantly white males, have in recent years attacked government programs aimed at "making whole" oppressed minorities and women. Conservatives have long worked vigorously and openly against most civil rights laws and sanction-oriented antidiscrimination programs. Many white-male liberals, although supporting programs prohibiting blatant race and sex discrimination, have increasingly opposed government and private programs which attempt to compensate for past discrimination by aggressive means which accelerate the mobility of minorities and women; removing blatant discrimination is as far as they seem willing to go. Indeed, more and more white-male liberals seem to be falling back into what has been termed a neoconservative ("benign neglect") position, one that believes the normal operation of this society will progressively liberate nonwhites and women, without government intervention. Thus in employment and education many white males have charged that discrimination against minorities and women is no longer serious, that "reverse discrimination" is now the more serious problem, that "merit" standards are going by the wayside as "unqualified" minorities and women are being hired for jobs and admitted to colleges in an arbitrary manner. (Note the unusually heavy emphasis on colleges.)

Symbolic of media coverage was *Newsweek* magazine's cover for a September 1977 issue focusing on "reverse discrimination": a black student and a white student pulling on each end of a rope tied to a giant college diploma. A major story on "reverse discrimination" followed. Moreover, in the 1970s a long series of books attacking private and government remedial programs (particularly those aimed at higher education) appeared, one after another, outnumbering pro-remedial action books. In his widely reviewed book *Affirmative Discrimination*, Nathan Glazer argues that affirmative action in employment, as well as government action in education, has become a means of "reverse discrimination." For example, he criticizes the idea of compensation for past discrimination:

Compensation for the past is a dangerous principle. It can be extended indefinitely and make for endless trouble. Who is to determine what is proper compensation for the American Indian, the black, the Mexican American, the Chinese or Japanese American? When it is established that the full status of equality is extended to every individual, regardless of race ... one has done all that justice and equity call for and that is consistent with a harmonious multigroup society.[23]

Here we have the now widespread view that equality of opportunity, as traditionally defined, is all that is required for a just society. Compensation tied to past race or sex discrimination is rejected.

In addition to rejecting the idea of compensation, neoconservative critics of remedial action worry a great deal about "merit" standards. The merit notion is linked to the notion of "qualified" persons, whether the persons concerned are students applying for some college program or job applicants. A basic argument is that affirmative action programs setting goals and timetables for the employment of minorities and women usually lead to the hiring of "unqualified" persons. Intense criticism also focuses on special admissions programs which accept minority applicants, many of whose test scores or grade-point averages are lower than those of whites with whom they are competing. Female and minority analysts have countered these criticisms of remedial action by noting that neoconservatives have generally ignored the fact that many white women, to take the most obvious example, have equal or better credentials than white men with whom they are or could be competing. It is interesting, to take one major example, that Glazer's sustained critique of affirmative action in employment totally focuses on minorities and ignores the point that women have been major beneficiaries of this remedial action. The reason seems obvious. Given their often equal or better educational and other traditional credentials, women can more easily meet attacks on affirmative action that stress lack of "merit," traditionally defined.

A number of female and minority writers have argued that this issue of merit must be probed more deeply than the usual superficial argument allows for. Let us consider the origin of the standard test-type measures of merit, which apparently lies in a shift in the practices of government bureaucracies. The first modern civil service apparatus was that of the British government in which, by the 1850s, participation was typically limited to university graduates.[24] Educational credentials thus became a major criterion for screening job applicants in government bureaucracies. In the United States, civil service tests were developed between the 1880s and the 1920s to reduce the amount of corrupt patronage at local, state, and federal government levels and to establish what came to be termed the "merit" system. In the 1920s a "scientific" management movement arose in public and private organizations, with a concern for measuring and classifying job skills; this movement gave further impetus to the rise of psychological (and other) testing and to a focus on "merit" in government and private sectors. Merit had become synonymous, by the 1930s, with higher scores on civil service tests devised by psychologists. In these decades, however, the merit criterion was manipulated, with separate lists of eligible candidates for employment for whites and nonwhites. "Greater merit" officially meant being white.[25] Merit systems involving test scores are tainted with racist thinking in their past use. Today many argue that merit systems involving test scores and education credentials can be liberated from their racist past and used objectively, so that nonwhites and women who have the appropriate test scores will no longer be screened out. The traditional merit system, so this argument runs, can be purged so that it will work on an equal opportunity basis.

Yet critics have suggested that there are a number of serious problems with this type of defense of the traditional merit criteria. First, educational credentials and test scores, taken alone, are questionable indices of ability, since, as a number of research studies suggest, they do not correlate well with on-the-job performance. While there is evidence that scores on college or university entrance tests fairly accurately predict performance in subsequent educational settings, such scores do not so accurately predict beyond those educational settings to on-the-job performance. What, then, do the standards of merit really mean if people who score lower than others do as well on the job as those scoring higher? Much research remains to be done on this point, but the vociferous advocates of merit tests and credentials must not assume that these measures of merit do indeed select the best people for any job: they should have to prove this common assumption. Moreover, critics of the neoconservative view have pointed out that even in the area of educational test scores, there is some evidence, odd as it may seem, that those scoring very high on certain tests are *less likely* than those scoring lower to finish the degree programs they enter. This has been found to be true by some law schools, for example, in regard to the common admissions (LSAT) tests given to prospective law students.[26]

From the subordinate group's perspective, government and private attempts to cope with discrimination in employment, housing, and education have, on the whole, been rather unsuccessful. Nothing having major national impact was done in any of these areas until the 1960s. Then the civil rights laws, increasing court litigation, and President Johnson's executive orders began to bring about the first modest changes of consequence in employment and education (with greater changes in the South) and some small, almost imperceptible changes in housing. Still, it is hard to demonstrate that government antidiscrimination action was more important in reshaping, for example, employment opportunities than the war-fed prosperity of the 1960s and early 1970s and the civil rights protests of minorities and women. Clearly, government pressure on federal contractors has so far had only modest and variable effects. By 1976 few employers failing to take affirmative action to desegregate their work forces—only fifteen out of thousands—had suffered serious penalties. Court decisions brought about some changes, but these usually applied to small groups of individuals or to plants and companies on a one-by-one basis. New arms of the federal bureaucracy were created; mounds of paper on affirmative action passed back and forth between private and government hands. Yet relatively little money and no massive effort was put into affirmative action programs at the corporate or university level. Things changed less than the recent dramatized concern over "reverse discrimination" suggests. Government action in regard to education was a bit different, for the focus on the South in the 1960s did bring changes there in the way minority children were treated. But when attempts to remedy the segregation of the North took place, few whites there continued to support desegregation. School desegregation seemed to go into a holding pattern, if not a tailspin.

WHAT MORE COULD BE DONE?

The authors agree with those critics who say that "too little" has been done by government and private agencies, and the individuals therein, to eradicate discrimination and make whole those harmed by it. But if what has been done is inadequate, what more could be done to eradicate discrimination and its effects? This bottom-line question has been answered in a number of ways. We can trace out here some ideas that have occurred to us and to others on this matter, suggestions which have at least heuristic value. We will, for the moment, assume that at least some of those with the power to implement such programs in fact want to do so. Perhaps the first step toward achieving adequate public and private action on discrimination is to establish clearer thinking about the different types of race and sex discrimination which persist in the United States. Recall the basic types of discrimination laid out in the beginning of the book:

1. Isolate discrimination
2. Small-group discrimination
3. Direct institutionalized discrimination
   a. Blatant type
   b. Covert type
4. Indirect institutionalized discrimination
   a. Past-in-present type
   b. Side-effect type

We have underscored throughout this book the point that Types 1, 2, and 3 can be tied to prejudiced motivation or intent to harm, while Type 4 is unintentional. In our view, different strategies are, and will be, required in order to eradicate these varied types of discrimination.

Coping with Prejudice

As we have noted before, past strategies attempting to deal with discrimination have often focused on the role of the bigot, the prejudiced individual, and the importance of prejudice-motivated, door-slamming discrimination. According to this point of view, prejudice-motivated discrimination is not so basic to society or human nature that it cannot be eradicated by a variety of traditional educational and psychological techniques. Such techniques emphasize reeducating bigoted individuals, on the assumption that the demise of prejudices and stereotypes will ultimately lead to the death of discrimination. In the United States we periodically have rhetorical campaigns and brotherhood dinners aimed at espousing human rights and deploring racial (and, less often, sex) prejudice. We have seen some emphasis on eradicating stereotyping and prejudice in schools, churches, and business organizations. In recent years a number of newly created private consulting organizations have tried to develop ways of helping concerned individuals in business ferret out prejudice, if not discrimination. Workshops and other consciousness-raising devices have been utilized by a number of business and government organizations in an attempt to get white and nonwhite workers—and less often male and female workers—to see each other's point of view.

Such techniques have probably reduced isolate and small-group discrimination by lessening prejudice, although in some cases the confrontations may have only intensified hostility. One basic problem with such psychologically oriented approaches is that they primarily focus on the prejudice of lower-level white (or white male) workers. Yet is is the prejudices of *higher-level* decision makers that are more critical, particularly with regard to subtle types of direct institutionalized discrimination. Additional efforts are needed to devise educational strategies which will bring to the forefront and expose prejudice and stereotyping all the way from the actions of teachers in grade-school classrooms to the actions of decision makers in corporate boardrooms.

An example of what imaginative effort could be made in exposing prejudice on a larger scale than has been tried so far can be seen in the systematic strategy Sedlacek and Brooks have worked out for educating teachers and principals about racism in their school programs. They have described their educational strategy and its actual application in an important resource book, *Racism in American Education.* Working with groups in on-site training programs, they bring teachers and administrators through ever-increasing levels of consciousness about the operation of attitudinal racism and racial discrimination in their own school environments. First open discussions of cultural and racial differences are developed to make participants aware of such differences. Attitudinal questionnaires are given before, during, and after the educational program both to assess its success and to stimulate the thinking of participants. Innovative situational questionnaires are given to develop an awareness among white participants of their own attitudes toward minorities. Sources of racial attitudes, as well as of institutional racism, are systematically explored by the participants under the guidance of experienced instructors. Finally, participants in the training sessions set up concrete goals for changing racial attitudes and discrimination back home, with provisions for actually evaluating the real-world implementation of these goals.[27] More innovative approaches such as this need to be developed and tried on a large scale, approaches which could be shaped to deal with sexism as well as racism.

The Need for Further Research

By the 1970s the reports of presidential and other investigatory commissions had become so numerous that it seemed almost a cliché to speak of the necessity of further research on social problems. Yet in the case of race and sex discrimination much additional investigation and research, particularly action-oriented research, is badly needed. In surveying the literature for this book it became clear to the authors just how little research has actually been done, and is being done, on the character and day-to-day operation of the mechanisms of race and sex discrimination. There is a serious need for researchers to examine and document in detail those types of discrimination which continue to have an adverse impact on the lives of women and minorities, especially the more subtle forms of institutionalized discrimination. This is easy enough to say, but extraordinarily difficult to carry out. One major difficulty resides in the hidden character and complexity of bureaucratized oppression. This means that many discriminatory mechanisms need to be examined and documented from *within* white–male–dominated organizations.

In many organizational settings there are numerous filtering points through which women and minorities must pass in order to secure higher-status positions. The previous sections on employment, housing, and education began the task of tracing out the various mechanisms of discrimination that operate as barriers. But since many barriers are concealed and little-studied, much research and analysis—on such things as internal promotion practices—remains to be done. Built into the foundation of this organizational society, the direct and indirect mechanisms shaping race and sex inequality have for a long time been accepted as normal and just. Now researchers must get behind the scenes to identify the specific sources of this type of inequality. The subtle real estate brokers' practice of "steering," documented so well in the recent Detroit study cited in Chapter 4, is a good example of routine discriminatory practices which usually remain hidden from public view. Here the researcher, Diana Pearce, sent out black and white couples as "testers" to check on differential treatment by real estate agents. This imaginative study could well become a model for further studies of routine discriminatory practices in banking, employment, and education. If the will to do this important documentation is present, the money to fund it can be found. Increasing documentation of and attacks on blatant forms of direct discrimination have characterized the period since the 1950s. Now it is time for such documentation to focus on the more covert, subtle, and indirect mechanisms. In addition, researchers would do well to develop better indices of the effects of both direct and indirect discrimination. Existing statistical work, such as that of the U.S. Census Bureau, should be expanded in order to develop new statistical indices specifically designed to measure the consequences of discrimination—as, for example, underutilization of minorities and women—in many types of organizations. The limited applicability of existing indices results in part from their not being developed originally to measure discrimination.

Making public both old and new research on and documentation of discrimination is also critical, for some now-unaware dominant group members may be moved to support changes once they become aware of how discrimination continues to operate. One reason for the apathy of some in regard to discrimination may be the misguided assumption that it has nearly been eradicated. Notions of "benign neglect" and attacks on such things as token affirmative action programs seem to be guided by the Pollyanna assumption that "liberty and justice for all" is reality, not rhetoric. A realistic appraisal, however, is that only the surface has changed. The tap roots of discrimination have seldom been touched. Extensive publicity on the hows and whys of continuing discrimination may have some effect—particularly if it "blows the cover," as it were, of those doing the discriminating. Of course, an acute awareness of the subtle and indirect patterns of discrimination will not *necessarily* lead to solutions. No remedial imperative is wedded to expanded knowledge. Nonetheless, expanding people's knowledge of discrimination seems a useful step in the direction of future and better solutions.

Action Strategies

Better educational programs and more sophisticated research procedures are not enough. In our view there must be sharply increased government and private *action* to eradicate race and sex discrimination in the United States, action aimed at covert intentional discrimination and indirect institutionalized discrimination as well as the more obvious types. School curricula and textbooks must be further revised to deal with the racist and sexist stereotyping which continues to fuel indirect discrimination. Training programs for future teachers and journalists must be expanded to include substantial, not superficial, education in racial and cultural differences, in the myths of racism and sexism, in overt and subtle patterns of discrimination, and in methods of eradicating discrimination.

Civil rights laws should be expanded beyond their present level to provide more effective regulation of, and more severe penalties for, discrimination against women and minorities in areas such as employment and housing. Perhaps more important, antidiscrimination penalties must be intensified and enforced. Many present penalties for intentional discrimination are either too weak or are applied only in token-to-modest numbers. As we have noted before, very few government contractors, including colleges and universities, have had their ties to the U.S. Treasury severed, even though it is obvious that race and sex discrimination by many of these contractors has been a routine way of life. A 1975 U.S. Civil Rights Commission report notes that the Office of Contract Compliance in the Department of Labor has

Failed to assure that sanctions be imposed for violations of the Executive orders. Sanctions authorized by the Executive orders include cancellation or termination of existing contracts or debarment from additional contracts, prohibiting the award of a contract, and withholding progress payments. In the 10 years of the contract compliance program, despite widespread noncompliance, only nine companies have been debarred.[28]

Serious enforcement would doubtless mean loss of government funds for hundreds of employers. Moreover, very few penalties have ever been suffered by private or public firms or other organizations involved in institutionalized race and sex discrimination in the sphere of housing. Significant penalties for educational discrimination in the form of school segregation have been limited to a few hundred school districts, mostly in the South.

The regular enforcement of antidiscrimination laws has often been left to hundreds of federal, state, and local bureaucracies, most of which already have other major duties which continue to command their attention. Relatively little time and money has gone into enforcing antidiscrimination laws. In those situations where new government bureaucracies have been specially created to implement antidiscrimination laws and regulations, such as the Equal Employment Opportunity Commission, they have typically been poorly funded and staffed, if not handcuffed by political intervention. The absence of a central, coordinated effort at the federal level signals the impotence of national antidiscrimination efforts, as one recent report on employment indicates:

> This fragmented [federal] administrative picture has resulted in duplication of effort, inconsistent findings, and a loss of public faith in the objectivity and efficiency of the [equal employment] program. This last deficiency is best exemplified by contrasting the opinion of many employers that they are being harassed by Federal bureaucrats with the belief of many minorities and women that the Government's equal employment program is totally unreliable.[29]

Race and sex discrimination were built into the society at a cost of trillions of dollars' worth of land and labor and incalculable loss of life over several hundred years. Token-to-modest governmental strategies over a decade or two, with a few million dollars of funding, are a pale reflection of the effort needed to eradicate race and sex discrimination of all types.

New laws are required to permit the massive effort required to eradicate discrimination. This will reduce the cost of fighting discrimination for individuals. All too often, what changes do occur are brought about by individuals in oppressed groups who go to the effort and expense of court suits, often to win redress for only one person, or a small number of persons. As a recent U.S. Civil Rights Commission report noted, "alterations are necessary in a number of provisions of Title VII of the Civil Rights Act of 1964, for example, in the sections which allow only court action to enforce the statute, require data to be confidential, and limit the authority of the Equal Employment Opportunity Commission to investigate and litigate matters involving patterns and practices of discrimination."[30]

Consolidating antidiscrimination activities into one national agency with several local offices would be one major step toward more effective remedial policies. For example, a National Employment Rights Board could be set up at the federal level to deal with patterns of employment discrimination rather than specific individual complaints. Several existing federal laws would need to be consolidated and amended to establish such an agency, which should have legal authority to enforce one strong, comprehensive federal law covering race and sex (and other) discrimination. The U.S Commission on Civil Rights has suggested that such a new agency be given "broad administrative, as well as litigative, authority to eliminate discriminatory employment practices in the United States."[31] Similarly, centralized agencies for antidiscrimination efforts in housing, education, and health care might also consolidate the presently fragmented, if not confused, government effort in these areas as well. Such consolidation would doubtless reveal new resources for fighting discrimination, and such a procedure could possibly generate relatively widespread support since it is at least compatible with the existing political system.

Much of what we have just discussed in terms of action strategies applies most directly to discrimination which is intentional, and most clearly to discrimination which can be shown to be intentional. Dealing with covert and indirect types of discrimination is much more difficult. Indeed, this is one reason we previously underscored the need for more probing research from within existing groups and organizations. We also have in mind some remedies for indirect discrimination which need to be tried, or need to be tried on a larger scale than has so far been attempted. In some cases remedies for indirect discrimination are less difficult than in others. The first step toward a remedy is that the discriminatory barrier must be recognized for what it is.

Consider, for example, recruitment networks. Some authors have suggested that one remedy for the discriminatory exclusion of nonwhites (or women) from job situations is for those excluded to develop informal communication networks among themselves to pass along job information. But as Granovetter has pointed out, this is very difficult for the victims of discrimination to do.[32] Most job information passes among people who already have the good jobs and who have known each other for several years. Developing such routinized ties into white male networks would thus be very difficult for most minorities and women. They have problems primarily because they are not now a major part of most higher levels in the existing job markets. Those with power, not the victims, must change an organization's dependence on traditional informal recruitment networks to hire new employees, as by imaginative recruiting and advertising procedures. Once a significant number of nonwhites and women are recruited and employed, a multiplier effect may set in as their own informal networks bring in yet more potential employees. It would seem that this type of indirect discrimination can readily be remedied. The cost to an employer, whether private or governmental, should not be great; indeed, there may even be a monetary return. Coming in via informal networks seems to reduce turnover; those who get jobs this way tend to find the workday more pleasant and also have greater access to information about how to perform their jobs.

Other cases of subtle intentional discrimination and indirect discrimination are considerably more difficult to remedy, since they involve time-honored practices considered to be sacred. In our previous discussion of traditional "merit" standards in hiring, promotions, and educational admissions procedures, we underscored the criticisms of those who question conventional screening criteria. We are not suggesting that tests and educational credentials, or job-specific work experience, should be discarded as screening criteria. We are suggesting that the heavy reliance on these conventional criteria, and the defense of these measures by critics of remedial programs, is naïve in the extreme. The framing of the debate in terms of "merit" versus "social justice" is not the real issue. The real issue is whether the systems we have that supposedly measure merit can be modified to generate more social justice.[33] The idea of merit must today be broadened to include a variety of other measures of individual potential and ability. Indeed, rethinking the definition of *merit* may provide a way out of the problems surrounding existing affirmative action programs. In the educational sphere, for example, minority students admitted under "special admissions" programs even though their scores on conventional tests are somewhat lower than those of competing whites are often viewed as cases proving that merit standards are being violated. Yet such minority students' average scores may often be higher than were average scores for whites only a few years earlier. Overall, test scores (and grade-point averages) necessary for admission to higher-rated colleges and professional schools have been going up since the 1950s and 1960s, in part because of increased applicants. So a test score that met a merit standard in 1965, when only whites (or white males) were applying, would not meet the merit standard in 1969 or 1976, when minorities were finally able to apply in significant numbers in many areas. Note too that a minority applicant with a modest law or medical school test score may not be considered as meeting the merit standards of Harvard or Yale, but may meet the merit entrance requirements of a state university professional school.

It seems clear from these examples that there is no such thing as a universally and objectively measured "merit" or "ability." One's ability is subjectively assessed by outsiders whose view of merit may be more affected by the supply and demand of students—or of potential employees—than by some carefully ascertained evaluation of job or school potential. If our current measures of merit are so greatly affected by a few years in time, by a few miles in geographical space, or by supply and demand, it is time such measures were carefully reexamined. Particularly since there is no objective, universal measure of job ability, and since conventional testing and other measures seldom accurately predict actual job performance, it is time we modify our screening practices in employment so as to give greater attention to the capabilities and experience of minorities and women.

Note too that the California Supreme Court, which in the celebrated *Bakke* case rejected a University of California medical school program for disadvantaged students, suggested that minority enrollment might be increased naturally *if grades received less emphasis.*[34] For example, social criteria—such as a medical school applicant's willingness to work for a long period of time in ghetto or rural southern areas where there are no doctors—might be added to the conventional criteria. With some imagination, potential for community service, particularly in those rural and urban areas which have poorer health care, legal services, and so on, could be adequately measured by screening processes. As for employment, scores on written tests and educational credentials should be supplemented, if not replaced, by specific on-the-job or job-relevant testing, perhaps even by measures of community service potential wherever that might be relevant.

Other factors which operate to screen out minorities and women might also be redrawn so as to accomplish a legitimate purpose without discrimination. In cases such as seniority and tenure systems in employment, innovative remedies are beginning to be suggested, if not extensively implemented. Typically, seniority systems were created to protect experienced workers. But in periods of layoffs, such as recessions, those women and minorities with less seniority are the first fired. The challenging task "is not simply to eliminate racist [or, we might add, sexist] arrangements, difficult as that alone would be, but to replace these arrangements with others that serve the same positive functions equally well without the racist [or, again, sexist] consequences."[35] A complex pattern of indirect discrimination requires a different remedy than a situation of direct discrimination, for the indirect mechanisms were typically not established for racist or sexist reasons. Transitional remedies may be necessary while more basic structural alterations are being planned and implemented. Thus, as we noted before, in the *Franks* v. *Bowman Transportation* (1976) decision the Supreme Court awarded *retroactive* seniority to specific minority persons who had actually been denied

employment because of their race after the date on which such discrimination had become unlawful.[36] But such retroactive seniority
is available only to persons who applied for jobs, and is calculated
from the time the applicant was first refused employment. Furthermore, it does not provide a remedy for more recently hired workers
who earlier failed to apply because of the employer's known discriminatory policies. Should they also be given retroactive seniority
so that layoffs will not have such a severe impact on them? This
more difficult problem requires some imaginative restructuring of
existing seniority practices. Two separate seniority lists may be
required, one for women and minorities and one for white males,
with the same proportion being fired from both lists in periods of
recession. This has been proposed in a number of debates on seniority,
both inside and outside courtrooms. In effect, it gives retroactive
seniority, for this one problem and no others, to all minority and
women employees. Whether there is a way to devise even more innovative seniority procedures remains to be seen.

Up to this point we have noted a number of specific ways in
which the antidiscrimination effort could be expanded, both by
government and by the private sector. But the why, where, and
how of implementing these actions often raise a number of other
questions that we need to discuss briefly. One issue is that of responsibility. This becomes most problematical in the case of indirect
(unintentional) discrimination, where consideration of solutions often
raises the issue of who bears the responsibility for remedies. Should
the organizational unit which practices indirect discrimination bear
the major share of responsibility for remedying that discrimination?
For example, where there are credential criteria realistically tied
to job performance, the question arises of who should train minorities or women who were unintentionally screened out. Should the
company immediately involved institute the major training program which may be necessary? Or should the local government
responsible for intentional discrimination in education take remedial
action? Indirect discrimination in one area is often so intricately
tied into problems in other areas that the dilemma of responsibility
for instituting remedies can be difficult to resolve. It seems evident
that all levels of government and the private sector must *share* the
responsibility for remedying this broad, interlocking discriminatory

situation. Much thought and greatly expanded action of an original sort is necessary to tackle these issues, probably with a view toward creating new institutional or societal arrangements.

Another issue to be confronted in implementation is the emergence of programs designed to stall significant or full-scale desegregation (including "de*sex*gregation"). Tokenism in employment is one example of a new barrier which can intentionally frustrate antidiscrimination strategies. The tokenism strategy is to place only one or two "token" nonwhites (or women) in jobs traditionally not held by them. Also common is the practice of placing the "token" in a conspicuous position. (Tragically, nonwhite women are sometimes considered "two-fers"—two "minorities" for the price of one.)

Consider tokenism at management levels, for example. In industrial and other business and government organizations the management levels have been and are composed almost entirely of white males. Those few women and minority men who have made their way into management ranks in recent years are usually viewed, whether they like it or not, as symbols of their entire group and thus are frequently singled out to the point that their workaday lives become difficult. Hiring and promotion processes sometimes select the "tokens" for front office, supervisory, or administrative levels in order to give a company or agency someone to point to, à la "Look at the dramatic progress we are making in hiring women and minorities." Moreover, the typical isolation of tokens in nontraditional jobs tends to reinforce the system of tokenism. Kanter argues that the tokens are caught in a dilemma: either they are successful in terms of conforming rigidly to white male (e.g., "good old boy") values, which usually means dissociating themselves from others in their own group, or because of intense isolation-type pressures they are unsuccessful and are used as examples by white males for not hiring more from their group. Often overlooked in discussions of equal opportunity strategies, by opponents and proponents alike, is the misery created for those minorities and women brought into previously all-white-male settings. Tokenism often involves the absence of social support to facilitate survival. Bringing in *larger* numbers of minorities and women is important, not just to provide equality of opportunity, but also because more-than-token numbers are necessary to provide a context in which many women and minorities can succeed, both in terms of greater work effectiveness and psychological survival.[37] Clearly, the major way to break this vicious cycle is to bring more-than-token numbers of women and minorities into a job setting within a reasonably short period of time. Tokenism, an insidious strategy, should not be allowed to forestall substantial desegregation of employment and other institutional settings.

Finally, we might reiterate that cynicism and pessimism over the possibility of future progress against discrimination are sometimes generated by a realization that inadequate resources have characterized government and private efforts. Many action programs recently begun have decayed or died after a fairly short time because they have not been allowed to become as well-institutionalized as the patterns of discrimination they attempt to eradicate. White (male) personnel in a mainstream organization seldom benefit themselves from vigorous antidiscriminatory actions, so footdragging should not be unexpected. To the extent that white males consider many job situations, as well as college situations, to be zero-sum games ("If you win, I lose"), it is inevitable that they will view the expansion of opportunity for minorities and women as harmful to white males. Indeed, some have argued that the neoconservative and liberal opposition to such programs as affirmative action is misplaced, that they really should be attacking the structure of a society which will not, perhaps cannot, provide enough jobs, housing, and education for all. Some have suggested that, however difficult it may be, one partial way out might be to expand dramatically the zero-sum game, to provide decent-paying jobs for *all* Americans, to provide college places for *all* those able to benefit from college.

WHAT WILL BE DONE?

The question of what *will* be done is fundamental. We have seen what government and private agencies have done in the past. We have underscored this recent progress to indicate that the first steps in eradicating race and sex discrimination have already been taken and that the potential for future change is indicated in these important first steps. We have also indicated some of the problems in existing remedies and have grappled with the question of what could be done. Obviously, our assessment of "What will be done?" has to be speculative. We do indeed expect something to be done in the near future in the direction of expanded antidiscrimination activity. But the degree and the pace of that change is hard to predict.

One major reason is that making further major breaches in the barriers of racism and sexism entails changing the system of privilege. In a system of entrenched privilege, achieving equitable redistribution of that privilege—or what is often called "social justice"—is not an easy task. White (male) privilege became enshrined in the United States legal and philosophical tradition in the distant past and has been basic to the founding documents and to many legislative acts, administrative decrees, and court decisions from then to the present. Even the Constitution institutionalized racism in its recognition and acceptance of slavery and the slave trade and sexism in its determination of who could vote. Not only did the Constitution fail to prohibit race and sex discrimination, it fundamentally contributed to the institutionalization of such discrimination. Given this fundamental racist and sexist tradition, it is not surprising that great resistance mounts when antidiscrimination procedures begin to cut significantly into the benefits that members of dominant groups derive from the existence of discrimination. And such resistance may well explain the token-to-modest character of many remedial programs.

'As Herbert Gans has noted in his pioneering book *More Equality,* pie-in-the-sky equality as a goal has to be replaced by the goal of substantially greater social justice, of substantially greater equality for nonwhites and women.[38] Historically, equality has had different meanings, ranging from equality before the law, to equality of opportunity, to equality of results. Equality of results is a relatively new idea in the context of this society. Even substantially increased (not complete) equality of results is a principle which is still not widely accepted. The United States is still a society whose dominant groups still believe in inequality along race, sex, and class lines. Increasing equality before the law and equality of opportunity has much broader support than increasing equality of income, wealth, power, or prestige.

Yet as we have seen, even support for equality of opportunity and equality before the law has its limits. White and male privileges, once entrenched, are rationalized by ideologies of preserving the status quo, individual "merit," and genetically superior ability. The fact that these privileges have been enjoyed for a long time not only ensures that the descendants of the privileged will have greater access to them but also gives rise to notions that these privileges have come "by right." Those with greater economic and political resources can often insure the same for their descendants. Discrimination reduces, if not excludes, the possibility of white males suffering competition from women and minorities. If 60 percent of the people, or more are hamstrung by discrimination, tokenism, or ineffective remedies, the remainder will have higher profits, status, salaries, and benefits than they otherwise might have. Unhampered competition would reduce the role of white males in running the society. Attempts to accelerate removal of discrimination, or to compensate those groups which have suffered large-scale discrimination in the past, will likely continue to be vigorously attacked, particularly as those attempts reach into ever higher levels of privilege and power in the society. The underlying concern, however hidden, continues to be the protection of privilege. Indeed, there seems to be a social law of inertia in regard to structured-in privilege, namely that resources gained at the expense of a subordinate group remain massed until a subordinate group takes action to change things.

When looking at both old and new solutions for discrimination, one sometimes feels overwhelmed by questions. When one presses for moderate changes in existing patterns of economic and social discrimination, is one simply helping to perpetuate a decaying system? Can remedies for subtle and indirect discrimination be implemented on a large scale without truly *major* changes in the structure of the existing economic and social system? The destruction of the mechanisms of discrimination on a really large scale might well begin to dismantle the built-in patterns of race and sex inequality which constitute foundation pillars of the society. Major structural changes, as in revising the all-pervasive seniority and tenure systems so they do not have their present adverse effects on women and minorities, would certainly have an impact on the social system. Pyramiding a large number of institutional changes of this type might well alter the foundation of what is now a racist-capitalist and a sexist-capitalist society. Thus some argue that the basic socioeconomic system, now a type of modified capitalism, would be completely remade in this process. A humanistic, democratic socialism could result.

Others argue against this conclusion, suggesting instead that more vigorous antidiscrimination measures can be undertaken on an expanded scale while keeping the present system of capitalism more or less intact. True, discriminatory recruitment procedures, screening tests, and real estate procedures could be eliminated without affecting the fundamentally capitalistic nature of the society —that is, the ownership of businesses and industries could still be in private hands. Yet at the same time, massive infusions of minorities and women into the organizational structures of this society, particularly the highest decision-making levels, probably would alter the shape of this particular brand of capitalism, for no longer could it depend on certain groups for the cheap labor and other subordinate positions essential to its operations. Seen from this viewpoint, capitalism in some form might survive a thoroughgoing purging of race and sex discrimination, but some of the fundamental structural and cultural supports of that system would likely be changed, with perhaps the entire system being humanized in the process. Greater power and influence for groups now in subordinate positions would almost necessitate a measure of toleration for diverse ideas, perspectives, and practices that the top groups cannot now accept. Economic class differences might persist, but the existing criteria for mobility within the system would be significantly altered.

A realistic appraisal of the possibilities for change, we suspect, would doubtless downplay or question the possibility of large-scale revolution against racism and sexism in the United States. In the near future, say the next thirty years, major reform seems, at best, to be the likely occurrence. Those pressing for major reform will find that persuasion and negotiation backed by moral suasion have their limits. In order to be effective persuasion and negotiation require sanctions in the form of subordinate group lobbying and pressure. Confrontation potential is necessary, for without some *clout*, attempts at negotiating change often lead to a dead end. For example, the senior author was recently involved in one ongoing attempt at negotiating with a private agency to reduce institutionalized racial discrimination in many of its routine operations. That negotiation revealed that resistance to remedying institutional discrimination can take the form of bureaucratic runarounds and blocking. Dodges such as "I'm with you, but X isn't" and sophisticated strategies such as referral to a series of committees can frustrate the negotiation. The runaround procedure often stalls decision making until the decision dies a natural death. In that particular organizational setting, there was little organized clout behind the minority-oriented negotiators working for change.

Where will the necessary additional clout come from? In speculating about the future, that is perhaps the most basic question. Knowles, Prewitt, and their associates, in the pioneering volume *Institutional Racism in America*, briefly lay out possible sources of clout. They are pessimistic about the standard political process: "Liberals are discovering that these vast problems are not soluble through standard political process—through voting Democratic, through letters to Congress, through testimony at city council."[39] Rather, they suggest that those whites concerned with eradicating racial discrimination will have to organize in their own communities to deal with inadequate housing, inferior schooling, and discriminatory hiring. White antidiscrimination organizations could then work with minority organizations. A similar strategy could be tried by sympathetic males in the case of sex discrimination. Moreover, antiracists and antisexists in bureaucracies whose actions are discriminatory are weak points from the dominant group's point of view and can be valuable in antidiscrimination efforts.

In organizations where a few top decision makers sincerely desire changes in persisting patterns of discrimination at lower levels, some clout is readily at hand. Since many organizations are built on a hierarchical chain of command, higher-level decisions changing discriminatory practices can be accompanied by reinforcement. Nondiscriminatory behavior can be rewarded, while discriminatory behavior, of several types, can be punished. For example, substantial desegregation of U.S. Army ranks, particularly at the level of major and below, has come as a result of enforced orders from the highest levels. In less rigidly hierarchical organizations, such techniques may be less effective, but they are likely to have some payoff. The idea of rewarding decision makers whose divisions or departments show reasonable rates of hiring and promotion of minorities, and women is one with substantial appeal. A few pioneering organizations, for a time, have experimented with making supervisor salaries in part contingent on affirmative action success.

Most critical of all for the future of major reform seems to be the action of subordinate group individuals themselves. There are top-down pressures for change, and there are bottom-up pressures in the form of subordinate group protest. Indeed, in the recent past we have seen the periodic effectiveness of subordinate group individuals banding together in organized protest against oppressive conditions. Coalitions between subordinate groups will likely be required for future reform on a large scale. At a minimum, such groups as black Americans, Chicanos, Native Americans, and Puerto Ricans need to organize a coalition to fight discrimination, perhaps with certain allied women's groups. Such coalitions have been tried before, with a few successes and numerous failures. Problems creep in. The priorities of different groups are not the same; the resources vary; the leadership gets co-opted; the opposition of dominant groups works to split up coalitions.

Nonetheless, the likelihood of *substantial* future change probably depends for the most part on the willingness of minorities and women to keep the pressure on. When the entrenched system of institutionalized discrimination gives a bit, as in providing greater access to formerly off-limits entry-level positions in industry or government, that does not mean that discrimination, overt or covert, will not continue in job benefits, promotions, and the like. Even hard-won advances can be rolled back, as has been the case in periods of recession. Not only is eternal vigilance necessary in order to expand liberty, but eternal organization and effort as well.

1. This paragraph draws heavily on Joe R. Feagin, *Racial and Ethnic Relations* (Englewood Cliffs, N.J.: Prentice-Hall, 1978), chapter 11.

2. Ibid., chapter 7.

3. Ibid.

4. Ibid.

5. *U.S.* v. *Georgia Power Co.,* 474 F. 2d 906 (1973); *U.S.* v. *Central Motor Lines,* 338 F. Supp. 532 (1971); *Crockett* v. *Green,* 388 F. Supp. 912 (1975), upheld on appeal, 534 F. 2d 715 (1976). See also *U.S.* v. *City of Chicago,* 416 F. Supp. 788 (1976); *Arnold* v. *Ballard,* 390 F. Supp. 723 (1975).

6. *EEOC* v. *Local 14 International Union of Operating Engineers,* 415 F. Supp. 1155 (1976); *Albermarle Paper Co.* v. *Moody,* 95 S. Ct. 2362 (1975). See also *Griggs* v. *Duke Power Co.,* 401 U.S. 424 (1971).

7. *Franks* v. *Bowman Transportation Co.,* 96 S. Ct. 1251, 1265-66 (1976). This principle was first expounded in *Local 189, United Papermakers* v. *U.S.,* 416 F. 2d 980 (1969), cert. denied 397 U.S. 919 (1970).

8. *Watkins* v. *Scott Paper Co.,* 530 F. 2d 1159, 1173 (1976); *Patterson* v. *American Tobacco Co.,* 494 F. 2d 211 (1974).

9. *Albermarle Paper Co.* v. *Moody,* 95 S. Ct. 2362 (1975); *United Papermakers Local 189* v. *U.S.,* 416 F. 2d 980 (1969).

10. *Washington* v. *Davis,* 96 S. Ct. 2040, 2050 (1976).

11. George Cooper and Harriet Rabb, *Equal Employment Law and Litigation* (New York: Columbia Law School, Employment Rights Project, n.d.), p. 1.

12. *Buchanan* v. *Warley,* 245 U.S. 60 (1917).

13. *Shelly* v. *Kraemer,* 333 U.S. 1 (1948).

14. Davis McEntire, *Residence and Race* (Berkeley: University of California Press, 1960), pp. 267-69.

15. U.S. Commission on Civil Rights, *The Federal Civil Rights Enforcement Effort, 1974,* vol. 2, *To Provide ... for Fair Housing* (Washington, D.C.: U.S. Government Printing Office, 1974), pp. 4, 38.

16. Ibid., pp. 35-41.

17. Ibid., pp. 56-57.

18. See *Hills* v. *Gautreaux,* 425 U.S. 284 (1976); *U.S.* v. *American Institute of Real Estate Appraisers,* Civil No. 76-1448 (N.D. Ill., filed Apr. 16, 1976).

19. Kathy Cosseboom, *Grosse Point, Michigan: Race Against Race* (East Lansing: Michigan State University Press, 1972), p. 25.

20. Feagin, *Racial and Ethnic Relations,* chapter 11.

21. Joan Abramson, *The Invisible Woman* (San Francisco: Jossey-Bass Publishers, 1975), pp. 170-73.

22. "The Furor Over 'Reverse Discrimination,'" *Newsweek,* September 26, 1977, p. 54; also see *Allan Bakke* v. *Regents of the University of California,* 45 U.S.L.W. 2179 (1976).

23. Nathan Glazer, *Affirmative Discrimination* (New York: Basic Books, 1975), p. 201.

24. Samuel Krislov, *Representative Bureaucracy* (Englewood Cliffs, N.J.: Prentice-Hall, 1974), p. 17.

25. Lewis Mainzer, *Political Bureaucracy* (Glenview, Ill.: Scott, Foresman, 1973).

26. Robert M. O'Neil, *Discriminating Against Discrimination* (Bloomington: Indiana University Press, 1975), p. 49. See also William E. Sedlacek and Glenwood C. Brooks, Jr., *Racism in American Education: A Model for Change* (Chicago: Nelson-Hall, 1976).

27. Sedlacek and Brooks, *Racism in American Education*, pp. 5-10.

28. U.S. Commission on Civil Rights, *The Federal Civil Rights Enforcement Effort, 1974*, vol. 5, *To Eliminate Employment Discrimination* (Washington, D.C.: U.S. Government Printing Office, 1975), p. 637.

29. Ibid., p. 618.

30. Ibid., pp. 617-18.

31. Ibid., p. 649.

32. Mark S. Granovetter, *Getting a Job: A Study of Contact and Careers* (Cambridge: Harvard University Press, 1974).

33. Krislov, *Representative Bureaucracy*, pp. 135-36.

34. "The Furor Over 'Reverse Discrimination,' " p. 54.

35. Thomas F. Pettigrew, "Racism and the Mental Health of White Americans: A Social Psychological View," in *Racism in Mental Health*, edited by Charles V. Willie, Bernard M Kramer, and Betram S. Brown (Pittsburgh: University of Pittsburgh Press, 1973), pp. 275-76.

36. *Franks* v. *Bowman Transportation Co.*, 96 S. Ct. 1251 (1976).

37. Rosabeth Moss Kanter, *Men and Women of the Corporation* (New York: Basic Books, 1977), pp. 212-13, 242.

38. Herbert Gans, *More Equality* (New York: Vintage Books, 1974).

39. Louis L. Knowles and Kenneth Prewitt (eds.), *Institutional Racism in America* (Englewood Cliffs, N.J.: Prentice-Hall, 1969), p. 129.

Race and Sex Discrimination Today: Conceptual and Research Studies

(with Nijole Benokraitis, Rose Brewer, and Beth Anne Shelton

chapter seven

CONCEPTIONS AND THEORIES OF DISCRIMINATION: AN OVERVIEW

This new chapter reviews recent data and research on the many types of discrimination that we discussed in previous chapters. We will also examine remedial action for discrimination. But first we can turn to conceptions of discrimination.

Reverse Discrimination: Problems of Poor Conceptualization

Since the late 1970s relatively little work has been done on theories of discrimination beyond that discussed in Chap-

185

ter 1. This lack of conceptual work has serious policy implications. For example, in recent years much scholarly and public policy discussion has focused on *affirmative action* programs, those programs discussed in Chapter 6 which grew out
of the civil rights laws and presidential executive orders in the
1960s. Most of this discussion has been negative, with phrases
such as "reverse discrimination" being coined in the attack on
the modest remedial programs we call affirmative action. In
the 1980s under the Ronald Reagan administration, the theory
of reverse discrimination was used to help legitimate a restructuring of the U.S. Commission on Civil Rights and of the
U.S. Department of Justice, so that both formerly pro–affirmative action agencies became opponents of affirmative action
programs set up by corporations and by government agencies.

Public discussion of affirmative action and its eradication tends to ignore the background and contemporary reality
of everyday race and sex discrimination in the United States.
This public discussion of equal opportunity often uses the
word *discrimination*, but few analysts have given attention to
the definition and dimensions of discrimination. Apart from a
few words about sharp declines in discrimination, critics focus
on the operation and effects of remedial action and ignore the
background of real-world discrimination. An adequate defense of affirmative action requires a thoroughgoing problem-
remedy approach, since it is the discriminatory problem that
requires the remedy. Compare the situation to that of cancer
and its remedies. Frequently, policy makers and other analysts have not distinguished the different types of race and sex
"cancers" and the different types of remedies that those
cancers may require. Talking about affirmative action without talking about discrimination is like assessing chemother-
apy without examining the cancers involved. Discrimination
is the *problem* for which affirmative action is the *remedy*.

Public Conceptions of Race Discrimination

A polarization of white and nonwhite views of discrimination is characteristic of public opinion in the 1980s. White

and nonwhite Americans have long disagreed over the conditions facing nonwhite people, but the polarization of views is particularly striking given that it has been more than two decades since the pathbreaking 1964 and 1965 Civil Rights Acts were passed into law.

Not long before President Ronald Reagan took office in the early 1980s, the Mathematica survey research firm interviewed three thousand black households nationwide. Two-thirds of the three thousand black heads of household felt that black Americans are discriminated against "a great deal" in this country. Moreover, a survey by *Black Enterprise* magazine found most of their middle- and upper-income black readers to be critical of the current racial situation. For example, 85 percent of the *Black Enterprise* readers agreed that "most lending institutions still discriminate against potential black borrowers."[1] In reply to an early 1980s Gallup poll question, "Looking back over the last ten years, do you think the quality of life of blacks in the U.S. has gotten better, stayed the same, or gotten worse?" over half of the nonwhites in the sample (mostly blacks) said "gotten worse" or "stayed the same."[2] Yet only a fifth of the *white* respondents answered in a negative way. Three-quarters of the whites said, "gotten better." Thus a majority of rank-and-file white Americans seem to agree with the more conservative white leaders in academia, government, and business. Black problems and disadvantages tend to be blamed on blacks themselves. Two-thirds of whites in a NORC survey blamed black disadvantages on blacks' lack of "motivation or will power to pull themselves up out of poverty."[3] The aforementioned Gallup survey also asked this question: "In your opinion, how well do you think blacks are treated in this community: the same as whites are, not very well, or badly?" In this nationwide sample, 68 percent of the whites said blacks were treated the same as whites; only 20 percent felt they were not well treated or were badly treated. Public opinion poll data suggest a clear polarization of the views of blacks and whites on issues of discrimination and inequality.

Moreover, the policy implications of polarized attitudes

are serious. The riots in Miami and other cities in the early 1980s make it clear that the price of racial injustice can be very high. In a 1980 Gallup poll (after the Miami riot), when asked about the likelihood of serious racial conflict in their local community in the future, 37 percent of nonwhites surveyed said racial conflict was likely or expressed uncertainty about that violent possibility. (Rioting by poor blacks in several areas of London, England in 1985 suggested that high unemployment in various parts of the English-speaking world fosters militant protests.)

Only a few public opinion surveys have asked women about sex-based discrimination. An early 1980s Roper poll did ask a sample of 3,000 women some relevant questions. Six women in ten in that survey said there was discrimination against women in jobs, including three-quarters of women in cities.[4] Majorities saw discrimination in business, government, and the professions. These surveys of minorities and women show clearly that substantial majorities of the victims perceive race and sex discrimination as serious problems in this society in the 1980s.

The Dimensions of Discrimination

In Chapter 2 we defined discrimination as *actions or practices carried out by members of dominant (race and sex) groups which have a differential and negative impact on members of subordinate (race and sex) groups.* This definition of discrimination remains an acceptable working definition for those working in the area of civil rights and equal opportunity. We highlight some of the dimensions of this discrimination in Figure 1.

The major dimensions of discrimination include (a) motivation, (b) discriminatory action, (c) effects, (d) the relation between motivation and action, (e) the relation between action and effects, (f) the immediate institutional context, and (g) the larger societal context. In the social science and policy literatures, a few of these components have been given the

Figure 1
The Dimensions of Discrimination

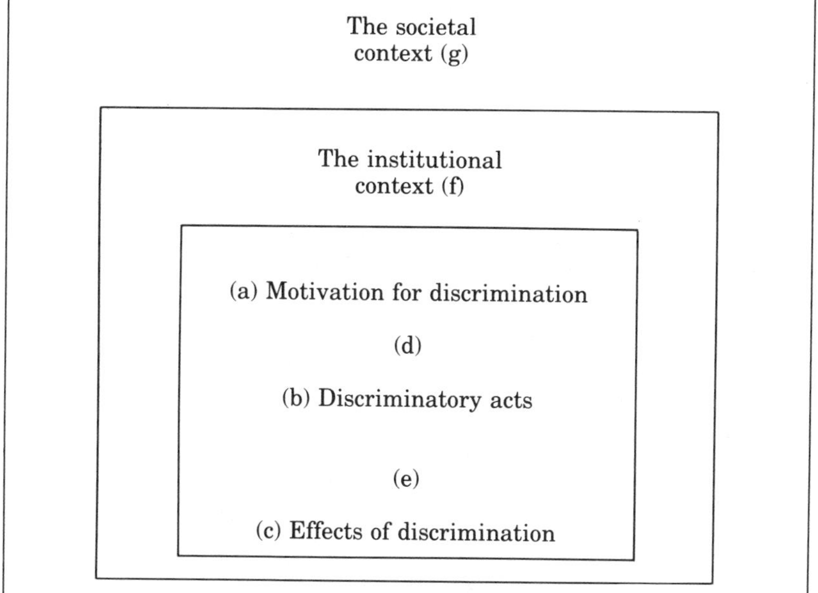

The societal
context (g)

> The institutional
> context (f)
>
> > (a) Motivation for discrimination
> >
> > (d)
> >
> > (b) Discriminatory acts
> >
> > (e)
> >
> > (c) Effects of discrimination

Source: Adapted from Joe R. Feagin and Douglas Lee Eckberg, "Discrimination Motivation, Action, Effects, and Context," *Annual Review of Sociology 6* (1980), p. 2.

greatest attention: motivation (a), effects (c), and the relation of motivation to action (d). The discriminatory practices or mechanisms themselves (b) and the larger institutional and societal contexts (f,g) have received less theoretical and empirical attention.

Discrimination: Motivation

As we explained in Chapter 1, much research and much discussion on discrimination are focused on one type of motivation (as in Figure 1)—on prejudice—to the virtual exclusion of other types of motivation. Traditional analysis emphasizes the relation between prejudice and discrimination (d in Figure 1), with prejudice seen as the critical causal factor underlying discriminatory treatment of a singled-out subordinate group. Recent research on white prejudice directed at nonwhites suggests that there is still a lot of blatant racism just below the surface. Our own observations in college settings and a study of southwestern medical schools suggests that "old-fashioned" prejudice-motivated discrimination, practiced by whites and males, is much more widespread than we usually admit. Some of this discrimination is camouflaged by a thin veil of equal opportunity rhetoric.[5] Most of the social science and policy literatures have adopted some variation of a prejudice-causes-discrimination theory. Gunnar Myrdal, in his study *An American Dilemma*, viewed racial prejudice as a complex of beliefs "which are behind discriminatory behavior on the part of the majority group."[6] But, in fact, today's race and sex discrimination involves more than the actions of bigoted individuals. Several authors have pointed out that the intent to harm lying behind much discrimination may not reflect prejudice or antipathy, but simply a desire to protect one's own privileges. Some discriminate because they gain economically or politically from racial and sexual restrictions on the competition.

Discrimination: Effects

Much discrimination literature concentrates on the psychological and statistical effects of discrimination (c in Figure 1). There are a number of social-psychological studies of the effects of discrimination on the personalities of black Americans, such as the famous Clark studies of black identity problems. And there are numerous studies, often utilizing government demographic data, that analyze such statistical effects of discrimination as income inequality or residential segregation. There are many research analyses in the social science literature, legal briefs, court cases, and affirmative action plans that examine differentials in income, occupation, education, and residence by race and sex. Most look at the effects of discrimination, with much too brief attention to the concrete discriminatory mechanisms that lie behind those effects.[7]

Discrimination: Mechanisms

As we detailed in Chapter 2, discriminatory actions take different forms in this society, both individual and institutional (organizational) forms. Given the public policy debate over discrimination, reverse discrimination, and affirmative action, it continues to be important to distinguish the basic types of discrimination laid out in Chapter 2, what we term isolate discrimination (Type A), small group discrimination (Type B), direct institutionalized discrimination (Type C), and indirect institutionalized discrimination (Type D). Some recent conceptual work has probed the more covert and subtle types of institutionalized (mostly Type C) discrimination, with a particular focus on differential treatment in the workplace.

Covert and Subtle Types of Institutionalized Discrimination

Let us now examine research on the more covert and subtle types of race and sex discrimination. According to Nijole Benokraitis, *covert* discrimination refers to unequal and injurious treatment of women and minorities which is hidden, clandestine, maliciously motivated and very difficult to document.[8] Common types of covert discrimination include manipulation, tokenism, and sabotage. We will illustrate the usefulness of these concepts in the area of employment.

One popular type of covert discrimination is *manipulation*; women and minority males are skillfully maneuvered to serve the (white) male manipulator's purposes. For example, one mid-level female administrator reported that once a month her male supervisor would give her a last-minute job that was impossible to complete by the assigned deadline. In his evaluations, he would praise her (generally well-known reputation) for being intelligent, hard-working, efficient, and innovative. However, he would cite the unfinished assignments as a major reason for not promoting or rewarding her. She had no way of proving that he was manipulating her work assignments to justify not promoting her. Black male managers in traditionally all-white organizations have reported similar acts of covert manipulation designed to slow their progress.

Tokenism is another type. Typically, tokens are seen and treated as "window dressing" and are stereotyped in terms of their race ("a credit to his race") or sex (as mother, sexpot) rather than being evaluated in terms of their abilities, talents, and accomplishments. Tokens are not taken seriously by supervisors or peers. In terms of the latter, for example, a woman in a male-dominated math department said that she had stopped going to lunch with her colleagues because, whenever she joined them, the conversations would shift from professional issues to personal comments and questions about her family, interests, and experiences. Thus, she was effectively isolated and excluded from almost all of the informal situations where much of the departmental decision making was conducted. Similarly, black male employees in traditionally white male job settings are often marketed as tokens, being moved from one committee to another, or from one organizational setting to another, to show that the organization is integrated. It is not uncommon for such black tokens to go unrewarded (in terms of pay, for example) for the added job burden of "window dressing." Some eventually quit because of the burden of tokenism.

A common type of covert discrimination is *sabotage*: employers or fellow employees purposely undermine a minority male's, or a woman's, work or self-esteem, or both. In many cases, the victims never realize they've been sabotaged. Even if they do find out, they are typically powerless to obtain the necessary documentation to prove discrimination. For example, one mid-level manager at a nationally known company reported that she had gotten excellent ratings from her supervisors throughout her first year of employment. In the meantime, the company psychologist had called her about once a month and inquired "how things were going." She was pleased by the company's interest in its employees. At the end of the year, one of her male peers whose evaluations were known to be very mediocre got a promotion and she didn't. When she pursued the reasons for her nonpromotion, she was told by one of the company's vice presidents that "anyone who had to see the company psychologist once a month is clearly not management material." She had no way of proving that she had been sabotaged by someone higher up in company management. Minority males have reported similar types of sabotage by white male managers above them.

Benokraitis has defined *subtle* discrimination as the unequal and injurious treatment of women or minority males which is neither immediately visible nor covert; it may be innocent or manipulative, intentional or unintentional, but can be documented. Whereas covert discrimination refers to discrimination that we suspect but do not see, subtle discrimination refers to inequality that we see but do not suspect because we have internalized sexist or racist behavior as acceptable. This type of discrimination seems to be more common today in the case of sex discrimination than race discrimination. For example, in a recent interview a woman faculty member at a university reported that she had served on a search committee where the two women candidates were treated "differently" from the four male candidates. The women were asked many factual questions, more specific questions, and were often interrupted during their responses. Male candidates were allowed to ramble, to talk about nonacademic issues (e.g. sports), and to digress. They were encouraged to ask—rather than answer—questions, and were rarely interrupted. Because women are more likely to be grilled, they are more likely to make mistakes, to become worn-down earlier in the day and to be perceived as not being "collegial" (an important trait in higher education) because there is minimal relaxed interaction. Black candidates, male as well as female, have reported similar problems in job interview settings where the interviewers are all white males. It is very difficult to be relaxed where the cultural characteristics of those interviewing are not the same as those of the candidates. The frequently tense responses of nontraditional candidates are later used against them.

Examples of subtle sex discrimination abound in every sector. According to women politicians, for example, their male counterparts sometimes "forget" to forward materials necessary for committee meetings, or they schedule informal get-togethers (where much of the business is done) when they know the women will be unavailable because of professional or personal commitments. Women in corporate sales and marketing departments are similarly "kept in their place" by supervisors, clients, and peers through "gentlemanly" overtures, paternalism, chivalrous and condescending behavior, and comments which exclude women from serious participation in group deliberations. For example, one mid-level manager in marketing said that she was in an important meeting where she and a comparable-level manager in another department disagreed on a critical issue. As the discussion grew more heated, her male counterpart exploded: "Look here, little girl . . . " She was so taken aback and embarrassed that she responded in a "typically female" way—she withdrew from the debate. The woman was clearly "put in her place." In most of the above examples, the women didn't immediately see the situation as discriminatory because most have internalized the notion that women are inferior and subordinate. Thus, women often unknowingly participate in their own victimization.

The major difference between these new concepts of "subtle" and "covert" discrimination is that, although both types of barriers are not immediately visible, subtle discrimination can be documented and challenged. Covert discrimination cannot (so far). A major effort needs to be made to document these concepts. Solutions also differ. Subtle discrimination practices might be remedied by changing everyday behaviors and institutional policies; covert discrimination will not be visible until there is widespread "whistle blowing" and until substantial numbers of whistle blowers (i.e., women) move into decision-making positions.

These concepts extend our conceptualization of institutionalized discrimination in that they force us to think about subtle and covert forms of race and sex discrimination in U.S. society.

EMPLOYMENT DISCRIMINATION

We will now examine recent evidence on employment discrimination in more detail (cf. Chapter 3). Recent studies have examined both public and private employment.

Recent Research: A Public Employment Setting

A study conducted by Beth Anne Shelton examined persisting patterns of race discrimination at a major state university in the Sunbelt.[9] She found that, even in the last 15 years of "equal opportunity", specific occupational classifications were segregated, with the majority of black employees concentrated in service or maintenance positions. While there was some racial diversity in the composition of each major occupational classification at the university, blacks had only token representation in the professional, managerial, and technical sectors. In the service and maintenance sector, for example, black employees were concentrated in custodial, food services, and grounds-keeping jobs, while white service and maintenance employees were concentrated in different and better paying positions. Most wage inequality at the university was a product of discriminatory occupational assignment, rather than different pay for the same jobs.

Looking beyond the basic racial inequality in wages and job assignments, Shelton carefully studied the internal organizational *mechanisms* that have perpetuated racially segregated work forces into the 1970s and 1980s. She studied job notice procedures, job referral practices, personnel interviewing practices, and hiring procedures. The job notice and referral mechanisms at the initial point of organizational contact were found to be the most important determinants of the overall and job-specific location of the university's black and white employees.

Job notices were not widely disseminated to the local job market in the city and county where this university is located. Limited job posting and the operation of informal networks for the dissemination of job information produced racially unequal access to job information. Information on jobs held by white employees already employed at the university was more readily available to white potential applicants, while information on the usually lower paying jobs held by blacks was primarily available to black potential applicants. The spread of job information within racially homogeneous information networks resulted in potential black applicants being screened out of the job selection process for traditionally white jobs at a very early point in the hiring process. This is a clear example of the institutionalized discrimination accented in Chapter 2.

When information on "white" jobs was made available outside the segregated information networks, the nature of that information was often such that the minority applicant would be discouraged from applying. The subtle racial typing of jobs at the university was a process that also tended to exclude black applicants. The message of "blacks need not apply" was implicit in some job notices, as in the description of, as well as the history of, traditionally white positions. Subtle messages about the requirements for a job, as well as information indicating that the present jobholder was white, would characterize a job publicly as "white" or "black." The self-selection resulting from this subtle racial advertising was a significant factor in the maintenance of racially homogeneous applicant pools.

Once applicants were accepted, the initial referral processes further handicapped black applicants through the channeling of applicants into racially homogeneous pools. Whatever their qualifications, most black applicants were channeled into referral pools for custodial, food services, and grounds positions, while white applicants were placed in clerical, bookkeeping, and miscellaneous referral pools. Informal referral practices were more intentionally exclusionary than other allocation mechanisms. At the place of referral, racial designations (e.g., "n" for Negro) were found to be placed on some application and referral sheets in a covert manner; and the internal referral lists in the university for specific job openings were, in the majority of instances, racially homogeneous. The predispositions of white personnel staff operated to limit employment options for black applicants.

Shelton also found differential treatment in the interview and hiring process—treatment favoring whites for better paying jobs. The decentralized interview and hiring process at the university allowed for significant personal discretion by hiring agents. Additional job requirements could be added at the interview. White interviewers might, consciously or unconsciously, emphasize certain "cultural" requirements such as traditionally white (and middle-class) dress, appearance, or language. To consolidate their position, white supervisors select others (whites primarily) with cultural characteristics similar to their own. Blacks were differentially eliminated through these exclusionary mechanisms. Cultural credentials can serve as a proxy for race, as they do in many employment settings in U.S. society today. We will see this cultural proxy for race operating in the realm of education in a later section. Intentional, institutionalized discrimination remains a part of the American workplace.

The Business World: Continuing Problems

Institutionalized discrimination in private workplaces has been documented in the 1980s. Significant numbers of minority men and women have moved into corporate America in recent years, especially at entry-level jobs such as low-level managers. But the success of some at the entry level has not carried through to everyday life, or to promotions in corporate workplaces. Thus, Jones's research on black managers has found that the predominantly white corporate environment, with its intense pressures for conformity, created regular problems. Jones describes one black manager (Charlie) who was working his way up the lower executive ranks. One day he met with other black managers who wanted his advice on coping with racial discrimination. This was the result:

> Charlie concluded that this should be shared with senior management and agreed to arrange a meeting with the appropriate officers. Two days before the scheduled meeting, while chatting with the President at a cocktail affair, Charlie was sombered by the President's disturbed look as he said, "Charlie, I am disappointed that you met with those black managers. I thought we could trust you."[10]

It is clear from numerous examples of this type that black managers in the business world are under heavy pressure *not* to cooperate, not to support one another even in the fact of blatant and subtle discrimination. Yet, without mutual support some (many?) may not make it in the long run. Moreover, examples such as this also point up a continuing problem in organizations. The leaders in white (male) oriented organizations are willing, often grudgingly, to bring blacks and women into important positions, but in token numbers and under the existing rules. New people are expected to change, not the organizations with their racist and sexist traditions.

In addition, Jones has reported dramatic racial-climate data from his nationwide survey of a large number of black managers with graduate-level business degrees. Nearly all (98 percent) felt that black managers had not achieved equal opportunity with white managers. More than 90 percent felt there was much antiblack hostility, either subtle or blatant, in corporations; more than 90 percent felt black managers had less opprotunity than whites, or no chance, compared with whites, to succeed in their firms solely on the basis of ability. Two-thirds felt that many whites in corporations still believe blacks are intellectually inferior, and most reported that this adverse racial climate had a negative impact on the evaluations, assignments, and promotions of black managers. This research on blacks who have moved up into nontraditional managerial positions documents the firm entrenchment of discrimination in the private sector in the 1980s. Entry-level changes have not brought about the necessary internal changes in corporate climate, in evaluation procedures, in assignments, and in promotions. As a result, blacks are rarely found in middle management and virtually never among the top corporate executives. There is still a double standard favoring whites (especially white males) who fit the dominant white-male mold.[11]

Continuing Inequality in the Mass Media

Limited progress in employment desegregation can be seen in the newspaper and broadcast journalism industries. A recent study of black owners and employers in the mass media found significant underrepresentation. Blacks own less than 1 percent of the 1,138 commercial television stations and only one of the 50 programming companies. Moreover, blacks own only 1.5 percent of the nation's nearly nine thousand radio stations. Only one of the 1,710 general circulation daily newspapers is black owned. Among newspaper news executives, 97 percent are white. Black representation increases among lower level employees in the newspaper and broadcast industries. In 1983 in the radio-television industry, for example, blacks were 16 percent of the clerical workers and 43 percent of the service (e.g., janitorial) workers, but only 8 percent of professional workers. Much of the progress at the professional level has come from the 1971 FCC equal employment guidelines, yet this pressure has *decreased* in the 1980s.[12]

DISCRIMINATION IN HOUSING

Research on residential segregation in U.S. cities in the 1980s has revealed that high levels of racial separation persist. A study of Taeuber in 28 central cities in larger metropolitan areas found only small declines in residential segregation between 1970 and 1980. There has been some increase in blacks living in suburban areas, but researchers note that this is mostly because of the spillover of black residents of central cities into adjacent suburbs. A recent study of the St. Louis metropolitan area confirms this finding. Most black suburbanization extended out from the traditional black residential areas, with many such suburban areas being "zones of transition" from white to black residence. This research suggests that there is more contact between blacks and whites than a decade ago, but that contact is often the short-lived result of turnover and resegregation. Racial isolation is still the norm in the 1980s.[13]

A 1980 study of black and white areas of Newark and East Orange, New Jersey, found a pattern of racial leapfrogging. Both of these cities are slightly more than half black, but East Orange is generally a more affluent area with a better educated population. Newark has distinctive white areas which resist the entrance of black families. In the late 1960s a citizens committee was formed in the part of Newark near East Orange to oppose attempts by blacks to achieve economic and residential equality in the city. Such organizations continue to protect white areas in the 1970s and 1980s. As a result, blacks who moved to East Orange leapfrogged the white areas of Newark to live in the more hospitable areas of East Orange, which had better services than the city of Newark. These black families were not more affluent than the white families they leapfrogged; thus, those blacks who wish to flee the toubled, crime-ridden city of Newark sought "housing in the predominantly black neighborhoods in nearby municipalities where they will not be greeted with hostility."[14]

Since the late 1970s there have been a number of important "audit" studies of housing discrimination mechanisms.

The best studies have used a black auditor and a white auditor of similar backgrounds, who were sent separately to realtors and apartment rental agents. Studies done in Dallas, Boston, and Denver between 1978 and 1983 found differential treatment favoring the white auditors looking for housing, whether they were owners or renters. In all studies whites were likely to be shown or told about more housing units than blacks. In a 1981 Boston study white auditors were invited to inspect 17 units on the average, 81 percent more than their black (matched) teammates. A 1983 Boston study found a similar pattern of differential treatment for blacks, as well as for Hispanics and Asian Americans. A 1982 Denver study found extensive discrimination against Hispanic owners and black renters across the city, while Hispanic renters and black owners faced high levels of discrimination in certain areas of Denver. In addition, these studies have found that some agents reserve certain housing units to show to whites and certain others for minorities. A common pattern is for minorities to be shown the advertised housing units, but not to be shown or told about other housing units that are made available to whites.[15]

The Boston studies reported significant discrimination against blacks in information about financing. Whites got much more information about financing. The same was true in the Denver study. The Boston and Denver studies also found some evidence of black housing seekers being steered away from traditionally white residential areas. Whites were more likely to be encouraged to seek housing in suburban areas, and agents sometimes encouraged blacks to seek housing away from the agent's own territory. Thus, recent housing studies confirm that there is still widespread housing discrimination in U.S. cities, North and South.

SCHOOL SEGREGATION AND DESEGREGATION

Proving Intent to Discriminate

Since the late 1970s a new factor in school desegregation has been the shift away from an emphasis on racial balance in local schools on the part of black leaders in numerous major cities. For example, in Atlanta, with its 80 percent black school population, black groups agreed to settle their school desegregation suit without a racial balance plan in exchange for complete desegregation of teachers and administrators.[16] Similar compromises were made in cities such as Detroit and Dallas, cities with large black school systems. Many local black leaders have given up on comprehensive school desegregation. Nonetheless, most civil rights organizations and leading civil rights lawyers have remained steadfast in pressing for comprehensive school desegregation plans, in spite of the massive white resistance.

In recent years, particularly in employment discrimination and school segregation cases, the Supreme Court and some other federal courts have fueled this white resistance, in part by requiring a new standard for proving racial discrimination. The major 1971 *Griggs* v. *Duke Power Co.* case (see Chapter 3) set up the standard of remediable discrimination to include practices "neutral on their face" and "neutral in terms of intent," if those practices had a differential and negative effect on black Americans and thus froze the "status quo of prior discriminatory employment practices." However, the more conservative Supreme Court of the late 1970s and 1980s has generally required proof that a particular employment policy was *intentionally* established to discriminate against *individual* members of minority groups. This standard is often difficult and expensive to prove, and thus less progress in fighting discrimination has been made since the mid-1970s. For example, in a 1977–1978 case the Supreme Court upheld the use of a teacher examination in South Carolina that disqualified 83 percent of blacks, but only 18 percent of white teachers, because intent to discriminate had not been proven.[17] Similar reasoning was used in a Mobile, Alabama decision in which a federal court approved an at-large election system in which no blacks could be elected in a city that is 35 percent black.[18]

In a 1974 *Miliken* decision the U.S. Supreme Court overturned, by a close 5–4 vote, a lower court order requiring a combining of the Detroit school system and surrounding (white) suburban school systems in one metropolitan-wide desegregation plan.[19] The Supreme Court ruled that it had not been proven that the segregation in Detroit was caused by the actions of surrounding school boards. As a result, only a few metropolitan-wide desegregation plans have cleared this Supreme Court hurdle. Meanwhile, half of all minority students still go to school districts which are 60–90 percent minority, central city districts where substantial desegregation is not possible without bringing in the white suburbs. Since the mid-1970s the U.S. Supreme Court has set up a standard of proof that requires minority plaintiffs in desegregation cases to prove that school officials intentionally acted to segregate a school system before dramatic remedies such as busing can be used to desegregate the schools.[20] Protest against busing around the country, and appointments to the Supreme Court by conservative Republican Presidents, have created this shift of policy by the Supreme Court. Still, in some cases, plaintiffs' lawyers have been able to show such intentional discrimination by school boards, and some school desegregation plans have been implemented.

In the 1980s a variety of school aid programs designed to aid poor, black, and other minority children were cut back by the Reagan administration, on the grounds that such programs were no longer necessary and also were too expensive. These cutbacks have reduced the schooling "safety net" for minority children. The Reagan administration also moved to support private schools, in such ways as providing tax deductions for parents who pay private school tuition. This action works to reduce public support for the public schools, particularly in central cities.

The Impact of Schools

Job discrimination in the outside world is well known to black and other minority students. Indeed, a number of scholars have argued that the poor or mediocre school performance of many minority children is directly linked to that outside reality, that black children "realize that they face a job ceiling in the larger world and they develop a variety of coping mechanisms that do not enhance school success. Also, an antagonism and distrust has developed between blacks and the schools based on a history of segregated and inferior education."[22]

It is not only the outside reality that causes problems for minority children. It is also the character of the desegregated schools themselves. Because desegregation has been carried out primarily by white officials, it has often had a negative impact on minority children, minority teachers, and minority communities. Research by Rose Brewer on black adolescent girls in a central city San Antonio school has examined the clash of two worlds, of two cultures, which minority students face as they move into white-oriented or white-dominated school settings.[23] Brewer found that a significant number of the black girls resisted this school culture and its distinctive values. There was the white middle-class school culture the black girls were expected to live up to—being neat, obedient, ladylike, docile, and doing their schoolwork. As a result, there was conflict with this school envirnoment. Most tension stemmed from very strong values and expectations these young black women possessed regarding fairness and unfairness on the part of white teachers and administrators. Instead of conforming meekly like many of their white counterparts, many blacks chose to question and challenge. This got them into trouble. The school culture emphasized a distinction between "nice" (well-behaved) girls and "bad" girls who caused "trouble." But many black girls could not be "nice" in the face of unfairness according to their perceptions. This can be seen in the reactions of one student named Carol. Frequent questioning of rule application by teachers landed her in trouble. As a result, Carol's hope of becoming an airline attendant was undermined by the many times she had been sent to the principal's office or sent home. Carol's process of school exclusion was well underway by the time she was fifteen.

Even the black students who did not get labeled as "bad" or troublesome by the white administration questioned the school culture. Although Nina, another black student, functioned fairly well in school, she was bothered enough by her experiences to envision a different school environment, if she had the opportunity to run her school:

> I think, if I could run a school, I think I'd try to please the kids instead of trying to please myself, knowing that I've had an education and what I didn't learn I'd make sure that they learn and like what I don't get and what I'm not able to get, I think that, like the way I am, I would want my kids to be higher than what I am, and have their kids be higher than what they are. So, I try to make a child be higher than what I am instead of putting myself in front of a child, but I guess some people just don't know.

Nina was particularly disturbed when her name appeared unjustly on the board with others who were disturbing her math class. Like her fellow black students, Nina had a strong sense of fairness, unfairness, and what a teacher should and should not do. Moreover, like the so-called bad girls, she will resist openly when she perceives herself as being treated unfairly. This overt resistance distinguishes the black adolescents from most of their white counterparts.

When these black girls resisted procedures in desegregated settings, they reacted quite humanly, but not always wisely. They had developed a partially independent way of life within a restrictive educational setting; they introduced complexity into school authority relations. As a result, they subsequently got themselves differentiated out as troublesome disrupters. While they did not fully realize it, this resistance to the school setting was placing many of them on a track to poor jobs and restricted life opportunities beyond the school setting. To a substantial extent, they have long been aware that their job and life chances beyond school would be limited. But their resistance to the *real* injustices in the school setting itself increased the labeling and tracking that all but guarantees racial inequalities for them in the future.

Moreover, a number of studies have found that in desegregated school settings, black children are more likely to be punished for infraction of the rules than are white children. For example, one study of recently desegregated schools found that black children were two to five times more likely to be suspended or expelled. This study also discovered that black children are particularly likely to be suspended for "subjective" offenses such as disobedience, disrespect for teachers, and personal appearance (dress), rather than for drugs or assault ("objective") offenses. This, again, suggests a *clash of worlds*, a conflict of values and subcultures. The white-dominated school is not expected to alter its structure or culture; the adaptation is one-way, with the expectation that black children will conform to the white way of doing things. When they rebel, they are punished. Black American values, beliefs, and dress are punished. Of course, such a situation is very likely to reduce the academic achievement of many black children, since white teachers' views and values affect that achievement. Moreover, in many schools with large black population, many white teachers leave as soon as they can, leaving such schools for the least experienced, and even minimally qualified, teachers.[24]

Losing Teachers: White Dominance in Desegregated Schools

Russell and Jacqueline Jordan Irvine have suggested that school desegregation has had effects not only on black achievement but also on the interpersonal relationships between black children and their teachers, on schools as black community institutions, and on black communities more generally.[25] In regard to pupil-teacher relationships, one result of school desegregation in many areas has been to reduce significantly the number of black teachers with whom a black child comes into contact. Most often, black children have been desegregated into formerly white schools, and in many areas, the number of black teachers and principals has been reduced. Picott's research found that between 1964 and 1973 the number of black principals in southern school systems had decreased to only two hundred, from a prior level of two thousand. Fewer black principals and teachers means fewer role models for black children. A number of research studies have shown that black teachers expect greater educational achievement from black pupils than white teachers do, both in schools with high average levels of academic achievement and in schools with lower levels of achievement. Thus, the absence of black teachers can mean not only an absence of role models, but also decreased expectations for achievement from black children.[26]

Community Effects

Irvine and Irvine have noted two broad effects of school desegregation on black communities and institutions, particularly in the southern areas. One broad effect has been to dismantle black schools which have long been an important institutional resource in black communities. Such schools once employed large numbers of black principals and teachers, who were dismissed or demoted with school desegregation. Since white authorities have controlled the actual implementation at the local level, it is not surprising that this took place. This dismantling of black schools has resulted in a loss of black professionals, both teachers and administrators, to black communities as role models and as the heart of the black community's institutional complex. These professionals have long served informally in communities as a source of support for young people growing up. Moreover, support for Afro-American culture was centered in the segregated schools in black communities. In white schools black children are expected to imitate white ways, to (in effect) reject their own cultural background.[27]

Desegregation in Suburbia

Research studies of desegregated public schools in suburban situations have found that desegregation under certain conditions speeds black achievement in a white world. Thus, a 15-year study by Robert Crain in Hartford, Connecticut found that black children in desegregated (formerly all-white suburban) schools made greater strides in a number of areas than comparable students in predominantly black city schools. Blacks in these desegregated schools were more likely to graduate from high school and to attend desegregated colleges. They were less likely to get into trouble with the police and were more self-confident in white settings. As adults, they were more likely to live in desegregated neighborhoods. One basic conclusion one might draw from his research is that the experience of learning in formerly all-white schools with excellent resources and facilities gives black children better coping skills for dealing with colleges, police officers, and white-dominated employment settings.[28]

However, it is clear from the problems of desegregated schools in the central cities (cf. Brewer's previously mentioned research) that this type of suburban desegregation is relatively unusual. The Hartford findings do not seem to apply to most minority children in the desegregated, but still heavily minority, central city schools across the nation. Nor does the Hartford study deal with the problems which one-way desegregation brings to black (and white) teachers, administrators, and communities.

Minorities and Women in Higher Education

Discrimination persists in higher education. In the last decade women and minority students have begun to penetrate such formerly all-male areas as medical schools. Once they have been admitted, however, the problems of discrimination do not disappear. Medical education has been tailored over the last eight decades almost exclusively for white male students. When women and minorities come up against this version of the "white male mold," there is often trouble.

An example of how cultural bias regarding the white male mold can inject itself into medical school evaluations of minority students is found in two evaluations of the same Puerto Rican woman medical student. The first evaluation is from an affluent, white male medical educator at a private hospital:[29]

This student consistently had difficulty relating to attendings, house staff and some patients. Her behavior, at times, was inappropriate and it was our feeling that she failed to appreciate her limitations as a student. She seemed to resent and have difficulty coping with authoritarian [sic] figures. Her manner, at times, was quite overbearing, demanding, and, quite frankly, inappropriate. Unfortunately, her personality problems tend to overshadow her work as a student. . . . Although intellectually we feel she could make it as a physician, unless she is able to correct her personality deficiencies, her future as a physican remains questionable.

In sharp contrast to this doctor's comments are the statements of other professors and physicians with whom this minority student had worked at neighborhood clinics—medical practitioners who had greater appreciation for the cultural diversity she brought to the setting as a minority woman. Excerpts from those comments include these:

She is clearly a bright, energetic and capable person and has demonstrated both independence and initiative in a situation where there is little supervision available. . . . Her relationship with others was good, she was cooperative and flexible in situations requiring teamwork, and she accepted direction and criticism willingly.

She demonstrates a broad intelligence, a refreshing

individuality, integrity, and most of all, courage in opposing pretense and rigidity.

[She], of all students, is very intent on the patient's welfare. She is not interested in power, in prestige, in making money. . . . She has the potential for being an unusual and outstanding doctor, the potential for being a doctor in settings that most students couldn't handle. Most of them are going to practice in white suburbia.

The first doctor's evaluation compared this Puerto Rican woman to a certain type of white male mold and concluded that she had "personality deficiencies." The second evaluation compared her to the sort of doctor needed for a more diverse set of minority patients and concluded that she was the sort of doctor that was needed. The important point to be derived from the two evaluations, however, is that her medical career was nearly terminated by her inability to fit that presecribed mold because of cultural, ethnic, and gender differences between her and the attending physician at the private hospital.

In her research on medical schools, Diana Kendall found that even where the double impact of being a minority woman in a "white male preserve" is not directly evidenced by poor teacher evaluations, that impact may exist in the way the individual "twofer" student feels she is perceived by faculty and other students, as in this comment by a third-year, Mexican-American student:

I think we [minority women students] get it from both directions. Some people "wonder" if we can make it here because we are "disadvantaged" students. Others think because we are women that we will "go make babies" and never practice medicine. I think there are a lot of people at this school who sincerely believe my chair should be filled by some white male student who was turned down.[30]

Similarly, a fourth-year black woman student stated that the way she was regarded at the teaching hospital was devastating to her self-concept and therefore extremely stressful, for physicians there frequently imagined that she was a nurse or cleaning lady instead of a doctor-in-training:

> I spend half my time on rotations explaining to everybody who I am. Some of the attending physicians and residents think I'm a nurse; others think I'm a ward clerk. Worse yet. . . . some of the patients think I'm there to clean up their room. I have to keep telling people I'm a medical student even though that's what my name tag says. White male students don't have this problem because they start to dress, walk and talk like the doctors and everybody says, "Oh yes, there's Dr. Smith," even when they really aren't doctors yet. They still call me by my first name.

In addition, Kendall found that cases of isolate and small-group disciminatory practices by white male students and faculty were seldom punished by the medical school authorities. Minority and female students criticized the medical schools for not hiring enough minority and female faculty members, whose presence would mean better role models for nontraditional students.

DISCRIMINATION IN POLITICS

Serious discrimination still confronts black and other minority voters in the United States. In his expert research, Chandler Davidson has noted that there are several major types of electoral discrimination: vote dilution, disenfranchisement, and candidate diminution. A major example of vote dilution is in the at-large electoral system of many cities. This commonplace at-large system has been demonstrated to reduce sharply the participation of minority candidates and minority voters in electoral campaigns. As long as blacks, for example, are a minority of local voters in a city, it can be difficult for them to elect officeholders from their own residential areas. The Supreme Court, in *City of Mobile* v. *Bolden* (1980), put a heavy burden on minority plaintiffs to prove that at-large electoral systems were *intentionally* set up to discriminate against minorities, not just to show that they have a severe negative impact which could be lessened by an alternative, more democratic system. In effect, the Supreme Court's ruling that indirect or subtle direct discrimination is constitutionally permissible demonstrates yet another backing away from the broad anti–institutionalized discrimination principles of the 1971 *Griggs* decision.[31]

A variety of other electoral strategies have had a disenfranchisement impact on minority candidates, including a run-off rule in at-large elections, gerrymandered districts, a decrease of the number of seats in a government body in a single-member-district system, and local (white) slating groups that handpick a token black or Mexican American candidate in order to prevent other minority candidates from having a chance at being elected. In addition to discriminatory vote dilution mechanisms, minority voters in some areas face discrimination in the form of such disenfranchisement practices as purging voter registration rolls, changing polling places with no notice or short notice, establishing difficult registration procedures, and threatening voters with retaliation. These practices have been documented in the states of Alabama, Mississippi, and Texas in recent years. Faced with minority dilution strategies, minority voters may further dilute their voting strength by giving up and staying away from the polls.[32]

Candidate diminution is yet another form of political discrimination that black and Hispanic Americans still face. This involves attempts to keep minority candidates from running for office. Davidson has noted these examples: changing an office from elective to appointive when a minority candidate has a chance to win (Georgia, Alabama); setting high filing and bonding fees to deter minority candidates

(Georgia); abolishing party primaries (Mississippi); and in-timidating minority candidates with threats of violence or of cutting off credit (Alabama, North Carolina, South Carolina, Georgia).[33]

As a result of these acts of discrimination (most of which are direct institutionalized discrimination), black and His-panic Americans have not yet achieved full representation in the political sphere, particularly in the Sunbelt. Indeed, a 1981 report of the U.S. Commission on Civil Rights found that blacks made up only 0.8 (Texas) to 7.7 (Louisiana) percent of the elected officials in the southern states, in every case far below their population proportions. In *every* state, black voters had a quarter or less of the representation among elected officials that one would have predicted on the basis of their population proportions. Hispanic voters in Texas, Cali-fornia, Colorado, and Arizona were better represented among elected officials, but still well below their population propor-tions (except in Arizona).[34]

REMEDYING RACE AND SEX DISCRIMINATION: THE LAST DECADE

Since the mid-1970s there has been an extended debate over affirmative action and reverse discrimination. We have devoted much of this chapter to demonstrating the critical point that race and sex discrimination is still a massive societal problem in the United States today and is a long way from being eradicated. Given the tenacity of so much of the mythology about equal opportunity programs and affirmative action, we will now examine several major misconceptions in detail.[35]

Misconception Number One: Affirmative action is reverse discrimination. The opponents of equal opportunity and affir-mative action have scored a brilliant coup by getting the mass media to discuss affirmative action in terms of the simplistic galvanizing phrase "reverse discrimination." For example, in

1976 *U.S. News and World Report* ran a feature story titled: "Growing Debate–Reverse Discrimination–Has It Gone Too Far?" and in 1977 *Newsweek* ran a cover story under a front page headline of "reverse discrimination." The cover showed a white student and a black student in a tug-of-war over a college diploma.[36]

Yet the term *reverse discrimination* is a grossly inaccurate label for the actions the critics deplore. This can be seen clearly if we follow the principle of keeping age-old patterns of institutionalized race and sex discrimination in mind. Think for a moment about patterns of discrimination against black Americans in the United States: Traditional discrimination by whites against blacks in most organizations in all major institutional areas of society—in housing, employment, education, health services, the legal system, and so on. For three centuries now, tens of millions of whites have participated directly in discrimination against millions of blacks, including routinized discrimination in the large-scale bureaucracies that now dominate this society. Traditional discrimination has meant extraordinarily heavy economic and social losses for blacks in all institutional sectors for hundreds of years. One result is that most black Americans today have little in the way of resources (economic and educational) that have been handed down to them by their parents and grandparents.

What would the *reverse* of this centuries-old race discrimination really look like? The reverse of the traditional discrimination by whites against blacks would mean reversing the power and resource inequalities for a long time: for several hundred years, massive institutionalized discrimination would be directed by dominant blacks against most whites. Most organizations in areas such as housing, education, and employment would be run at the top by a disproportionate number of blacks; middle- and lower-level decision makers would be disproportionately black. These decision-making blacks would have aimed much discrimination at *whites*. As a result, millions of whites would have suffered trillions of dollars in economic losses, lower wages, unemployment, political weakness, widespread housing segregation, inferior school facilities, and violent lynchings. That societal condition would be something one could reasonably call a condition of reverse discrimination. It does not exist, nor is it ever likely to exist.

Reverse discrimination is a mythological notion designed primarily to confuse and discredit, not to enlighten. Whatever cost a few brief years of affirmative action have meant for whites (or white males), those costs do not total anything close to the total cost of true reverse discrimination. To our knowledge, *no* affirmative action plan in industry, housing, higher education, or government has had the purpose or effect of establishing a system of black supremacy over whites or female supremacy over men. Affirmative action plans as currently set up do not make concrete a widespread antiwhite prejudice on the part of blacks nor a widespread antimale prejudice on the part of women. Affirmative action plans have been modest remedial efforts, designed for the most part by white males, to bring token-to-modest numbers of women and nonwhite males into those areas of our economic, social, and political institutions. After centuries of exclusion from these areas, women and nonwhite males had only 5–10 years of these modest remedial programs before they were largely retracted during the 1980s. Major affirmative action plans in the areas of education, housing, and employment were originally set up and largely implemented by white males who dominate the line decision-making positions in virtually all major organizations in the society.

A very small number of white males have paid a price for some affirmative action programs. If affirmative action were successful, particularly in a society with little economic growth, it would entail some cost. But to compare the scale of that modest cost to the scale of the suffering of minorities and women is absurd. A white male who suffers as an individual from remedial programs such as affirmative action in employment or education suffers because he is an *exception* to his privileged group. A black person who suffers from racial discrimination suffers because the whole group has been subordinated, not because he or she is an exception. MacKinnon suggests that:

> When a white charges race discrimination (for example, due to preferential admissions for blacks), he is protesting the cost on one sphere of his life of a rectification process of an entire system that has tried to destroy all blacks in every sphere of their lives for generations, and could afford to ignore their protests.[37]

Misconception Number Two: Affirmative action efforts have been so effective that white male resistance has been inconsequential. Much opposition to affirmative action seems to suggest the misconception that there has been little effective resistance, that white males have watched helplessly as affirmative action has sharply eroded their control of organizations and institutions. Given the fact that white males have virtually always been in substantial control of those affirmative action plans that exist in areas such as business and higher education, this view would seem to be problematical on its face.

Winning the statistical battle is a major focus in many organizations. In such organizations, minority and female workers have been reclassified in order to make it look like the employer has a good affirmative action record in reports filed with the government. For example, senior clerical workers have been reclassified to "managers," although the job and salary remain the same, and suddenly there were many more women in "management." Two management experts have noted these effective resistance activities by corporations:

> Instead of improving organizational climate and revamping human resource planning, legal staffs have been beefed up to fight discrimination cases. Instead of validating selection processes, more emphasis is placed on winning the statistical battle.[38]

Tokenism in affirmative action is another successful device used to slow down the process of dismantling institutionalized discrimination. Reluctantly tearing down the traditional exclusion barriers over the last two decades, the white (male) executives in many organizations have retreated to this second line of defense. Part of the tokenism strategy is to hire minorities and women for nontraditional jobs and put them in conspicuous and/or powerless positions. Given the weakness in governmental compliance efforts, even before the Reagan period, the majority of corporations, agencies, and colleges had seldom gone any farther than tokenism as a strategy. In such a situation most organizations should be able, with modest effort, to find well-qualified minorities and women for the small number of nontraditional positions they intend to fill. Yet, according to one survey, 70 percent of corporate executives report they cannot find qualified women and minorities. A top executive at Sears, Roebuck, and Co. has suggested that these executives are not being candid:

> We don't believe the 70 percent response to the Yankelovich survey that said that the biggest problem with affirmative action is the availability of qualified minorities and women. That's not the biggest problem. The biggest problem is acceptance—in getting management, which still happens to be white males, to accept the fact that if we start with the concept of individual differences and individual worth there are a lot of minorities and women out there who can do anything.[39]

The suggestion that there are a lot of qualified minorities and women who are not being tapped is here corroborated by an unlikely source, a top executive who himself is a white male. He further implies that for every corporation under close government scrutiny, there are two hundred employers who are ignoring affirmative action and "are laughing at the whole process."[40] While corporations such as Sears and AT&T have occasionally gotten a lot of scrutiny from the government and the media, the majority of corporations move along, at best, at a snail's pace of tokenism.

Misconception Number Three: Whites haven't benefited

from affirmative action. Kenneth Smallwood has argued that white America has historically benefited from huge federal "affirmative action" plans for whites only, programs which laid the foundation for much of white prosperity (and black inferiority in resources) in modern America.[41] For example, from the 1860s to the early 1900s, the Homestead Act provided much free land in the West for whites; because most blacks were still in the semi-slavery of debt and tenancy in southern agriculture, they could not participate in this massive government affirmative action program. That billion-dollar land giveaway became the basis of economic prosperity for many white Americans and their descendants. Recent affirmative action plans for black Americans pale in comparison with that single program. Moreover, the great U.S. railroad corporations got their start in huge giveaways of federal lands (amounting to acreage the size of France), plus $700 million in cash, all to assist private (white) enterprise in the task of linking the East with the West.

Most of the New Deal programs in the 1930s primarily subsidized white Americans and white-controlled corporations. The policies of the Federal Housing Administration (FHA) helped millions of white American families secure housing while (until the 1960s) the same agency's policies encouraged the segregation of black Americans in ghetto communities. Massive New Deal agricultural programs and the Reconstruction Finance Corporations kept many white American bankers, farmers, and corporate executives in business, again providing the basis for much postwar prosperity in white America. Yet, similar multibillion dollar aid programs have never been made available to most black Americans, even though they suffered tragically as the victims of chains for three centuries of unpaid work building up the wealth of white Americans, followed by more than a century of discrimination aimed at keeping them in their place (e.g., in low-wage work). Smallwood makes the important point that preferential treatment for white Americans has always been legitimate, an essential part of government development in U.S. society for more than three centuries. If so, one might add, why not provide three centuries of affirmative action to build up the wealth of those black American victims of white discrimination?

Misconception Number Four: Affirmative action plans for minorities are no longer necessary because the real problems facing minorities are problems of the "lower class," not race. Many critics suggest that affirmative action and equal opportunity programs have primarily benefited middle-income black Americans. They argue that, as a result, there is a growing polarization in the black community between a growing, affluent middle class and a poverty underclass. Since, in the critics' view, racial discrimination is rapidly being eradicated for middle-class blacks, and since the problems of the underclass have to do with "class culture," not racial discrimination, there is less need for affirmative action.

One problem with this argument is that the evidence on family income does not lend it support. The Bureau of Labor Statistics publishes data on three family budget levels, low, intermediate, and high. The proportion of white families with incomes at or above the intermediate budget level increased a little from 47 percent in 1970 to about half by 1980. The proportion of black families falling into this middle-income range rising or above it increased slightly from 24 to 26 percent. As Robert B. Hill puts it: "In short, the proportion of economically 'middle class' families is not significantly different among blacks (one-fourth) or whites (one-half) today than it was a decade ago—due to the unrelenting effects of recession and inflation."[42] And the gap between blacks and whites is even greater than these statistics suggest because wealth such as stocks, bonds, and real estate is omitted. By this measure, there has been little growth in the black middle class over the last decade.

In recent years, the plight of the black underclass has been discussed as though its high unemployment, underemployment, low income, and poor housing conditions had little to do with racial discrimination. Indeed, in a *New York Times Magazine* article which articulates a pervasive argument circulating in academia and policy circles in the 1970s and

1980s, Carl Gershman argues that it is the worsening condition of the underclass, *not* racial discrimination, which requires the greatest policy attention today.[43] Critical to his argument is the idea that the conditions of poorer black Americans are due to the "tangle of pathology" in which they find themselves. The suggestion is that poor black Americans have gotten locked into a lower class subculture, a culture of poverty, with its allegedly deviant value system of immorality, broken families, juvenile delinquency, and lack of emphasis on the work ethic. These arguments are not new, but are a resurrection of culture-of-poverty arguments made in the 1960s (for example, in Daniel Patrick Moynihan's *The Negro Family*). If this misconception were true, poor blacks should face the same conditions as poor whites. But this is not the case. Poor blacks do not live in integrated "slums" with poor whites. Poor and near-poor blacks are less likely than comparably poor whites to get unemployment compensation when they are unemployed. They hold even lower paying and less secure jobs than poor whites.

The role of past discrimination in current "tangles of poverty" needs to be reassessed. Much "past" discrimination is not something in the distant past; rather, it is recent. *Blatant* discrimination against blacks was very widespread until 15 to 20 years ago, particularly in the South. All blacks (and whites) now over the age of 21 years (half the population) were born when the United States still had massive color bars in both North and South. Most blacks over 35 years of age were educated in legally segregated schools of lower quality than those of whites, and many have felt the weight of tremendous racial discrimination in at least the early part of their employment careers. And the majority of those black Americans under the age of 21 have *parents* who have suffered from blatant racial discrimination. Moreover, most white Americans over the age of 30 have benefited, if only indirectly, from all types of racial discrimination in many institutional areas. Combine this recent past discrimination with today's overt and covert types of racial discrimination and one has a better understanding of the causes of much black poverty, unemployment, and underemployment than resurrected poverty-subculture theories provide. The *real* dilemma is the persisting tangle of interlocking and institutionalized race discrimination in this society.

We have noted previously that a substantial majority of black Americans surveyed in a Mathematica survey feel that there is a great deal of racial discrimination in this country. The supposed black beneficiaries of affirmative action (those with higher incomes) were somewhat more likely than the poor to report a great deal of discrimination. There is a consensus among large majorities of the poor and of the middle class that racial discrimination remains a serious problem. In the same survey a majority of the black respondents saw a declining national commitment to equal rights. The survey asked: "Is the push for equal rights for black people in this country moving too fast, at about the right pace, or too slow?" Fully three-quarters said, "too slow." This compared dramatically with the results of a similar question asked in a Harris survey in 1970; in that survey only 47 percent said "too slow," with 41 percent saying, "about right."[44] The overwhelming majority of black Americans believe that the U.S. commitment to racial equality has eroded.

Misconception Number Five: Blacks today are like white immigrants in the past. There is a notion among some affirmative action critics that "blacks today are like white immigrants yesterday," and thus "benign neglect" should suffice for public policy. That naive notion is simply wrong. In a famous article in the *New York Times Magazine* in 1966, social scientist Irving Kristol argued that "The Negro Today is Like the Immigrant of Yesterday."[45] His argument represents the view that the black experience is not greatly different from that of white immigrant groups who came in large numbers prior to 1925, that black Americans will move up just as those white immigrants of yesterday did. Nathan Glazer argues that there are some important differences between the experiences of blacks and those of white immigrants, but that there are probably more similarities than differences. In particular, he emphasizes that the difference is one of degree, not kind: " . . . the gap between the experience of the worst off of the [white] ethnic groups and the Negroes is one of degree rather than kind. Indeed, in some respects the Negro is better off than some other groups."[46] Glazer further argues that, for the most part, the employment conditions faced by black migrants to northern cities were not worse than those encountered by earlier immigrant groups.

An alternative to this view would emphasize the dramatically *different* experiences and economic conditions encountered by black immigrants moving up from the South to the North. Research by Theodore Hershberg, William Yancey, and their associates has underscored the importance of an approach emphasizing economic roots. Their research suggests that economic conditions at the time of entry into cities and the level of antiblack racism at that time made the experiences of blacks far more oppressive and difficult than those of white immigrant groups in northern cities. In the case of the pre-1925 white immigrant groups, and of their children and grandchildren, group mobility was possible because

1. Most arrived at a point in time when jobs were available, when capitalism was expanding and opportunities were more abundant for a significant period of time.
2. Most faced far less severe employment and housing discrimination than blacks did.
3. Most found housing, however inadequate, reasonably near the workplaces.[47]

During the major periods of white immigration, the major recipient cities (for example, New York, Philadelphia, Boston, and Chicago) were industrializing. Blue-collar (albeit unskilled) jobs were increasing and available, if not plentiful, in this critical period of industrial capitalism. Some upward mobility became possible for their children. It was into these booming areas that many European immigrants migrated prior to 1925. Research on cities such as Philadelphia has made it clear that Irish and German immigrants were clustered into neighborhoods with other immigrants, but that they did not live in highly segregated Irish or German ghettos. Half the people in such areas where they lived were *not* of their own ethnic background. *They were not nearly as segregated from the native population as blacks were then or now.*

The new white immigrants often resided within a mile or so of their workplaces, many of them crowded into tenement housing. Industrial workplaces were becoming larger and more concentrated in cities, thus encouraging immigrants to settle in congested residential areas near their employment. The children of these white ethnic Americans, over the next few decades, followed industrial plants to suburbs. This left many central cities with a disproportionate number of lower-wage employers. It was into this new employment situation that nonwhite Americans—blacks, Puerto Ricans, Chicanos, and Native Americans—moved, in the growing waves of migration after World War II. Many of the best job opportunities had moved away. Moreover, many blacks already in the cities from 1880 to 1920, prior to the great waves of black migration, often lived *near* the new manufacturing jobs being created in the factories, but they were *rarely hired.* In Philadelphia, for example, blacks were completely excluded from the better paying jobs; they were even forced out of their traditional unskilled jobs, which became the preserves of new white immigrants. Nonwhites have faced greater discrimination in housing and schooling than did earlier immigrant groups.[48]

Black immigrants to cities in the decades after World War II differed dramatically in their structural conditions and historical experiences from white groups. First, the white immigrants generally faced a better economic opportunity structure. They arrived when the expanding capitalist-directed industry was expanding in core cities. Later, blacks and other nonwhites arrived when many jobs, particularly better paying jobs, were leaving the central cities. Second, earlier white immigrant groups often could live near then-plentiful central city jobs; later black migrants to the cities generally had to (and have to) live in the central housing abandoned by whites, housing no longer near many better paying jobs in suburbia. And third, blacks have suffered from enormous, across-the-board residential, employment, and school segregation from the beginning of their urban experience to the present.

THE DECLINE OF AFFIRMATIVE ACTION/
EQUAL OPPORTUNITY EFFORTS: 1980–1986

End of Momentum

The momentum toward expanding employment, educational, and housing opportunity for minorities and women came to an end in the 1980–1986 period. Governmental policy makers and private sector officials had become preoccupied with matters other than race and sex discrimination; this is clearly indicated by the 1980 congressional rejection of a much-needed fair housing bill and by aggressive actions by the Reagan administration to destroy affirmative action programs, the EEOC, and the U.S. Commission on Civil Rights. Widely cited books by men such as Nathan Glazer and George Gilder have been heralded as demonstrating the need for government to pull back further from its already weakening commitment to equal rights. It was only a century ago that a decade or two of great progress in expanding opportunities for black Americans (1865–1885) called the "Reconstruction period" was followed all too soon by a dramatic resurgence of conservatism and reaction called the "Redemption period." While there are certainly major differences between then and now, only 20 years after the public policy shifted significantly in favor of expanded opportunities for minorities and women, we again see major movement in a conservative and reactionary direction. Many powerful leaders have taken action to restrict or to end effective (even token) affirmative action and equal opportunity programs. Today, white males overwhelmingly dominate, often alone, the upper-level and middle-level managerial and professional positions in virtually every major bureaucratic organization in the United States, from the Department of Defense to General Motors, state legislatures, local banks, and supermarkets. In the 1980s, governmental concern shifted away from trying to eradicate the significant patterns of institutionalized race and sex discrimination in U.S. society.

Defining the Terms

It is important to define the term *affirmative action*, which has been used to cover at least four different types of government and private actions:

1. Any increase in nonwhite or female employment
2. Voluntary remedial programs
3. Court-ordered employment remedies for race and sex discrimination (such as goals in hiring)
4. Administratively (government) coerced employment remedies for race and sex discrimination (such as goals in hiring).

The first usage is the most general, since it covers all situations where there have been increases in the numbers of nonwhites hired, even though such increases may be the result of subordinate group (e.g., black American) pressure rather than government action programs. The second type of usage refers to voluntary business programs not ordered by government.

Two categories that critics have been concerned with are (1) court-ordered programs and (2) administratively ordered programs. Court-ordered affirmative action programs are perhaps the more difficult for opponents to criticize, since in most cases *documentation* of past intentional discrimination by a company or organization has become part of the legal record. Frequently a severe imbalance in the nonwhite proportions of employees in skilled and unskilled work, compared with proportions in the available work force, has been enough to establish a prima facie case of discrimination. Then it is the responsibility of the employer to prove that such imbalances were not due to intentional discrimination. Where such a defense has been inadequate, courts have ordered affirmative action by employers to increase the proportions of nonwhites in their work force and to take other actions to upgrade or improve the working situations of nonwhites.

Administratively ordered affirmative action has also "taken the heat." Federal administrative agencies, particularly the Equal Employment Opportunity Commission (EEOC) and the Office of Federal Contract Compliance (OFCC), have pressured employers to develop and implement affirmative action programs. The authority of the EEOC pressure stems from the 1964 Civil Rights Act. The OFCC, part of the Department of Labor has been a major source of administrative pressure on employers. Two presidential Executive orders, issued in the mid-1960s, prohibited discrimination on the basis of race, national origin, and sex by private businesses with federal contracts and gave authority to the OFCC to supervise them. The OFCC has responsibility for supervising the implementation of its contract regulations, which spell out the intent of the orders.

Voluntary affirmative action plans have become very important in the last decade, particularly as governmental agencies have backed off from aggressive antidiscrimination litigation. Extensive publicity has been given to a few Supreme Court decisions dealing with voluntary affirmative action programs. In the 1978 *Bakke* v. *Regents of the University of California* case, a white male applicant to a university medical school argued that he had been excluded from consideration for a small number of openings which had been set aside for nonwhite applicants, with lesser academic credentials than his.[49] The medical school had voluntarily set aside sixteen of its one hundred openings for qualified candidates who were seen as victims of race discrimination. Bakke challenged this procedure, and the case went to the Supreme Court. The Justices decided the case with a five-to-four vote in favor of Bakke. Bakke was ordered to be admitted to the school, but five of the Justices agreed that such affirmative action plans *were* constitutional, if universities would show more clearly how their plans remedy past discrimination. A second case, *United Steelworkers of America* v. *Weber*, involved a voluntary affirmative action plan set up by the Kaiser Corporation and a union, which sought to raise black representation in skilled craft jobs from 2 percent to something closer to the black percentage (39 percent) of the local area work force.[50] The plan reserved half of the positions in a small job-training program for qualified black employees, some of whom had less seniority than white male workers like Brian Weber, who went to court to challenge the plan. The Supreme Court ruled, in 1979, by a five-to-four vote that racial preferences in this affirmative action plan was legal and that the plan was a lawful means of ending the proven racial discrimination in craft jobs in that part of the country.

In a court case dealing with Detroit, the evidence conclusively showed a history of race discrimination against black applicants for police jobs, as well as against black officers seeking to be promoted.[51] Under outside pressure, the Detroit Police Department had established, more or less voluntarily, a remedial plan for lieutenant promotions. Under this plan, separate lists of black and white officers eligible for promotion were set up, and promotions were made alternatively from each list until the proportion of blacks at the lieutenant level reflected the black proportion in the city's population. Some white officers were passed over and sued. The federal district and appellate courts upheld this voluntary affirmative action plan. The Supreme Court let the lower court rulings stand, even though the Reagan administration's chief civil rights lawyers attacked this voluntary affirmative action plan.

Another strategy of those seeking to insure equal opportunities for blacks and women has focused on voluntary affirmative action plans that would protect them from the "last hired, first fired" practice during hard economic times. Since women and minority men have only been hired in many organizations during the last 10 to 15 years, they suffer the most from cutbacks in jobs. They have less seniority only because of prominent discrimination in the past. Therefore, one strategy of antidiscrimination groups is to reform seniority systems, which perpetuate the discriminatory effects of past race and sex oppression. A number of school cases, such as *Wygant* v. *Jackson Board of Education*, have dealt with the problems of black teachers in school systems with past records of discrimination.[52] In the *Wygant* case, the federal district court and the appellate court ruled that such a collective bargaining agreement—which insured that there would be no greater percentage of minority personnel laid off than the current percentage of minority personnel—was constitutional, even though some white teachers were displaced. The appellate court reasoned that affirmative action in a layoff period was permissible "in light of [the] school board's interest in eliminating historic discrimination, promoting racial harmony in the community, and providing role models for minority students." It is being appealed to the higher courts by the whites affected.

COMPARABLE PAY FOR COMPARABLE WORK: A STRATEGY OF THE WOMEN'S MOVEMENT

A major public debate has arisen in the last decade over "comparable pay for comparable worth," which refers to giving men and women in comparable jobs the same pay. It is commonly said that market capitalism pays people what they are worth. Yet recent job evaluation studies looking at the skill, effort, responsibility, and productivity of male-dominated and female-dominated job categories show that this is a myth. Regardless of their worth in terms of objective job evaluations, women's jobs pay less than comparable male jobs. We can see this in two major studies in California and Washington[53]

In both studies, job categories dominated by women are paid substantially less than comparable, or less skilled, job categories dominated by men. This is a common pattern

	Monthly Salary	Job Evaluation Study Points
San Jose, California		
Librarian I (Female)	$ 750	288
Street Sweeper Operative (Male)	$ 758	124
Senior Legal Secretary (Female)	$ 665	210
Senior Carpenter (Male)	$1040	210
Washington (State)		
Laundry Worker (Female)	$ 884	105
Truck Driver (Male)	$1493	97
Secretary (Female)	$1122	197
Maintenance Carpenter (Male)	$1707	197

across the United States and reflects a long history of lower pay for women's jobs than for men's. Historically, for example, clerical workers before 1920 were predominantly male. When that job category became predominantly female in the 1930–1950 period, the wages declined.

The Washington study cited above was forced on the state government by organized women workers. Finally, a statewide study was done in the mid-1970s. That impressive study found that in 12 comparable job pairs the male-dominated jobs consistently paid more than the female-dominated jobs. Subsequently, an expanded study of 121 job classifications found that the female-dominated jobs averaged $175 less per month than the male-dominated jobs with equivalent skill and responsibility levels. When the state legislature did not take action to respond to its own state government study, the public employees union, AFSCME, filed a lawsuit in 1982. The federal district court judge ruled for the plaintiffs and thus for comparable pay for women doing work comparable to male workers. But in 1985 the Ninth Circuit Court of Appeals overturned the district court ruling. In the meantime, however, the Washington legislature had passed a comparable worth law and had appropriated millions of dollars to eradicate sex-based discrimination in wages and salaries among public employees.

The critical data in the comparable worth debate are those showing that *all* female job categories are paid less than comparable-skilled male-dominated categories. The issue is not that one job, such as that of a carpenter, is paid more than another, such as that of a secretary. It is that male-dominated categories are consistently (always?) paid a *lot* more than comparable female job categories. As an AFSCME lawyer put it: "It is not that Jane is being paid less than Joe that is the issue. It is that all Janes are being paid less than the Joes in jobs of equal value to the same employer."[54] It is likely that major organizing efforts on behalf of "comparable pay" will persist for at least the next decade.

THE NAIVE NOTION OF A COLOR-BLIND SOCIETY

Since the early 1970s there has been a sustained effort by American conservatives to destroy or reduce most equal opportunity and affirmative action efforts, whether they be voluntary, governmental, or court-ordered remedies for race and sex discrimination. Thus, in the early 1970s conservative President Richard Nixon packed the U.S. Supreme Court with conservative judges, who, in a number of decisions, have taken the position that U.S. society is now a color-blind society. In a recent *Harvard Civil Rights–Civil Liberties Law Review* article, Judge Damon J. Keith of the Sixth Circuit Court argues that by proclaiming the fiction that the United States is a color-blind society, the Supreme Court—in such cases as *Bakke*—has perpetrated a "cruel hoax" at the expense of black Americans. This "cruel hoax" has been perpetuated by subsequent presidential administrations, particularly the Reagan administration, and in a series of Supreme Court decisions.[55]

For example, in a recent court case, *Firefighters Local* v. *Stotts*, the conservative-dominated Supreme Court rejected the argument that a discriminatory seniority system is discrimination which must be legally redressed.[56] This is a striking defense of the indirect institutionalized discrimination that we discussed in Chapter 3. Such court decisions protect white male privileges that are locked into existing job structures, which are, in turn, grounded at their *base* in more than a century of overt discrimination against women and minorities. The discriminatory character of seniority systems was accented in the 1977 U.S. Commission on Civil Rights report entitled *Last Hired, First Fired*, a report endorsed by most civil rights groups in the United States. (But many labor union leaders, mostly white males, are adamantly opposed to any modifications of the seniority systems that were won in the militant union struggles with capitalists in the 1930s and 1940s.)[57]

The *Stotts* case began with a 1974 consent agreement under which the city of Memphis agreed to increase minority hiring in its fire department. In May 1981, because of a budget crisis, the city laid off fire fighters, announcing it would follow the "last in, first out" provisions of its contract with the fire fighters' union. But in this case, the federal court ordered the city to lay off workers in a way which would not reduce the percentage of minority workers, in effect setting up separate seniority lists for black and white workers. The Supreme Court overturned this lower court (involuntary) affirmative action plan. The majority of the Justices reasoned that the United States was essentially a color-blind society, at least in regard to such institutions as seniority systems. (This bodes ill for the aforementioned *Wygant* case.)

Perhaps the most important assertion of the color-blind philosophy can be seen in the Reagan administration, which dominated public civil rights policy in the 1980s. During this period, the Reagan administration sharply reduced the federal commitment to civil rights and equal opportunity efforts. Real (inflation-adjusted) federal outlays for agencies operating in these areas declined 9 percent between fiscal year 1981 and fiscal year 1983, with even sharper decreases for the Equal Employment Opportunity Commission (EEOC) and the Office of Federal Contract Compliance (OFCC). In addition, the 1980–1983 period saw a sharp drop in federal enforcement in employment, education, and housing.[58] In June 1984, a former assistant regional administrator of the OFCC, Colonel Samuel Lynn, testified that the Reagan administration was intentionally destroying the federal contract compliance program that had begun to desegregate employment in the 1970s. Enforcement action against contractors, once decentralized in 71 field offices, was centralized in Washington, D.C. The result was a huge file overload and a closing of most files without punitive or corrective action. Lynn described the Reagan actions as introducing a system of voluntary, unsupervised conformity to the law, a strategy which has historically been a failure as an approach to ending race and sex discrimination. Lynn noted that "I see the burden of affirmative action delegated to the individual worker through the complaint process. . . . I see change, a change to reverse the minimum progress made over the past 15 years."[59]

The number of administrative complaints filed against government contractors by the OFCC dropped from 53 to 18 between 1980 and 1983; and the number of disbarments from getting contracts dropped from five to zero. Employment discrimination cases brought by the Department of Justice and the EEOC also declined sharply in this period, even though complaints of discrimination from citizens increased by 50 percent. In the area of school desegregation, the Reagan administration cut back most federal efforts to desegregate schools. Yet it attempted to defend tax breaks for certain private schools (e.g., Bob Jones University) with racially discriminatory policies.[60]

The Reagan administration's top lawyers have been active in attacking affirmative action programs in situations where overt discrimination has been proven in court. Because of the administration's pressures on local governments with successful affirmative action programs, in recent years we have seen the strange phenomenon of local governments in the South telling the Reagan administration to "mind its own business." Local governments have discovered that the desegregation of local governmental agencies such as police departments can significantly reduce the race and conflict problems faced by local governments. In addition, the Reagan administration's appointments in its first two years were of significantly more white males than those in the Carter administration. In effect, as a recent Urban Institute report put it, the administration has brought about "a major change in the definition of federal responsibility for the enforcement of civil rights and equal opportunity."[61]

The Character of the Successes

A major reason for the attack on equal opportunity programs, affirmative action programs, and class action (and other antidiscrimination) legal suits is that these actions have had some impact on many business and governmental employers in U.S. society. Such action has been effective in opening up entry-level positions for women and minority men; even though progress beyond the entry level has often been difficult, the breakthrough here has been quite significant. Indeed, the vigorous attack on these employment desegregation programs in the 1970s and 1980s does suggest that the programs are to some extent effective.

Jonathan Leonard has done considerable research on questions about affirmative action and equal opportunity programs: Have federal antidiscrimination laws had an impact on increasing minority and female participation in manufacturing? Has employment discrimination decreased? Has productivity declined, as right-wing politicians such as Senator Orrin Hatch assert, because of the increased hiring of minorities and women? Leonard's careful analyses show that private antidiscrimination litigation, particularly class action suits based on antidiscrimination laws such as the 1964 Civil Rights Act (Title VII), has had a prominent role in accelerating the employment of blacks—and to a lesser extent, white females—in nontraditional jobs. When coupled with antidiscrimination pressures under federal executive orders such as Executive Order 11246, the litigation impact has been very significant in expanding minority employment in companies which formerly had few minority employees, particularly in nontraditional jobs.

Leonard's sophisticated analysis clearly suggests that the increase in equal employment has had *no* significant productivity or efficiency costs, that the relative productivity of minority and female workers increased with their integration into the work force. Leonard examined 1974–1980 data on five hundred large corporations and found *no* significant evidence that corporations which increased their employment of minorities and women suffered lower profit rates. Leonard's work also demonstrates the relatively small cost of equal opportunity paperwork on the corporations involved. On the whole, then, Leonard's research on the impact of civil rights litigation shows that it works to improve minority and female employment, particularly at entry levels, without significant dollar or productivity costs for the firms involved. This research, moreover, does not consider the additional long-term benefits to these firms of ending lawsuits and of improving their image among women and minority groups.[62]

Continuing Problems

Affirmative action programs seem to have been the most effective when court-ordered for (larger) firms with proven histories of race and sex discrimination. And these programs have been most effective in the sphere of entry-level jobs.

When it comes to promotions, massive discrimination hurdles remain. For example, in the 1970s many black Americans were hired for, or upgraded into, management positions by corporate executives under pressures from court suits, the OFCC, or civil rights protests. Yet recent research by Ed Jones on black managers reveals that well-educated blacks in professional and managerial settings still face many discriminatory barriers. His interviews with black managers revealed extensive complaints about capped upward mobility, shortened careers, difficulties in gaining top executives' support, and exclusion from the inner circles of managerial power in companies. Nearly 100 percent of a nationwide sample of black managers (with MBA degrees, mostly from major business schools) reported that equal opportunity did *not* exist in their corporations. Ninety percent felt less support than their white peers; more than 80 percent felt that there was still antiblack discrimination in assignments, evaluations, and promotions. One of Jones's respondents put it this way: "Black managers may be tolerated, but corporations make it very plain that we are not needed or desired any longer. Boy, a black manager will be the last promoted. Because there is no pressure from the federal government, companies are merely giving lip service, and some aren't even giving lip service anymore."[63]

Foot dragging, obstruction, and sabotage are constant problems. For example, a large corporation's lawyers and accountants may negotiate with the government's (e.g., OFCC) lawyers over a very long period, and the result may be an affirmative action plan which is not grounded in a careful study of race and sex discrimination within the organization. This may mean a poorly constructed affirmative action plan, issued with fanfare but bringing only token or modest results. A top Sears executive has complained about negotiations with the government: "We are forced to create mounds of paper to prove that people aren't available instead of creatively and innovatively developing techniques to make sure people are available."[64] Whether he would aggressively pursue the development of new techniques to find qualified women and minorities if he did not face the paperwork is open to question. But a number of observers of organizations, in assessing organizational reactions to affirmative action, have noted that too much of the effort often goes into paperwork, both statistical and legal, and too little into aggressively finding minorities and women for nontraditional positions. Two veteran management consultants have concluded from their experience not only that too much corporate effort is aimed at winning the statistical battle, but also that hostile overreactions, little budget money, and poor management have created "mongrel" affirmative action plans, which are particularly weak in dealing with race and sex discrimination beyond entry-level hiring.

The Rationale for Race-Conscious Action

The U.S. Constiution, in its thirteenth, fourteenth, and fifteenth Amendments, is *race-conscious*. The thirteenth Amendment explicitly authorizes Congress to eradicate the badges of slavery, which it attempted to do in the Civil Rights Acts of 1866, 1964, 1965, and 1968. Since race discrimination in the United States today is system-wide, institutionalized, and rooted in a 230-year history of legal slavery, and a 360-year history of legal slavery and semi-slavery, a race-conscious plan for relief is both necessary and constitutional. Color-blindness is not required by law or custom in the case of black Americans. If their condition is the result of institutionalized oppression along race-conscious lines, eradication can only be brought about by restructuring the system. Certainly desegregating segregated schools in the South required race-conscious action. Eliminating the effects of past discrimination is a major task which was just begun in the 1960s. The new theory of discrimination peddled by defenders of white privilege is that state-sanctioned relief should be limited only to those blacks who are identifiable victims of specific discriminatory acts. Yet this theory of discrimination has until recently been rejected in Supreme Court cases. Thus the 1954–1955 *Brown* decisions targeted the system of institutionalized discrimination. They were designed to restructure an institution with group-oriented relief, not to provide relief for each black student, one at a time. In *Williams* v. *City of New Orleans* (1984) Appellate court justice Wisdom has pointed out that without group-oriented relief, much discrimination "such as deterrence of unidentifiable black applicants even before they apply for jobs, would go unremedied . . . when the vice is in the system or the institution, the system or the institution must be restructured to eliminate the vice."

THE FUTURE: ETERNAL ORGANIZATION?

We do not have the space here to discuss more fully the many antidiscrimination strategies which women and minority men have developed in recent years. We have already noted a number of these vital strategies in the various sections of this chapter; some of the most important are the many court suits brought by minority and female victims, the development of voluntary affirmative action plans to remedy proven discrimination, and the "comparable pay for comparable worth (work)" programs of organized women's groups and unions. These efforts will need to be multiplied if the walls of race and sex discrimination are to fall.

The abolitionist movement to free blacks from slavery began in the 1820s and 1830s, helped generate the Civil War, and eventually led to the Thirteenth Amendment. That was an integrated movement of blacks and whites, of men and women. The same was true of the civil rights movement of the 1960s and the feminist movement of the 1850s–1920s and of the 1960s–1980s. These movements periodically revive in the United States and bring further motion in the direction of greater freedom and equality.

1. "Initial Black Pulse Findings," *Bulletin No. 1*, Research Dept., National Urban League, August, 1980, pp. 102; "Economics," *Black Enterprise*, August 1980, p. 70. This section draws on Joe R. Feagin, "Affirmative Action in an Era of Reaction," in *Consultations on the Affirmative Action Statement of the U.S. Commission on Civil Rights*, Vol. I (Washington, D.C.: Government Printing Office, 1981), pp. 44–61.

2. "Whites, Blacks Hold Different Views of Status of Blacks in U.S.," *Gallup Opinion Index*, Report No. 178, June 1980, p. 10.

3. Cited in John C. Livingston, *Fair Game?* (San Francisco, CA: W.H. Freeman, 1979), p. 78.

4. "1980 Virginia Slims American Women's Opinion Poll," *Data Sheet*, The Roper Center, Storrs, Connecticut.

5. Feagin, "Affirmative Action in an Era of Reaction," pp. 47–48.

6. Gunnar Myrdal, *An American Dilemma* (New York: McGraw-Hill, 1964), Vol. 1, p. 52n.

7. Cf. Kenneth B. Clark, *Prejudice and Your Child* (Boston: Beacon Press, 1955).

8. This section draws heavily on Nijole Benokraitis, "Sex Discrimination in the '80s," *Focal Point Newsletter*, Maryland Commission for Women, Summer 1983, pp. 1–4.

9. This section draws heavily on several sections in Beth Anne Shelton's *Formal and Informal Mechanisms of Discrimination: A Case Study*, Unpublished Ph.D. Dissertation, Austin, University of Texas, 1984.

10. Ed Jones, "What It's Like to Be a Black Manager," *Harvard Business Review*, forthcoming.

11. Ed Jones, "Beneficiaries or Victims? Progress or Process," Unpublished Research Report, South Orange, New Jersey, January 1985. Cited by permission.

12. Samuel L. Adams, "Blackening in the Media; the State of Blacks in the Press," in *The State of Black America: 1985*, edited by J.D. Williams (New York: National Urban League, Inc., 1984), p. 111.

13. Karl Taeuber, "Racial Residential Segregation, 28 Cities, 1970–1980." Working paper, Madison, Wisconsin, University of Wisconsin Center for Demography and Ecology; John E. Farley, "P* Segregation Indices: What Can They Tell Us About Housing Segregation in 1980?" *Urban Studies*, 21 (August 1984), pp. 7–15.

14. Jonathan Rich, "Municipal Boundaries in a Discriminatory Housing Market: An Example of Racial Leapfrogging," *Urban Studies*, 21 (February, 1984), p. 39.

15. We draw here on summaries of the Boston, Denver, and other research studies in John Yinger, "Measuring Racial and Ethnic Discrimination with Fair Housing Audits: A Review of Existing Evidence and Research Methodology," HUD Conference on Fair Housing Testing, Washington, D.C., December 1984.

16. *Calhoun* v. *Cook*, 362 F. Supp. 1249 (N.D. Ga 1973), affirmed 522 F. 2d 717 (5th Cir. 1975), 525 F. 2d 1203 (5th Cir. 1975).

17. *U.S.* v. *South Carolina*, 445 F. Supp 1094 (D.S.C. 1977),

affirmed mem. sub nom. *National Educ. Assn.* v. *South Carolina*, 434 U.S. 1026 (1978).

18. cf. Derrick Bell, "A Thirty Year Perspective on the Law and Race," in *The State of Black America 1984*, ed. J.D. Williams (New York: National Urban League, Inc., 1984), pp. 132–133.

19. *Miliken* v. *Bradley*, 418 U.S. 717 (1974).

20. Cf. *Columbus Board of Education* v. *Pennick*, 443 U.S. 449 (1979).

21. Cf. *Brennan* v. *Armstrong*, 433 U.S. 672 (1977).

22. Faustine Jones-Wilson, "The State of Urban Education," in *The State of Black America: 1984*, edited by J.D. Williams (New York: National Urban League, Inc., 1984), p. 111.

23. This section draws heavily on Rose M. Brewer, "Schooling, family, and Work: A Look at Afro-American Girls," Paper presented to the Southern Sociological Society, Atlanta, Georgia, April 6–9.

24. J. Eyler, V. Cook. and L. Ward, "Resegregation: Desegregation Within Desegregated Schools," Paper presented at Annual Meeting of American Education Research Association, as summarized in Russell W. Irvine and Jacqueline Jordan Irvine, "The Impact of the Desegregation Process on the Education of Black Students: Key Variables," *Journal of Negro Education*, 53 (1983), p. 415.

25. Irvine and Irvine, "The Impact of the Desegregation Process," pp. 410–415.

26. R. Picott, *A Quarter Century of Elementary and Secondary Education* (Washington: Association for the Study of Negro Life and History, 1976; Charles Beady and Stephens Hansell, "Teacher Race and Expectations for Student Achievement," *American Education Research Journal*, 19 (1981), pp. 191–206.

27. Irvine and Irvine, "The Impact of the Desegregation Process," pp. 416–421.

28. Study Shows Social Mix Good for Blacks," *Daily Texan*, September 18, 1985, p. 3.

29. The discussion is this section is adapted from passages and quotes in Diana Kendall and Joe R. Feagin, "Blatant and Subtle Patterns of Discrimination," *The Journal of Intergroup Relations*, 11 (Summer 1983), pp. 21–28.

30. *Ibid.*

31. Chandler Davidson, "Minority Vote Dilution: An Over-

view." Reprint 85–1, Institute for Policy Analysis, Rice University, Houston, Texas.

32. *Ibid.*, p. 3.

33. *Ibid.*, p. 3.

34. U.S. Commission on Civil Rights, *The Voting Rights Act: Unfulfilled Goals* (Washington, D.C.: U.S. Government Printing Office, 1981), pp. 31–39.

35. This section draws heavily on Feagin, "Affirmative Action in an Era of Reaction," pp. 52–60.

36. Cf. Nathan Glazer, *Affirmative Action Discrimination* (New York: Basic Books, 1975).

37. Catherine A. McKinnon, *Sexual Harassment of Working Women* (New Haven: Yale University Press, 1979), p. 132.

38. Gopal C. Pati and C.W. Reilly, "Reversing Discrimination: A Perspective," *Labor Law Journal* (January 1978), p. 23.

39. Max Benavidez, "The Sears Interview: Roy Graham," *Forum*, October 1980, p. 16.

40. *Ibid.*, p. 17.

41. Kenneth W. Smallwood, "The Folklore of Preferential Treatment," Southfield, Michigan, Unpublished manuscript, 1985.

42. Robert B. Hill, "The Economic Status of Black America," in *The State of Black America, 1981* (New York: National Urban League, 1981), p. 34. The BLS data are cited by Hill.

43. Carl Gershman, "A Matter of Class," *New York Times Magazine*, October 5, 1980, pp. 24–30.

44. "Initial Black Pulse Findings."

45. Irving Kristol, "The Negro Today is Like the Immigrant of Yesterday," *New York Times Magazine*, September 11, 1966, pp. 50–51, 124–142.

46. Nathan Glazer, "Blacks and Ethnic Groups," *Social Problems* 18 (Spring 1971), pp. 458–459.

47. Theodore Hershberg et al., "A Tale of Three Cities: Blacks, Immigrants, and Opportunity in Philadelphia: 1850–1880, 1930, 1970," in *Philadelphia*, edited by T. Hershberg (New York: Oxford University Press), pp. 426–464.

48. *Ibid.*, pp. 469–480.

49. 438 U.S. 265 (1978).

50. 443 U.S. 193 (1979).

51. *Baker* v. *Detroit*, 483 F. Supp 930 (E.D. Mich., 1979), cert. denied, 104 S. Ot. 703 (1984).

52. *Wygant* v. *Jackson Board of Education*, 746 F2d 1152 (6th Cir. 1984).

53. Hay Associates, *State of Minnesota Report*, March 1982; Hay Associates, City of San Jose, November 1980; State of Washington Study, *Public Personnel Management Journal*, Winter 1981–1982; we draw on summaries of these studies in National Committee on Pay Equity, *The Wage Gap* (Washington, D.C., 1983), p. 5.

54. Quoted in Beth Paulin, "Comparable Worth Reduced Job Discrimination," *Daily Texan*, September 18, 1985, p. 2.

55. Damon J. Keith, "What Happens to a Dream Deferred: An Assessment of Civil Rights Law Twenty Years After the March on Washington," *Harvard Civil Rights-Civil Liberties Review*, Summer 1984, Vol. 19, No. 2, pp. 469–495.

56. *Firefighters* v. *Stotts*. 104 U.S. S. Ct. 2576 (1984).

57. For a defense of seniority systems, see Arch Puddington, "Seniority: Not for Whites Only," *New Perspectives*, Vol. 16 (Fall 1984), pp. 8–13.

58. D. Lee Bawden and John L. Palmer, "Social Policy: Challenging the Welfare State," in *The Reagan Record*, edited by J.L. Palmer and I.V. Sawhill (Cambridge, Mass: Ballinger, 1984), pp. 204–208.

59. Statement of Samuel Lynn, former assistant regional administrator, Office of Federal Contract Compliance Programs (OFCCP), New York region (now retired), before the Committee on Education and Labor, Subcommittee on Employment Opportunities, United States House of Representatives, June 27, 1984.

60. Bawden and Palmer, "Social Policy," pp. 204–208.

61. *Ibid.*, p. 208.

62. Jonathan S. Leonard, "Antidiscrimination or Reverse Discrimination: The Impact of Changing Demographics, Title VII, and Affirmative action on Productivity," *Journal of Human Resources*, 19 (1984), pp. 145–174; Jonathan S. Leonard, "Employment and Occupational Advance under Affirmative action," *The Review of Economics and Statistics*, 66 (August 1984), pp. 377–385.

63. Jones, "What It's Like to be a Black Manager," p. 6.

64. Benavidez, "The Sears Interview," p. 16.

Index